Deconstructing Flexicurity and Developing Alternative Approaches

In recent years, the concept of flexicurity has come to occupy a central place in political and academic debates regarding employment and social policy. It fosters a view in which the need for continuously increasing flexibility is the basic assumption, and the understanding of security increasingly moves from social protection to self-insurance or individual adaptability. Moreover, it rejects the traditional contradictions between flexibility and security, blending the two into a single notion and thus depoliticizing the relationships between capital and labour. This volume provides a critical discussion of the flexicurity concept, the theories upon which it is built and the ideas that it transmits about work, unemployment and social justice. It shows that flexicurity fosters the further individualization of social protection, an increase in precariousness and the further weakening of labour in relation to capital. The authors present a series of alternative theoretical, normative and policy approaches that provide due attention to the collective and political dimension of vulnerability and allow for the development of new societal projects based on alternative values and assumptions.

Maarten Keune is Professor of Social Security and Labour Relations and Co-Director of the Amsterdam Institute of Advanced Labour Studies at the University of Amsterdam.

Amparo Serrano is Professor of Social Psychology and Sociology at the University Complutense of Madrid.

Routledge Advances in Sociology

For a full list of titles in this series, please visit www.routledge.com

92 **Solidarity in Individualized Societies**
Recognition, Justice and Good Judgement
Søren Juul

93 **Heritage in the Digital Era**
Cinematic Tourism and the Activist Cause
Rodanthi Tzanelli

94 **Generation, Discourse, and Social Change**
Karen R. Foster

95 **Sustainable Practices**
Social Theory and Climate Change
Elizabeth Shove and Nicola Spurling

96 **The Transformative Capacity of New Technologies**
A Theory of Sociotechnical Change
Ulrich Dolata

97 **Consuming Families**
Buying, Making, Producing Family Life in the 21st Century
Jo Lindsay and JaneMaree Maher

98 **Migrant Marginality**
A Transnational Perspective
Edited by Philip Kretsedemas, Jorge Capetillo-Ponce and Glenn Jacobs

99 **Changing Gay Male Identities**
Andrew Cooper

100 **Perspectives on Genetic Discrimination**
Thomas Lemke

101 **Social Sustainability**
A Multilevel Approach to Social Inclusion
Edited by Veronica Dujon, Jesse Dillard, and Eileen M. Brennan

102 **Capitalism**
A Companion to Marx's Economy Critique
Johan Fornäs

103 **Understanding European Movements**
New Social Movements, Global Justice Struggles, Anti-Austerity Protest
Edited by Cristina Flesher Fominaya and Laurence Cox

104 **Applying Ibn Khaldūn**
The Recovery of a Lost Tradition in Sociology
Syed Farid Alatas

105 **Children in Crisis**
Ethnographic Studies in International Contexts
Edited by Manata Hashemi and Martín Sánchez-Jankowski

106 **The Digital Divide**
The internet and social inequality
in international perspective
*Edited by Massimo Ragnedda
and Glenn W. Muschert*

107 **Emotion and Social Structures**
The Affective Foundations of
Social Order
Christian von Scheve

108 **Social Capital and Its
Institutional Contingency**
A Study of the United States,
China and Taiwan
*Edited by Nan Lin, Yang-chih Fu
and Chih-jou Jay Chen*

109 **The Longings and Limits of
Global Citizenship Education**
The Moral Pedagogy of
Schooling in a Cosmopolitan Age
Jeffrey S. Dill

110 **Irish Insanity 1800–2000**
Damien Brennan

111 **Cities of Culture**
A Global Perspective
Deborah Stevenson

112 **Racism, Governance, and
Public Policy**
Beyond Human Rights
Katy Sian, Ian Law and S. Sayyid

113 **Understanding Aging and
Diversity**
Theories and Concepts
Patricia Kolb

114 **Hybrid Media Culture**
Sensing Place in a World of
Flows
Edited by Simon Lindgren

115 **Centers and Peripheries in
Knowledge Production**
Leandro Rodriguez Medina

116 **Revisiting Institutionalism in
Sociology**
Putting the "Institution" Back in
Institutional Analysis
Seth Abrutyn

117 **National Policy-Making**
Domestication of Global Trends
Pertti Alasuutari and Ali Qadir

118 **The Meanings of Europe**
Changes and Exchanges of a
Contested Concept
*Edited by Claudia Wiesner and
Meike Schmidt-Gleim*

119 **Between Islam and the
American Dream**
An Immigrant Muslim
Community in Post-9/11 America
Yuting Wang

120 **Call Centers and the Global
Division of Labor**
A Political Economy of Post-
Industrial Employment and
Union Organizing
Andrew J.R. Stevens

121 **Academic Capitalism**
Universities in the Global
Struggle for Excellence
Richard Münch

122 **Deconstructing Flexicurity
and Developing Alternative
Approaches**
Towards New Concepts and
Approaches for Employment and
Social Policy
*Edited by Maarten Keune and
Amparo Serrano*

Deconstructing Flexicurity and Developing Alternative Approaches

Towards New Concepts and Approaches for Employment and Social Policy

Edited by
Maarten Keune and Amparo Serrano

Routledge
Taylor & Francis Group
NEW YORK   LONDON

First published 2014
by Routledge
711 Third Avenue, New York, NY 10017

and by Routledge
2 Park Square, Milton Park, Abingdon, Oxon OX14 4RN

*Routledge is an imprint of the Taylor & Francis Group,
an informa business*

Library of Congress Cataloging-in-Publication Data
   Deconstructing flexicurity and developing alternative approaches :
towards new concepts and approaches for employment and social policy /
edited by Maarten Keune and Amparo Serrano. — 1st Edition.
      pages cm. — (Routledge advances in sociology ; 122)
   Includes bibliographical references and index.
   1. Manpower policy. 2. Social policy. I. Keune, Maarten, 1966–
editor of compilation.
   HD5713.D436 2014
   332.12'042—dc23
   2013031159

ISBN: 978-0-415-63426-7 (hbk)
ISBN: 978-0-203-09457-0 (ebk)

Typeset in Sabon
by IBT Global.

Contents

List of Figures   ix

List of Tables   xi

1   The Power to Name and Struggles over Meaning:
    The Concept of Flexicurity   1
    MAARTEN KEUNE AND AMPARO SERRANO

2   Class Relations and Labour-Market Reforms   27
    COLIN CROUCH

3   From Flexicurity to Social Employment Regimes   47
    CARLOS PRIETO

4   Inequality as a Central Component in the
    Redefinition of Security: The Case of Gender   68
    MARIA JEPSEN

5   Beyond Flexibility: Active Securities for
    Flexible Employment Relationships   88
    GÜNTHER SCHMID

6   Labour, Capabilities, and Situated Democracy   116
    ROBERT SALAIS

7   From Flexicurity to Capabilities:
    In Search of Professional Development   135
    BÉNÉDICTE ZIMMERMANN

8   Life-First Welfare and the Scope
    for a "Eudemonic Ethic" of Social Security   152
    HARTLEY DEAN

9   Quality of Employment: An Alternative to Flexicurity?   173
    DOMINIQUE MÉDA

    Contributors   197
    Index   201

Figures

3.1   Social regime of employment.   51

4.1   Correlation between overall EPL and EUGEI, 2005.   77

4.2   Correlation between participation in any LLL and EUGEI, 2005.   78

4.3   Correlation between % of GDP spent on ALMP and EUGEI, 2005.   79

4.4   Correlation between % of GDP spent on unemployment benefits and EUGEI, 2005.   80

4.5   Correlation between childcare enrolment for children 3–5 years of age and EUGEI, 2005.   81

4.6   Correlation between childcare enrolment for children below 3 years of age and EUGEI, 2005.   81

5.1   Part-time employees (only with open-ended contracts, and without self-employed) as per cent of working age population (age 15–64), 1998 and 2008.   93

5.2   Temporary employees (including part-timers) as per cent of working age population (15–64 years), 1998 and 2008.   94

5.3   Self-employed (full-time or part-time, own-account workers) as per cent of working age population (15–64 years), 1998 and 2008.   95

5.4   Aggregate non-standard employment rates in Europe, 1998 and 2008.   96

Tables

1.1 Confronting the Views of Employers and Unions on
Flexicurity 13

2.1 Debt Burdens for Lower-Income Groups, Various Countries,
mid-2000s 33

2.2 Basic Variables for Study of Labour Markets 39

2.3 Countries Grouped for Independent Variables 40

2.4 Countries Grouped for Dependent Variables 40

2.5 Countries Grouped on Independent and Dependent
Variables 41

2.6 Union Membership Decline 42

2.7 Employment Levels by Tables 2.3 and 2.4 Categories 44

3.1 Average Annual Wages in PPP in Some European Countries
(Euros p.a., 2005) 50

3.2 Social Spending as a Percentage of GDP in Some European
Countries, 2005 54

3.3 Employment Segments Broken Down by Sectors of Activity
and Size of Firms 55

3.4 Wage-Earners Employed by Firms with Less Than Ten
Employees as a Percentage of Total Wage-Earners and Self-
Employed Workers as a Percentage of Total Job-Holders, 2005 55

3.5 Trade Union Membership Rates and Proportion of
Employees on Fixed-Term Contracts Broken Down by Size
of Firms 57

3.6 Proportion of Fixed-Term Contracts in Spain and Other EU
Countries, 2008 58

3.7 Forms of Organisation of Work in Some European
Countries (Percentage of Wage-Earners in Each Country
Employed in Each Type of Organisation of Work) 59

3.8 Percentage of Job-Holders Employed in Some Job Groups in
Spain and EU-15, 2006 59

3.9 Employment Segments per Proportion of Fixed-Term
Contracts and Qualification Levels 59

3.10 Socioeconomic Factors Conditioning the Segmentation of
Quality of Employment in Spain and the EU-15 61

3.11 Employment Segments per Hierarchical Tier for Types of
Job-Holders 62

3.12 Proportion of Job-Holders Aged 15–64 per Country and
Gender, 2008 63

3.13 Average Number of Minutes per Day Spent by Men and
Women on Work outside and inside the Home in Some
European Countries; Population Aged 20–74, 2000 63

1 The Power to Name and Struggles over Meaning
The Concept of Flexicurity

Maarten Keune and Amparo Serrano

INTRODUCTION

Employment and social policies may be understood as a set of techniques devised for the governance of a society (Donzelot, 1994). The notion of governance has two different meanings in this context. First, the policies in question play an important role in efforts to create employment, to curb unemployment, to determine the quality of jobs, and to provide support to the needy. Second, these policies play a key role in the struggle over how these phenomena are to be named and judged. Inherent to employment programmes are ethical theories concerning the objects of policy intervention. They transmit shared ideas about what is meant by work, employment, and unemployment, about what is socially just or unfair, and about the type of actions that are required to achieve the desired objectives and the respective order of responsibilities.

In recent decades, in the wake of profound changes in the production model, a major semantic shift has taken place in ideas concerning employment and social policies in Europe. This shift is exemplified by the spread of a new vocabulary (including such terms as *employability, entrepreneurship, activation, benchmarking,* and *flexicurity*) within policy discourses concerning employment. One of the most recent additions to this new rhetoric, the concept of flexicurity, has come to occupy a central place in political and academic debates regarding new modes of employment and social policy regulation. Flexicurity—a contraction of *flexi*bility and se*curity*—entered the academic and political discourse in the late 1990s, surging to prominence in Europe after the European Commission placed it at the core of the European Employment Strategy in the mid-2000s. Since then, it has been the subject of an increasing number of academic publications, as evidenced by some ten thousand hits in Google Scholar in 2012. It continues to hold a prominent position in more recent European policy, e.g., in the EU's long-term economic and social strategy Europe 2020, adopted in 2010, and in the 2012 communication of the European Commission entitled *Towards a Job-Rich Recovery*.

This volume aims to provide a critical discussion of the flexicurity concept, the ethical theories upon which it is built, and the ideas that it transmits about work, unemployment, and social justice, as well as the policy programmes that it fosters. The book also addresses various alternative and innovative approaches to the conceptualisation and analysis of employment and social policy in contemporary European societies. In doing so, this volume aims to fill a twofold gap in the contemporary debate on employment and social policy. First, many academics and politicians tend to adopt the concept of flexicurity uncritically, readily emphasising its virtues while scarcely questioning its assumptions, providing a clear and unambiguous definition of the notion or critically examining the reforms that are proposed under its flag. Second, the academic community seems to suffer from a lack of alternative concepts and ideas that could reorient the debate on employment and social policies and help to overcome the weaknesses of the flexicurity paradigm. Moreover, alternative concepts and approaches that do exist are often debated in isolation and are rarely brought together.

In the first part of this book, we analyse the prevailing discourses on flexicurity. First of all we will focus on the broad contours of the concept and on its interpretation by its dominant promoter, the European Commission. In this way, we will show how such a new concept can change the understanding of social phenomena and that of the role and objectives of employment and social policy. The flexicurity concept does indeed contribute to the production of alternative interpretative frameworks within which it is possible to think about work. Characteristic features of these alternative frameworks are their emphasis on individual autonomy and responsibility and their lack of attention to the interdependent nature of social relations and to the fact that the affirmation of interpersonal dependence (one of the essential pillars of social protection) is a precondition for the exercise of autonomy (see Dean, this volume). In this way, as will be discussed in detail below, the appeal to autonomy and individual responsibility is accompanied by a trend towards ever-increasing vulnerability.

There is no one single flexicurity discourse, however, and not all actors understand or employ concepts like flexicurity in the same way. Actors can adopt, reject, or instrumentalise such concepts to serve their interests and ideas, for example, by giving them a different meaning. We will illustrate this with the example of the European trade unions and employers' organisations and the different meanings they attribute to flexicurity, reflecting their different political positions. The diversity in the way concepts are interpreted and used by actors with different interests means that concepts become part of a struggle over their meaning and translation into policy. This leads us to stress the importance of incorporating power relations into any analysis of the emergence and use of concepts (see also Prieto and Crouch, this volume). The dominant interpretative model in a society at a given point in time can be seen as the product of symbolic and political strategies adopted by a variety of actors in search of discursive hegemony within a permanently conflict-ridden field: the labour market. Particular types of knowledge and concepts concerning work, unemployment, and social justice result from a series of struggles and confrontations. The *epistemes* that are used to name these concepts are essentially open, and they are liable to be challenged, interpreted, and/or refuted. Changes in the balance of power thus play a fundamental role, resulting in changes to the framework used for interpreting the problem. In addition, actors can instrumentalise concepts that are both hegemonic and open in order to pursue their own interests and political projects. Employment and social policies can thus be regarded as a broad nexus of struggles aimed at imposing (or challenging) a defined set of rules and principles that can be legitimately used to organise the field (Bourdieu, 1985: 28). The content and meaning of these concepts are the result of permanent struggles and a fluctuating balance of power.

The chapters in this book contain discussions of several of the most important characteristics of the concept of flexicurity and in particular of the European Commission's interpretation of the concept: a limited, work-first view of labour that is driven by market efficiency; individual responsibility for one's own employment and income situation; and contribution to economic growth as the main indicator of effectiveness. The chapters show how the implementation of this paradigm has enhanced some of the negative trends that have been observed in Europe's labour markets and welfare states in recent years, including the growth of income inequality, insecurity, and precariousness, accompanied by an erosion of social rights, a decline in job quality, reduced possibilities for development and life-course navigation, and a weakening of the workers' voice.

Curbing these trends requires reconsidering the dominant discourses on employment and social policies. This volume aims to contribute to this process by highlighting the importance of concepts and indicators, as well as the ways in which these express and reinforce prevailing power differences and social inequalities. We reconsider the concepts and indicators that are in use in order to broaden the prevailing view of employment and work and reconceptualise the meaning of social justice and our representation of the society in which we wish to live. We also analyse the background, characteristics, effects, and problematic features of the dominant discourses on the labour market and welfare (particularly with regard to the flexicurity paradigm) and present alternative theoretical, normative, and policy approaches to work and social justice. In particular, we emphasise the importance of alternative epistemic frameworks that provide due attention to the collective and political dimension of vulnerability.

This introductory chapter begins with an elaboration of the importance of considering the power to name, proceeding from the observation that the concepts used to define the terms of the labour-market debate are not neutral: Each imposes a specific view of the problem, as well as of possible solutions. The second section of this introductory chapter consists of a semantic analysis of the concept of flexicurity. The analysis focuses on two features of the concept. One is the semantic shift that it creates, illustrated by the example of the European Commission's flexicurity discourse. Strongly promoted by the Commission, flexicurity sparked a metonymic shift in the concept of security by stressing its individualising features, with clear repercussions on the social representation of what the problem is and whose responsibility is involved. The second feature is the ambiguity of the flexicurity concept, which enables its appropriation and instrumentalisation by political actors. Indeed, in the battle for symbolic power, the ambiguity of this concept allows it to be used as an expression of the asymmetrical power relations in specific social contexts. The third section of the chapter outlines the main arguments and alternative approaches developed in the contributions to this volume. This chapter ends with some concluding reflections.

THE POWER TO NAME

Employment policies and the concepts they build upon incorporate interpretative frameworks that orient the gaze directed at work issues, simultaneously contributing to their production and transformation. Analysis of the evolution of the terms used to designate work and the lack of work reveals continuously shifting meanings. The emergence of the concept of unemployment in the late nineteenth century is a good example. This concept assigned a new meaning to the situation 'lack of work', which had previously been construed largely as a result of individual failure. Expressing 'lack of work' as unemployment emphasised interdependency between the fate of the individual, the state of the labour market, and public policy, and radically altered the political capacity for social intervention (Lecerf, 2002). The appropriation of this concept by the social movements of the time and its incorporation into the trade union lexicon transformed the risk of unemployment and the associated loss of income into a collective responsibility, in contrast to the earlier hegemonic notions associated with individual blame (Castel, 1997; Bilbao, 1997). The concept of unemployment also emphasised the inter-connectedness of 'lack of work' with asymmetrical power relations and political inequality. This development supported the hegemony of a socialised conception of risk, a notion stemming from the asymmetry of power inherent in labour relations, the vulnerability of the worker, the intrinsically interdependent nature of social relations, and their character of contingent equilibrium. In a similar way, the quality of employment was transformed into a collective responsibility and became regulated through labour legislation and collective agreements.

The emerging labour legislation and social protection systems enabled the reconciliation of two seemingly irreconcilable premises of the liberal system: (a) the condition of heteronomy and subordination that characterises waged relationships and (b) the recognition of the formal principle of political sovereignty (Donzelot, 1994). This produced a new type of subject: the protected subject. This protected subject is insured against risk (e.g., of old age, unemployment, sickness) and is entitled to collective support. The creation of social and labour legislation called into question some of the most important principles that prevailed in the regulation of the waged relationship under conditions of liberalism (Martin Valverde, 1987): the principle of the equality of contracting parties (and, as such, of subjects governed by free will); the need for abstention on the part of the state (the myth of the self-regulated and self-regulating market; see Polanyi, 1989); and the direct understanding between individual contracting parties (individuals as de-socialised atomised entities). These assumptions were reconstructed in accordance with three principles: the imbalance inherent in every waged relationship, the need for state intervention through social protection, and the collective dimension of labour relations (Palomeque López, 2002). These three premises are the most important pillars upon which the social and political regulation of labour and the socialisation of risk were founded. In most European countries, this regulation of the social condition of workers abated the wage conflict, which was a necessary condition for ensuring social peace and guaranteeing the viability of the industrial productive model.

These pillars thus provided the foundations for the welfare state in Western societies. They also revealed key features of the *epistemes* of the industrial world order: power imbalances in labour relations, vulnerability as a constitutive feature of the labourer, and the interdependence inherent in social relations. The individualistic notion of personal failing was replaced by the notion of social risk and its socialisation: collective solidarity (see Salais, this volume). The question of social risk came to occupy a central position in the way people thought about work, thus relegating aspects related to individual attitudes (e.g., personal negligence, lack of foresight, weak will) and the judgement of such failings (e.g., blame and responsibilities) to the secondary level (Castel, 1997). Instead of the ethical diagnosis that had previously been dominant, its political regulation came to be fostered. The civil contract between labour and capital became a political and socially regulated contract entailing rights and duties between the subject and the collective entity. It was upon this foundation that the edifice of social and labour legislation came to be built.

The notions of employment, unemployment, and social justice are hence subject to continual reconfiguration and, rather than abstract categories or social phenomena, they become social constructions. Employment policy concepts play a key role in interpreting the truth with regard to employment, unemployment or social justice, but also in the configuration of this reality (Serrano, 2009). They also entail ethical theories about how things ought to be (Prieto, 2007). Policy intervention aimed at addressing employment issues accordingly entails a continuous process of constructing and deconstructing a *shared meaning* pertaining to the nature of work.

This points to a need to analyse the ways in which reality is produced through concepts and truths that are presented as rational, meaningful, and beyond doubt. Such an analytical approach entails studying the practices through which meaning is assigned to labour and employment issues, as well as the ways in which knowledge is circulated and fed into collective consciousness and symbolism. It demands that particular attention be paid to the historical dimension when studying social practices and to consideration of the dialectical relationship between discursive practices and the institutional frameworks and social structures in which they are rooted, as well as to the individual and collective struggles that establish the definition of social categories (e.g., *need* or *security*). In other words, they emphasise the need to understand the social as the product of a strategy-based and conflict-ridden dialectical process.

It is therefore important to stress two issues: first, the role played by employment and social policies in the creation of epistemic frameworks that enable knowledge of reality, and, second, the open and political nature of such policies. Employment and social policies can thus be understood and analysed as a field and interplay of forces in which different *voices* fight to gain symbolic hegemony, or the power to name.

CONSTRUCTING FLEXICURITY: THE EUROPEAN COMMISSION AND THE METONYMIC DISPLACEMENT OF THE MEANING OF SECURITY

In recent years, the notion of the protected subject, as developed within industrial societies, is being challenged by the increasing use of 'flexicurity' and similar concepts in the social lexicon. The dominant version of this discourse, as it is put forward by the European Commission, several other European and international institutions, and a number of academics, conjures up a new and alternative epistemic framework for interpreting the state of the labour market. It provides an alternative way of naming problems and assigning responsibility for addressing them. Flexicurity can be seen as an expression of a new political order that has been under construction since the 1980s. This new order is characterised by the flexibilisation of the labour market, the strengthening of the control of capital over the employment relationship, activation and reduction of welfare state dependency, the prioritisation of the quantity of jobs over the quality of jobs, and an increasingly individualised and psychology-soaked notion of work (Crouch and Keune, 2012; Crespo and Serrano, 2011). The notions of flexibility and security had previously occupied contrasting and opposing semantic spaces, which largely enabled the articulation of political antagonisms between the voices of employers and those of workers. Such antagonisms were rooted in the power imbalance and inequality inherent in the respective economic conditions of workers and employers. The hybrid notion of flexicurity restates this antagonism in new terms, allowing the co-existence of different (and unequal) components, thus eliminating their apparently mutually exclusive features.

The concept of flexicurity aims to reconstitute the relationship between flexibility and security within the labour market. It also aims to overcome their traditional contraposition by arguing that, instead of being contradictory, flexibility and security can also reinforce each other and produce important complementarities (Wilthagen and Tros, 2004; Wilthagen, 2005). In the dominant flexicurity discourse, therefore, flexibility and security cease to be distinct categories. Flexicurity is thus proposed as a policy strategy that aims to increase flexibility and security simultaneously. More flexibility *and* more security should lead to 'win-win solutions', which could be expected to further the interests of both workers and employers while overcoming traditional divisions between capital and labour. Indeed, flexicurity is posited as a form of coalescence and synchronisation of economic and social policy, as well as a system of joint and mutual risk management for workers and employers (Wilthagen and Bekker, 2008). In this sense, it attempts to de-politicise employment policy through the *a priori* claim that consensus and common interest can and should prevail.

Within the hybrid notion of flexicurity, increasing *flexi*bility is considered necessary and goes unquestioned. With regard to se*curity*, the issue has less to do with ascertaining how much security should be guaranteed given a higher degree of inevitable flexibility than it does with the types of security that are needed to foster the growing flexibility. It opens the meaning of the notion of 'security' to discussion, thereby downplaying its collective and protective dimensions and advocating individualised risk-containment strategies (Serrano, Fernández, and Artiaga, 2012). Consider the following example from one of the key statements of the European Commission on flexicurity:

> Flexibility, on the one hand, is about successful moves ('transitions') during one's life course (. . .) Security, on the other hand, is more than just the security to maintain one's job. It is about equipping people with the skills that enable them to progress in their working lives, and helping them to find new employment. It is also about adequate unemployment benefits to facilitate transitions. Finally, it encompasses training opportunities for all workers, especially the low-skilled and older workers. (European Commission, 2007: 10)

The notion of security thus undergoes a *metonymic shift*: from social protection to self-insurance. Consequently, security through self-insurance (the adaptability of the worker) becomes the subjective correlation of flexibility (of the labour market).The technology of flexible regulation is presented as an ideal model to ensure the optimal functioning of the labour market and as a remedy for the mismatches that detract from its effective operation. This diagnosis is quite at odds with the original grounds for introducing labour regulation. It suggests that legal regulation, rather than protecting workers, makes them vulnerable. Considerably different founding principles and criteria are cited in order to proclaim the failure of established social and labour legislation to adjust to the flexibility required by the economy.[1] These new principles and criteria are used to justify the continual increase of flexibility and deregulation of labour relations, on the pretext of removing rigidities that are allegedly harmful *to all*. Economic growth then becomes the main criterion for evaluating social performance (see Salais and Méda, this volume).

Incentives for 'self-insurance' are also regarded as an essential facet of the self-regulation promoted by the paradigm of activation.[2] Activation entails the promotion of insurance techniques (i.e., techniques of self-governance), which are intended to prevent welfare dependency by producing subjects who will be active, employable, and adapted to the new economic conditions (see Zimmermann, this volume). The problem comes to be framed in terms of the attitudes displayed by the worker. Policy measures are supposed to focus on these attitudes,[3] thus making it possible to question the ontological and epistemic foundations that had previously supported the paradigm of social protection, thereby enabling the production of alternative *epistemes* (Serrano and Magnusson, 2007):

1) The individual subject becomes the principal locus towards which policy measures are geared, thereby coming to be regarded as constituting part of the problem.
2) There is an increasing tendency to promote the participation of individuals in their own processes of integration. A political contract between the subject and the public services becomes a formal reality: an *activity agreement* regulates the conditionality of entitlement to unemployment benefits, entailing the obligation on the part of jobseekers to take part in active measures and accept available jobs, beginning upon the signature of an *accountability agreement* testifying to the unemployed individual's availability for work. Both of these aspects are fused into the growing emphasis on demanding that 'clients' behave like responsible citizens.

Combating welfare dependency and passivity is pursued through a two-pronged approach in which pressure is exerted from the outside, as well as from within. On the one hand, an attempt is made to influence the behaviour of subjects through penalties (e.g., by restricting access to social protection). On the other hand, biopolitical practices are deployed for the production of 'normalised' subjects through three types of technologies: discipline/normalisation, surveillance, and therapeutic intervention (a paternalistic mode of intervention fundamentally akin to 'therapeutic medicalisation') (Schram, 2000; Méda, this volume). In this manner, dependency is transformed into a form of pathology. Economic and political problems are reframed as questions of personal competences, motives and wills, thus encouraging a process of *de-politicisation* with regard to the management of the social conflict. The sociopolitical character of social exclusion is not allowed to emerge, the new object of policy intervention is the 'inactive' subject (which has been semantically converted into a passive element), and the new problem to be addressed is the risk of dependency.

This new policy rationale gives rise to several major *contradictions*: Whereas the type of policy advocated is aimed at restoring the capacity of self-governance and the power of agency, what is actually being promoted is adaptation to a situation imposed from outside (Crespo and Serrano, 2005). It proclaims empowerment while fostering models of policy intervention that allow no power of decision other than adaptation to the market. *Activation* is presented as the effort to foster adaptability (self-improvement in order to achieve a state of self-insurance), to educate the goodwill of the worker, and to strengthen the subject's responsibility and agency. It is pursued, however, under conditions that the subject cannot and must not change. This approach might actually undermine the collective resources (both conceptual and political) that could enable workers to exercise some control over the asymmetrical and vulnerability-inducing conditions of certain employment situations. As Schmid shows in Chapter 5, active policies should guarantee social rights that allow workers to participate in decisions about work and share the outcomes equally. The exercise of autonomy and responsibility requires freedom, and thus the power and institutional capacities that support such freedom (Zimmermann, this volume). Furthermore, the call for activation is accompanied by an ideological tendency to transform dependency into a moral pathology. The dependency (or, rather, interdependency) that derives from belonging to collective entities (e.g., the state or society itself) is condemned. At the same time, the vulnerability-inducing dependency on the market is concealed and hence made invisible, thus being understood as 'independence' (see Dean, this volume).

Finally, this model of policy intervention understands security and equality in terms of the needs of the labour market. Flexicurity involves ways of adjusting social needs (in terms of equality or adequate jobs) to suit labour-market demands (Jepsen, this volume). This raises and encourages significant *paradoxes* (Serrano, Fernández, and Artiaga, 2012). It involves seeking to induce psychological autonomy in spite of the deeply rooted economic and political heteronomy that characterises the condition of a large proportion of the unemployed and socially excluded. It involves reinforcing the government of wills ('corporate social responsibility' and 'encouraging autonomy on the part of job-seekers') parallel to increasing corporate greed, misgovernance, and the naturalisation of the political interests served by corporate behaviour. The actual shapes that these paradoxes take, however, cannot be disassociated from the power relations and values that are characteristic of individual countries. They are inevitably influenced by a range of factors, including labour and social legislation, the role of social partners, company strategies, and labour-market dynamics, as well as the dominant values and conceptions regarding the role of the welfare state and the functioning of the labour market. This explains how and why the epistemic frameworks described here (which give rise to such notions such as flexicurity) can be translated into highly diverse forms of policy, which subsequently engender highly variable political consequences (see Prieto, this volume).

AMBIGUITY AND STRUGGLES OVER MEANING

The de-politicised representation of work-related regulation that characterises the discourse of the European Commission on flexicurity is matched by the concept's ambiguity with regard to how it should be translated into policy (Burroni and Keune, 2011; see also Schmid, this volume). The flexicurity discourse argues that the labour market can be conceived as a field characterised by the interaction of several different types of flexibility (external-numerical flexibility, internal-numerical flexibility, functional flexibility, and wage flexibility) and security (job security, employment security, income security, and combination security) (Wilthagen and Tros, 2004: 171). These types of flexibility and security can be used for describing the configurations of a labour market, outlining their respective weights, and discussing the interactions between them. Drawing upon such descriptions, the concept of flexicurity is often illustrated and legitimised with examples from the labour-market models in the Netherlands and Denmark, which have had the lowest unemployment rates and highest employment rates in the EU for several years. The Dutch flexicurity model is portrayed as promoting the use of atypical, flexible types of employment while providing these flexible types of employment with rights ('securities') in terms of conditions of employment and social security that are similar to those of standard employment. In contrast, the Danish flexicurity model is presented as a 'golden triangle' that builds upon (a) flexible standard employment resulting from low employment protection, (b) extensive unemployment benefits providing income security to the unemployed, and (c) active labour-market policies aimed at upgrading the skills of and activating the unemployed (Madsen, 2006). The explicit links that are made with these two countries (which are presented as the two 'original' flexicurity countries), along with the position of flexicurity at the core of EU employment policy, have provided the concept with ample legitimacy and placed it high on the policy agenda across the EU.

At the same time, the flexicurity discourse does not provide political actors with any well-defined policy programme (see Crouch, this volume). Even though the European Commission, for example, through its recommendations to the individual EU member states, clearly promotes increased external numerical flexibility combined with active labour-market policies and (limited) unemployment benefits subject to strict conditions, it carefully refrains from explicitly prescribing a single model made up of specific types of flexibility or security over others. Moreover, it does not specify what levels of flexibility or security are appropriate or which types of flexibility and security are compatible or incompatible. In fact, in line with the prevalence of widely different national labour-market models, the Commission's discourse explicitly claims that it does not promote any particular labour-market model, arguing that the policies and outcomes of flexicurity can be produced through various combinations or pathways composed of different types of flexibility and security. This point is further emphasised by the fact that the 'flexicurity models' of the Netherlands and Denmark (i.e., the 'exemplary' models of flexicurity) are constituted of different constellations of flexibility and security. Flexicurity thus emerges as an ambiguous discourse, as it remains unclear which constellations of labour-market institutions do and do not qualify as examples of flexicurity (Keune, 2008; Burroni and Keune, 2011). Indeed, in theory, a labour-market model characterised by high levels of dismissal protection and within-firm flexibility can be argued to fit the flexicurity discourse just as well as a model constituted of low levels of dismissal protection and high-income security through unemployment benefits (Keune and Jepsen, 2007). Alternatively, if in the latter model income security was replaced by training (which is supposed to provide more 'employment security'), it could still plausibly be argued that it follows the flexicurity philosophy. In sum, almost any empirical reality can be described as fitting the flexicurity discourse in one way or another. Flexicurity thus emerges as a 'composite resolution', a purely linguistic combination of opposites that can be applied to virtually any policy mix (Hyman, 2005). Indeed, it is hard to recognise a 'true' flexicurity programme, given that we lack the parameters to make the necessary judgement effectively. This calls into question the usefulness of the flexicurity concept.

The ambiguous and open nature of the flexicurity discourse, paradoxically combined with its high level of political legitimacy, has generated a situation in which flexicurity is a widely accepted concept but in which there is no agreement regarding how it should be translated into actual employment policy. As a result, flexicurity has become a field of struggle, in which different (national and transnational) actors with different opinions on this translation confront each other. This is clearly demonstrated by developments at the European level. Whereas almost all European-level actors (e.g., the Commission, Council, European Parliament, European Trade Union Confederation [ETUC], BusinessEurope) endorse the importance of flexicurity in addressing Europe's labour-market problems, they have very different views on how to translate the abstract concept into policy. In many cases, their respective positions are actually their traditional positions, but now presented under the heading of flexicurity (Keune, 2008).

The positions on flexicurity of the ETUC and the most important European employers' organisation (BusinessEurope) provide a good illustration. In 2007, several months after the Commission produced the communication on flexicurity, the European social partners presented a joint analysis of the challenges facing the European labour market (ETUC et al., 2007). In this document, it is stated that "European Social Partners recognise that in today's labour market it is necessary to improve policy measures which address both the flexibility and security dimensions for workers and employers alike. Applied in the right way, the flexicurity approach can create a win-win situation and be equally beneficial for employers and employees" (53). This would seem to express consensus with regard to the importance of flexicurity for labour-market reform, as well as a willingness to engage in social dialogue on this issue.

However, detailed examination of the position of the two sides on the various elements of the flexicurity debate (Table 1.1) makes it clear that they actually seem to be in complete disagreement on most of the key aspects of the flexicurity debate. The disagreement begins with their general diagnosis of the problems of the labour markets in the EU. For example, BusinessEurope claims that Europe's labour markets need more flexibility in order to allow companies to be competitive, whereas the ETUC claims that companies already have extensive flexibility and that the main problem is excessive flexibility, which leads to precariousness. BusinessEurope perceives flexicurity to involve adaptation to the market; the ETUC considers it to involve human, social, and sustainable development, as well as better jobs. BusinessEurope perceives employment-protection legislation (a key issue in the flexicurity debate) as hampering job creation, whereas the ETUC sees it as a factor that facilitates proper adaptation to changes in the labour market, prevents unfair dismissals, and acts as an incentive for investment in human resources. In addition, BusinessEurope emphasises the need for and advantages of flexible contracts, whereas the ETUC prefers for such contracts to remain an exception. BusinessEurope argues for employment-friendly unemployment benefit systems that foster the quick re-entry of unemployed people into the labour market. The ETUC argues for comprehensive and generous welfare systems.

The positions of the two social partners concerning flexicurity and its elements are clearly worlds apart, representing the 'traditional' views of capital and labour. The flexicurity discourse has not managed to overcome this labour–capital divide, nor has it brought the two sides closer to each other, even though both have stressed the importance of flexicurity. Moreover, several years after these documents were published, it was confirmed that flexicurity had failed to serve as a new impulse for social dialogue in Europe, as it had not managed to bring the two sides any closer

Table 1.1   Confronting the Views of Employers and Unions on Flexicurity

Issue	BusinessEurope	ETUC
General diagnosis EU labour market	Structural reforms are required in order to increase labour-market flexibility and allow companies to be competitive. Workers need employment security rather than job security.	Businesses already enjoy high adaptability. The problem is the increase of precarious jobs with 'excessive' flexibility. Moreover, a flexible labour market does not create more jobs.
On flexicurity	Flexicurity involves facilitating the creation of new jobs, not preserving existing ones. It implies removing obstacles to the creation of new jobs while equipping workers to maximise their chances on the labour market.	Flexicurity involves finding a socially acceptable balance between the needs of adaptable enterprises and the long-term objective of human, social, and sustainable development, in addition to creating more and better jobs.
Employment protection legislation	Stringent EPL hampers the creation and growth of new businesses and jobs. It also has a negative impact on the entry of the less advantaged into the labour market and increases the average duration of unemployment.	Job protection functions as an 'early warning' system, giving workers that have been fired time to look for new jobs or be retrained. This reduces the time spent in unemployment makes it easier for workers to find new jobs.
Flexible contracts	In order to stimulate job creation, it is essential to have access to a variety of contractual arrangements. Part-time, fixed-term, agency work, and other forms of employment enable employers to adapt to changes in demand while allowing workers to respond to their personal needs and preferences.	The principle of the Directive 1999/70/EC is that atypical forms of work should remain exceptions. The ETUC's policy is also to integrate 'non-standard' contracts fully into labour law, collective agreements, as well as into systems of social security and lifelong learning.
Work organisation	In addition to strengthening external flexibility, there is a need to increase internal flexibility (e.g., internal mobility and variations in working patterns and working-time arrangements).	Internal flexibility is an alternative to external flexibility. It aims to advance productivity, innovation and competitiveness, while improving the combination of work with other activities.

(continued)

Table 1.1 (continued)

Issue	BusinessEurope	ETUC
Labour costs	High levels of employment require that labour costs remain contained. The reduction of non-wage labour costs is crucial to job creation.	Wages should be fair, and competitiveness should focus on productivity instead of wage competition.
Lifelong learning, training	Lifelong learning is crucial to competitiveness and the employability of individuals, but legislation is not the appropriate instrument for influencing learning behaviours.	An educated workforce with updated skills is a flexible one, both internally and externally. Nevertheless, businesses continue to decrease their investment in training. They should take responsibility in this regard.
Active labour-market policies	Active labour markets aim to spur unemployed people to be more active in looking for work and/or to improve their employability.	Active labour markets are crucial to building bridges from job to job. With generous benefits, they allow workers to prepare for and seek new employment that is suitable and rewarding.
Unemployment benefits and social security	Employment-friendly social security systems that do not discourage the quick re-entry of unemployed people into the labour market.	Comprehensive and generous welfare systems that limit loss of income and allow workers to prepare for and suitable new jobs.

Sources: ETUC (2007a, 2007b); BusinessEurope (2007).

together (Keune, 2012). The parties continue to represent the interests of their constituents, and any consensus or cross-class alliances with regard to the reform of the labour market seem as far away as ever. More generally, this situation shows how actors can agree on the general discourse on flexicurity while having strong disagreements with regard to the measures that should be taken to balance flexibility and security. It is the ambiguous nature of the flexicurity concept that makes it possible for actors with widely differing views on employment and labour-market policy to subscribe to it. When a precise and operative specification of the concept is needed, however, many of its contradictions come to light, and the cleavages between different views re-emerge.

As illustrated by this example, instead of being guided by flexicurity, political actors tend to shift the focus of political struggles to the interpretation of what flexicurity is and what it is not, attempting to impose their views by using the concept to justify political positions.

ALTERNATIVE VIEWS

This volume proceeds from the assumption that concepts play an important role in the articulation of epistemic frameworks that channel views on work, unemployment, and social justice, becoming not only objects of knowledge, but also instruments for political struggle and change. The concept of flexicurity entails its own particular ways of perceiving work, unemployment, and social justice, and it has created its own struggle concerning the ways in which it should be translated into policy. As emphasised by the authors in this volume, it is therefore of prime importance to analyse which epistemic frameworks the concept shapes and which semantic frameworks it activates.

The first part of this volume discusses the problematic assumptions underlying flexicurity from different perspectives. Flexicurity has been presented as an adequate tool for addressing the three main pillars of the European social contract: labour-market performance, quality of work, and social equality. Colin Crouch discusses the first pillar (labour-market performance), Carlos Prieto focuses on the second pillar (quality of work), and Maria Jepsen addresses the third pillar (gender equality).

In Chapter 2, Colin Crouch discusses (a) why different countries (or groups of countries) adopt different combinations of flexibility and security, as operationalised by employment-protection legislation and unemployment pay-replacement levels, and (b) the respective effects of these combinations on employment performance. With regard to the first question, Crouch stresses the importance of including class relations in the analysis, particularly through indicators that express inequality in collective power (expressed as the strength of employee interest representation), property, and income. He concludes that higher levels of inequality in class power reduce the likelihood of reaching positive-sum compromises in the balance between flexibility and security. With regard to the second question, Crouch examines the central argument behind the debate on worker security (which developed in the 1990s within the OECD, IMF, the European Commission, and a growing number of national governments), which holds that high levels of security have a negative effect on employment levels and increase unemployment. Contrary to the neoliberal thesis, Crouch shows that poor employment performance is also concentrated amongst countries with low levels of unemployment compensation, whereas there are no clear differences between countries with high and with low levels of employment-protection legislation. He therefore concludes that a primarily punitive approach to workers is unlikely to succeed in reducing unemployment. Finally, he demonstrates a link between the policy and employment outcomes of different countries and the balance of class relations. His primary conclusion in this regard is that there is no evidence that employee power has a negative effect on employment performance, as suggested by neoliberal arguments.

In Chapter 3, Carlos Prieto discusses the extent to which the flexicurity approach is capable of tackling problems relating to quality of work and the segmentation of the labour market. He stresses that the focus of the current discussion about the labour market and social protection is in need of adjustment and shows that the focus needs to shift from the current, nearly exclusive emphasis on the quantity of employment towards the crucial dimension of quality of work. Closer attention to the quality of work helps to reveal the complex and multidimensional nature of the interrelationships that structure a specific *employment regime*. Prieto stresses that employment and social policies form just one of the dimensions that shape the performance of the labour market. A broader, multidimensional approach is needed, which includes in its analysis the key roles played by factors such as the production model, competitive strategies of firms, the level of technology, the level of productivity, the size of enterprises, etc. Prieto uses the example of Spain to illustrate this point. The Spanish employment regime places workers in a very vulnerable position, because of an institutional framework that encourages external numerical flexibility, a production regime that promotes low-productivity sectors, trade unions that have limited capacity to counterbalance the power of firms, and competitiveness strategies that are based on temporary employment, intensification of work, high job turnover, low-skilled jobs, low wages, and small firms working as subcontractors. These factors explain the poor performance of the Spanish labour market (in terms of quantity and quality), as well as its strong segmentation. Immigrants and women are over-represented in the precarious work segment. Prieto further shows that, in addition to being a consequence of this employment regime, the high level of vulnerability of Spanish workers is also one of its causes, as it limits the power of workers to influence its characteristics. He also demonstrates that, rather than reducing segmentation, employment policies based on enhancing numerical flexibility contribute to its reinforcement and legitimation. He concludes that, although flexicurity might be suitable for countries with well-balanced power structures (e.g., Denmark), countries like Spain require transversal empowerment interventions, in addition to new social and productive contracts.

Maria Jepsen (Chapter 4) explores the potential of flexicurity to enable greater gender equality and a new gender contract. The chapter is divided into two sections. In the first, Jepsen analyses how gender equality is addressed in the flexicurity paradigm as it is expressed in the policy documents of the European Commission. She argues that the Commission's approach fails to address the roots of gender inequality. It is assumed that gender equality means helping women to combine paid and unpaid work, without any discussion about the basic power imbalances between men and women caused by the unequal distribution of work and care, labour-market discrimination, unequal access to certain employment statuses, gender-segregated labour markets, etc. The understanding of this issue is reduced to ensuring the creation of jobs (i.e., increasing employment rates) that enable women to combine work and family life. In the second section, Jepsen presents an empirical analysis of the correlation between gender equality and five indicators that represent the four dimensions of flexicurity identified by the European Commission (employment protection legislation [EPL], lifelong learning [LLL], active labour-market policies [ALMPs], unemployment benefits, and childcare). She shows that, although some of these measures (e.g., childcare and ALMPs) might increase female employment, they do not necessarily ensure gender equality. Gender-equality policy should go beyond merely implementing supply-side measures and fostering the employment of mothers; it requires a new definition of security and the recognition of the prevalence of an unbalanced gender–power relationship in the labour market, in addition to the need for a broad range of public care services, changes in workplace practices, and the redistribution of paid and unpaid work, among other things. Jepsen concludes that a flexicurity strategy based on supply-side measures and on the assumption that women and men have equal power in the labour market is bound to exacerbate inequality rather than to reduce it.

The second part of this volume includes discussions of a series of alternative views on labour market and social policy that aim to overcome the limits and problematic features of flexicurity and related approaches. The discussions focus on four main alternatives: the transitional labour-market (TLM) approach (Schmid), the capabilities perspective (Salais, Zimmermann), the life-first approach or the eudemonic ethic of social welfare (Dean), and the quality-of-work approach (Méda). In Chapter 5, Günther Schmid develops the TLM perspective as an alternative to the conceptually weak notion of flexicurity. The TLM perspective proposes a gender-sensible life-course perspective as the new orientation for labour market and social policy. TLM theory redefines the social dimension of the labour market by focusing on solidarity through *ex ante* risk sharing as a way to enhance transition capacity, instead of merely providing *ex post* compensation to the losers in the game of market dynamics, through transfers. This *ex ante* solidarity distinguishes the social market economy from the liberal market economy for which the 'social' consists only in charity. Schmid argues that most people accept changes (including transitions) more readily if risks are shared in a just way, thereby grounding the TLM approach on four principles of justice: justice as fairness, justice as solidarity, justice as agency, and justice as inclusion. TLM theory also redefines the allocation function or matching dimension of the labour market by focusing on sustainable transitions (work-life careers) over the life course, instead of optimising only single job-to-job matches. The core idea of TLM thus involves empowering individuals by enabling them to change from one work situation to another in the event of economic and social change or of shifting individual preferences. This approach aims to foster 'freedom from want', as well as 'freedom to act', which means 'positive freedom' to determine one's own life through the endowment of capabilities.

Schmid then draws upon the European Labour Force Survey to offer an empirical comparison of non-standard employment relationships as the alleged core of flexible employment relationships in Europe. From this analysis, he concludes that the contractual variety of employment relationships is increasing and that there is a tendency to shift the related risks to the weakest members of the workforce, combined with low productivity gains. He claims that labour-market policies oriented towards TLM are aimed at providing 'social bridges' that compensate for the higher risks of increasing contractual variety and which ensure that non-standard jobs will either serve as intermediate stages in the work-life or become 'stepping stones' to sustainable jobs and careers. 'Active securities', understood as legally guaranteed social rights to participate in decisions about work and employment and to have equal share in their fruits, as well as in their risks, are an essential precondition for bringing flexibility and security to a right balance. In addition, TLM theory suggests the need to extend the expectation horizon, and therefore the willingness to take risks, through a set of opportunity structures available during the most critical events people encounter during their life course. Finally, Schmid argues that the classic employment contract should be transformed into a citizen-based labour-market status that broadens the flexibility-security nexus by providing further elements of active securities. He then elaborates on two regulatory ideas: (a) rights and obligations with regard to capacity building and (b) coordinated flexibility, both as functional equivalents for numerical or other forms of external flexibility.

In Chapter 6, Robert Salais discusses the potential of the capabilities approach to build the foundation for a new economic and social model aimed at full employment. This model systematically reallocates public resources towards the development of capabilities for people (both within and outside of work) throughout their lives. Salais argues that, in order to be socially just and economically efficient, such policies should be defined and implemented through the profound democratisation of economic, political and social life, with collective decisions taken closer to situations of life and work. The pillars of such a model are a universalistic approach that abandons old divisions between social groups; a concept of identity in which individuals' own lives and work are seen in unity rather than divided up into separate identities (e.g., worker, caregiver, consumer, owner, voter); a new understanding of what policies should achieve (i.e., not only security, but also the freedom to choose one's own way of life); a new definition of citizenship, in which citizens are not merely potential workers, but also capable of voicing their opinions; a 'situated' democracy, in which democratic practices combine representative democracy (especially at the national level) with forms of participatory democracy at the lower levels; and decreased centrality for labour markets in deciding the social and economic future of people, accompanied by increased responsibility for firms, public agencies, and collective bargaining with regard to capability development. Salais outlines a number of challenges. One is to develop negative freedoms (i.e., 'freedom from want') into positive freedoms aimed at preventing social hazards and providing people with the capability of controlling their lives. Another challenge involves replacing the current model of development based on economic growth, accelerated capital accumulation, the mobilisation of labour power, and the rise of hourly labour productivity with a model that incorporates its potential costs and benefits from the perspective of human capabilities and the development of nature. Yet another challenge involves the horizontal reorientation of the representation of labour, thereby representing individuals in their entirety (including their claims as workers, consumers, users of public services, voters, and so on) and finding synergies between them at a 'situated' level. To this end, unions should either seek to cooperate with civil society associations or to include wider claims within their scope.

Salais argues that the capability approach places democracy and its full exercise at the core of collective decision making in every field, in the cognitive and social mechanisms of representation as well as in the production of public knowledge. Moreover, the search for efficient solutions from the perspective of development and its needs should rely on deliberative democratic procedures. Achieving both social justice and economic efficiency requires deliberative procedures in the production of knowledge, including a plurality of voices, as well as a debate on the goals to be achieved and the criteria to be applied. A situated state that bases its policies on the premise that people are autonomous and capable of acting in favour of the common good should therefore provide the institutional frameworks that foster the emergence of the capabilities and collective learning of citizens and, ultimately, individual and collective control of development.

In Chapter 7, Bénédicte Zimmermann calls into question the way in which the flexicurity approach conceives the role of firms with regard to the reconciliation of flexibility and security, as well as with regard to fostering security through employability. Zimmermann argues that, rather than being an individual issue of personal competences, security by employability largely depends upon the conditions and opportunities for professional and competency development in the workplace. She discusses the meaning and political conditions of employee security and proposes going beyond the discussion of transitions to include the issue of professional development. The exercise of responsibility, which is a cornerstone of the flexicurity paradigm, depends on more than individual willingness, competency, and self-regulation alone; it requires appropriate institutional, social, and political conditions in order to allow individuals to determine their own futures.

Zimmermann uses the capabilities approach to place the company and the worker at the heart of the debate, rather than factors outside the enterprise, drawing upon the example of professional development practices developed within the enterprise Bigtrucks. She illustrates the key role that the company plays in creating spaces for deliberation and participation, in providing opportunities and means for fostering individual employability, and in strengthening basic capabilities for professional development (the capability to perform a quality job, to find a balance between different life activities, to be trained, to give an opinion, and to be heard), all of which are beneficial to economic development as well as to worker security. Zimmermann stresses the collective dimension of security and the link with the possibilities offered by the enterprise. Rather than placing security outside the firm (as assumed by the flexicurity paradigm), in order to strike a balance between flexibility and security, the latter should thus also get a place inside the firm.

In Chapter 8, Hartley Dean discusses the need to reconstruct the currently dominant meaning of welfare and work, proposing a life-first approach. He begins by highlighting the key role that paid employment plays in the construction and prevalent meaning of citizenship in industrial societies. In recent years, the emphasis on paid employment has been radicalised, and labour-market participation has emerged as the primary means of access to welfare. In the main conceptions of welfare and work, work is placed before welfare, which shapes the goals of social policy. Rather than aiming to decommodify citizens, social intervention focuses on governing individual responsibilities. Formal paid employment becomes the prevalent and recognised form of work, subordinating to its logics other forms of work (e.g., care work, recreational work, voluntary work, and informal work) that shape individuals as human beings. Dean stresses the need to turn these prevailing neoliberal assumptions around and to reconstruct social policy approaches from an alternative ethical perspective, articulated with reference to the following two dimensions: reinforcement of a eudaimonic welfare ethic and a life-first approach with regard to employment policies.

Strengthening the responsibilities of both employers and the state to meet people's need to work, to provide decent work, and to meet the needs of workers who cannot become immediately productive is a key premise of this alternative approach. Key dimensions include the redefinition of the ethics of employment practices, a reconstruction of popular and political understandings of work and welfare, a greater acceptance of the value of forms of work other than paid employment, and the commitment of nation-states to embracing fairness and security. The central contention of Dean is that people need to work and that we share a collective responsibility to let them work, whether or not their work takes the form of paid employment. This amounts to an inversion of the prevailing neoliberal assumption that work is an individual responsibility and that people must be made to work.

In Chapter 9, Dominique Méda analyses the reasons underlying the consensus in the political and scientific domains with regard to flexicurity. She highlights three main reasons. The first involves the symbolic efficiency of some scientific disciplines (particularly economics), combined with the political authority of certain institutions (e.g., the OECD) to incorporate the role of institutions (EPL, rigidity of wages, generosity of unemployment benefits) into their reasoning and equations, developing the argument that protective institutions obstruct flexibility, and hence employment creation and growth, and foster labour-market segmentation. The second reason concerns the practice of using countries with high levels of social protection as reference models (and thus as an alternative path to the liberal regime of modernisation) and the perception of this paradigm as the proper way to reconcile social goals (high employment performance) with economic goals (high competitiveness) through high unemployment benefits (providing security) and low employment protection (providing flexibility).

Méda analyses how the implementation of flexicurity has resulted in the development of policies that are aimed primarily at the increase of flexibility while the security dimension is translated into work-first policies designed to enhance labour participation. She also shows how the inappropriateness and unsustainability of this flexicurity model has become particularly evident during the economic crisis, as it has least affected the countries that offer high social protection and stable employment. Finally, Méda emphasises the need for alternatives to flexicurity, proposing the concepts of decent work and quality of employment as key concepts for an alternative approach, in which economic development depends upon social rights and not the other way around. Establishing these principles requires an alternative model of development, as well as new and broader indicators (that go beyond the GDP growth rate) to measure development, especially including social justice and the preservation of natural heritage.

DISCUSSION

Several general points emerge from these chapters. First, the orthodoxy of work and welfare analysis and policymaking has been dominated by economic and psychological approaches that emphasise the precedence of market coordination and the responsibility of the individual. These approaches suffer from deficits in both the sociological and political realms. They overstate the possibilities of individuals to influence their own situations and to be responsible for their fates; they have an unrealistic belief in the capacity of the market to produce beneficial outcomes; and they obscure the interdependency between vulnerability and asymmetrical power relations. They also downplay the importance of such political questions as social justice, democracy, collective responsibility, and solidarity. The alternative approaches advanced by the authors in this volume aim to move away from this orthodoxy in several ways. They underline the need to assign greater importance to the institutional and political conditions of work and welfare in our analyses, as well as in assessing the empowerment capacity of employment policies.

With its primary emphasis on economic growth, self-regulating markets, and related supply-side and activation policies, the orthodox approach has a very simplistic, one-dimensional conception of the labour market. This severely limits our understanding of its actual functioning. Insufficient attention is paid to a series of crucial aspects that play key roles in determining the creation of employment, the quality of work, and the extent to which the labour market promotes equality. In his chapter, Prieto argues for a more complex and multidimensional view that considers all dimensions of what he calls the employment regime: all factors that directly or indirectly affect the quality and quantity of employment and its distribution over social groups. Other authors emphasise the importance of specific dimensions, including macroeconomic policies (Schmid, Salais), power asymmetries (Jepsen, Crouch, Prieto), or the role of the firm (Zimmermann, Dean, Méda).

The exclusive focus on economic growth and market efficiency also diverts political attention away from important dimensions of human well-being, including the quality and 'decency' of jobs (Méda, Prieto, Schmid), the eudemonic dimension of work (Dean), the freedom to act (Zimmermann, Salais), the adjustment of the market to the needs of workers rather than adjusting workers to the needs of the market (Schmid, Jepsen), unity of life as opposed to fragmented human beings (Salais, Prieto, Méda), the sustainability of development and the safeguarding of our environment and natural heritage (Méda), and the empowerment of both employers and employees (Schmid, Crouch, Zimmermann).

The authors further emphasise the need to rely on the right informational base and political procedures, in addition to addressing the right questions. The present practice of considering only a limited number of standardised, quantitative economic and financial indicators in the evaluation of socioeconomic development in general, and labour-market performance in particular, is insufficient and fosters a developmental model based on economic benchmarking and low costs. It should be complemented by the evaluation of the additional aspects here developed, including quality of work, the sustainability of the developmental model, social justice, and equality. Key procedural issues include the construction of institutional capacity through the establishment of learning communities (Schmid and Salais) or the establishment of procedures of public deliberation (Méda) and deliberative democracy (Salais). Deliberative enquiry and participatory representation (instead of representative democracy alone) are key conditions for the deconstruction of scientific data and political dogmas, as well as for the construction of well-informed and broadly supported policies representing the ideas and interests of different social groups. As argued by Salais, situated democracy and collective learning involve voicing several different perspectives at the same time.

Another issue stressed by several authors in this volume is the need to ensure the responsibility of enterprises in the task of finding an adequate balance between flexibility and security. As noted by Zimmermann and Dean, enterprises play a key role in determining the actual levels and shape of flexibility and security through their social and HRM policies and practices.

However, they are hardly ever held accountable for their actions in this respect, except for their obligation to respect the law, and it is by and large accepted that their primary pursuits are profits and growth. At the same time, individuals are invested with important responsibilities to be flexible, act flexibly, and moderate their wages in the service of these enterprise goals, and are expected to strengthen their own security by improving their employability. This imbalance should be redressed by achieving a more even distribution of responsibilities and gains between capital and labour.

An additional issue raised by some of the authors involves the need to revise the underlying assumptions of the prevalent scientific and political debate on flexicurity, which is often based on general empirical presuppositions that are not necessarily correct. Examples include the supposed trade-off between employment protection and unemployment (Crouch) and the supposedly positive relationship between unemployment and the level of institutional protection of unemployment (Méda), between labour-market segmentation and strictness of employment of institutional protection in general (Prieto) and between economic participation and gender equality (Jepsen). These assumptions have turned into axioms, even though they are empirically and theoretically unfounded. According to Salais and Méda, this perverse development can be attributed in part to the questionable objectivity of many experts.

CONCLUSIONS

Concepts play an important part in the articulation of the epistemic frameworks that channel prevailing views on work and unemployment. Over time, new concepts have advocated new ways of understanding work, the lack of work, social justice, and the responsibilities of the individual and the collective, as well as appropriate policy interventions in these areas. In recent years, the concept of flexicurity has been the core concept used for transmitting a new view of the labour market. Promoted vigorously by the European Commission, it fosters a view in which the need for continuously increasing flexibility is the basic and inevitable assumption, and the understanding of security is acquiring an increasingly individualistic quality, moving from social protection to self-insurance or individual adaptability. Moreover, it is assumed that flexicurity is able to overcome the traditional contradictions between flexibility and security, aiming to blend the two into a single notion, de-politicising the relationships between capital and labour in the process.

Flexicurity is now a core concept in the European labour-market debate, and it enjoys a high level of legitimacy. As demonstrated in this volume, however, this does not mean that the concept is undisputed. On the one hand, although most political actors proclaim their support for flexicurity, some reject it, refusing to take for granted the eternal need for more flexibility, the abandonment of collective social protection, and the individualisation of security. On the other hand, as we have shown, the ambiguous nature of the concept allows political actors to assign their own interpretations, thus instrumentalising it for the promotion of their own political projects. Rather than rejecting flexicurity, these political actors are involved in a struggle over its meaning at the national and European levels. The outcome of this struggle then depends upon the prevailing power relations.

The pursuit of flexicurity is most likely to result in the further weakening of labour in relation to capital, the further individualisation of social protection, and an increase in the vulnerability and precariousness of the individual. It is therefore important to identify alternative concepts and approaches that make it possible to question the de-politicising and decontextualised *doxa* that is shaped by the notion of flexicurity, as well as allowing the development of various societal projects based on alternative values and assumptions. This book is intended as a contribution to this endeavour.

NOTES

1. 'Adequate social protection systems that at the same time provide incentives to work are necessary to smooth transitions and keep up consumer demand. The following actions are of particular importance in the short and long term: contractual arrangements: reduce segmentation, harmonise conditions for temporary and permanent contracts (. . .) Modernise social security systems: reduce high marginal effective tax rate on the low paid, boosting demand in the economy and reducing unemployment/inactivity traps' (Council of the European Union, 2008/2009: 8).
2. 'Modern social security systems offering adequate unemployment benefits, as well as active labour market policies, are essential components providing income security and support during job changes. Good unemployment benefit systems are necessary to offset negative income consequences during job transfers, but they may have a negative effect on the intensity of job search activities and may reduce financial incentives to accept work. This can be largely offset by setting up efficient job search support and work incentives, ensuring a balance between rights and obligations (. . .) Active labour market policies, too, have a positive effect on the feeling of security among workers' (European Commission, 2007: 14).
3. 'Effective labour market policies (ALMP) that help people cope with rapid change and ease transitions to new jobs (. . .) By implementing ALMP such as an efficient job search support and good work incentives, jobseekers can be encouraged to find new employment. Job search courses and job clubs have been shown to be among the most effective measures to help the unemployed find a job' (European Commission, 2007: 12–13).

BIBLIOGRAPHY

Bilbao, Andrés. *El accidente del trabajo: entre lo negativo y lo irreformable.* Madrid: Siglo XXI, 1997.
Bourdieu, Pierre. *¿Qué significa hablar?* Madrid: Akal, 1985.

Burroni, Luigi and Maarten Keune. "Flexicurity: A Conceptual Critique." *European Journal of Industrial Relations* 17(1) (2011): 75–91.

BusinessEurope. *Commission Communication: Towards Common Principles of Flexicurity.* BusinessEurope Position Paper, 2007http://www.businesseurope. eu/DocShareNoFrame/docs/2/ONJAKENCJDHGAHIFOCIFGIBKPDB39D-W1269LTE4Q/UNICE/docs/DLS/2007–01553-E.pdf.

Castel, Robert. *Las metamorfosis de la cuestión social: una crónica del salariado.* Buenos Aires: Paidós, 1997.

Council of the European Union, *Joint Employment Report 2008/9,* 6452/09, 2009.

Crespo, Eduardo and Amparo Serrano. "The Paradoxes of the Active Subject in the Discourse of the EU Institutions." In *Making It Personal. Individualising Activation Services in the EU,* edited by Rik van Berkel and Ben Valkenburg, 107–127. Bristol: Policy Press, 2005.

Crespo, Eduardo and Amparo Serrano. "The Psychologization of Work: The Deregulation of Work and the Government of Wills." *Annual Review of Critical Psychology* 8 (2011): 43–61.

Crouch, Colin and Maarten Keune. "The Governance of Economic Uncertainty: Beyond the 'New Social Risks' Analysis." In *The Politics of the New Welfare States in Western Europe,* edited by Giuliano Bonoli and David Natali, 45–67. Oxford: Oxford University Press, 2012.

Donzelot, Jacques. *L'invention du social. Essai sur le déclin des passions politiques.* Paris: Edition du Seuil, 1994.

European Commission. *Towards a Job-Rich Recovery..* Communication from the Commission to the European Parliament, the Council, the European economic and social committee and the committee of the regions, COM(2012) 173 final, Strasbourg, 2012.

European Commission. *Council Conclusions towards Common Principles of Flexicurity.* Brussels: COM(2007) 359 final, 2007.

European Trade Union Confederation. "Collective Bargaining Information Bulletin 2007/4: The European Strategy for Flexicurity: How the OECD Indicator on Employment Protection Legislation Will Undermine Social Europe and Transitional Security." 2007a. http://www.etuc.org/IMG/pdf_EPLOECD.pdf.

European Trade Union Confederation. "The Flexicurity Debate and the Challenges for the Trade Union Movement." 2007b. http://www.etuc.org/IMG/pdf/ Depliant_Flexicurity_EN.pdf.

European Trade Union Confederation, BusinessEurope, UEAPME, and CEEP. *Key Challenges Facing European Labour Markets: A Joint Analysis of European Social Partners.* 2007. www.businesseurope.eu.

Hyman, Richard. "Trade Unions and the Politics of European Integration." *Economic and Industrial Democracy* 26(1) (2005): 9–40.

Jørgensen, Henning and Per Kongshøj Madsen. "Flexicurity and Beyond— Reflections on the Nature and Future of a Political Celebrity". In *Flexicurity and Beyond: Finding a New Agenda for the European Social Model,* edited by Henning Jørgensen and Per Kongshøj Madsen, 7–35. Copenhagen: DJØF Publishing, 2007.

Keune, Maarten. "Flexicurity: A Contested Concept at the Core of the European Labour Market Debate." *Intereconomics* 43(2) (2008): 92–98.

Keune, Maarten. "Flexicurity: A New Impulse for Social Dialogue in Europe?" In *The European Union and Industrial Relations—New Procedures, New Context,* edited by Stijn Smismans, 206–224. Manchester: Manchester University Press, 2012.

Keune, Maarten and Maria Jepsen. "Not Balanced and Hardly New: The European Comission's Quest for Flexicurity." In *Flexicurity and Beyond,* edited by

Henning Jørgensen and Per Kongshøj Madsen, 189–211. Copenhagen: DJØF Publishing, 2007.

Lecerf, Eric. *Le sujet du chômage*. Paris: L'Harmattan, 2002.

Madsen, Per Kongshøj. "How Can It Possibly Fly? The Paradox of a Dynamic Labour Market in a Scandinavian Welfare State." In *National Identity and the Varieties of Capitalism: The Danish Experience*, edited by John Campbell, John Hall, and Ove Pedersen, 321–355. Montreal: McGill-Queen's University Press, 2006.

Martin Valverde, Antonio. "La formación del Derecho del Trabajo en España." In *La legislación social en la historia de España. De la revolución liberal a 1936*, edited by A.A.V.V, 32–48. Madrid: Congreso de los Diputados, 1987.

Palomeque López, Manuel Carlos. *Derecho del trabajo e ideología*. Madrid: Tecnos, 2002.

Polanyi, Karl. *La gran transformación: crítica del liberalismo económico*. Madrid: Ediciones La Piqueta, 1989.

Prieto, Carlos. "Del estudio del empleo como norma social al de la sociedad como orden social." *Papeles del CEIC* 1 (2007): 2–27.

Rogowski, Ralf. "Governance of the European Social Model: The Case of Flexicurity." *Intereconomics* 43(2) (2008): 82–91.

Schram, Sanford. "The Medicalisation of Welfare." *Social Text* 18(1) (2000): 81–107.

Serrano, Amparo. "The Battle of Ideas in the European Field: The Combat to Defeat Unemployment and the Struggle to Give It a Name." *Transfer—European Review of Labour and Research* 15(1) (2009): 53–71.

Serrano, Amparo, Carlos Jesús Fernández, and Alba Artiaga. "Ingenierías de la subjetividad: el caso de la orientación para el desempleo." *Revista Española de Investigaciones Sociológicas* 138 (2012): 41–62.

Serrano, Amparo and Lars Magnusson. *Reshaping Welfare States and Activation Regimes*. New York: Peter Lang, 2007.

Wilthagen, Ton. "Striking a Balance? Flexibility and Security in European Labour Markets." In *Employment Policy from Different Angles*, edited by Thomas Bredgaard and Flemming Larsen, 253–267. Copenhagen: DJØF Publishing, 2005.

Wilthagen, Ton and Sonja Bekker. "Flexicurity: Is Europe on the Right Track?" In *Flexicurity and the Lisbon Agenda: A Cross-Disciplinary Reflection*, edited by Frank Hendrickx International Studies on Social Security series, 33–48. Antwerp: Intersentia, 2008.

Wilthagen, Ton and Frank Tros. "The Concept of Flexicurity: A New Approach to Regulating Employment and Labour Markets." *Transfer—European Review of Labour and Research* 10(2) (2004): 166–186.

2   Class Relations and Labour-Market Reforms

Colin Crouch

INTRODUCTION

A major consequence of the decline of Keynesian economic policy and its replacement by neoliberalism from the late 1970s onwards was to change the institutional and policy location of the search for high levels of employment. Keynesianism had made this a central economic policy responsibility of government, with the implication that measures that secured the jobs of individual employees had no negative consequences for those who did not have jobs; government would take measures to expand employment to soak up the unmet demand for employment. Workers' search for secure employment was not seen as a zero-sum game, although it needs to be remembered that full employment was implicitly defined in terms of men's jobs only.

Under neoliberal regimes, governments changed their priority to the maintenance of price stability. They remained concerned about employment levels, as their re-election chances were affected by them, but areas of policymaking other than core macro-economic policy had to bear the main responsibility: in particular the labour-market behaviour of employers and workers. This produced the now well-known emphasis on the supply side of labour policy. In its strict form, as enacted by US governments and originally recommended by the OECD (1994) and other international institutions, this meant little more than the elimination of both legal measures and collective bargaining outcomes that gave workers some assurance of security in their jobs. It also meant an attack on the level of benefits for unemployed, sick, and disabled workers in order to reduce the reservation wage and persuade such people to take work at low wages. Further, removal of full employment as a direct policy goal turned job protection measures into zero-sum games: One worker's protected status became another's unemployment or relegation to an inferior, segmented temporary labour market. Temporary employment can be a direct consequence of labour-market protection; if it is difficult for employers to make employees with established status redundant, they are likely to avoid taking on new workers with such status, especially if they are not confident about future levels of demand. If they could not take on temporary workers, then they might not take on any at all, indirectly producing an increase in unemployment.

By the mid-1990s, neoliberal economists and international organisations like the OECD and European Commission began to produce evidence to show that, true to their expectations of an insider–outsider problem in protected labour markets, overall employment levels were higher in countries with lower levels of employment protection legislation (EPL). Labour flexibility, in the crude sense of the ease by which employers could hire and fire workers, seemed to produce greater overall *de facto* employment security than attempts to protect people's positions in specific jobs. This unleashed a wave of so-called reforms to labour protection, which is continuing today. Some of the newly democratic countries of Central and Eastern Europe often took to such measures in a radical way, producing some of the least protected labour markets in the industrial world. More recently, advantage has been taken of the European sovereign debt crisis to impose labour-market reforms on countries with major public debts. Meanwhile, however, more recent empirical studies have thrown doubt on the confidence of the original deregulation programme. Various tests of the effectiveness of liberalising reforms have sometimes found no trace of improvements, whereas the OECD (2008) has started to revise some of its earlier extreme support for such measures, particularly in the face of growing inequality. A more positive form of the supply-side approach developed under the slogan of active labour-market policy (ALMP), a concept that had been initiated by Swedish policymakers as early as the 1950s. Under its new form, this approach included measures such as increased attention to education and training, in order to upgrade the quality of the labour force (Morel, Palier, and Palme, 2012). The approach could come in various forms; in some cases (as in the UK after 1997) it came in a combination of 'carrot and stick' with 'workfare' policies; in others the emphasis was more supportive towards unemployed people (Bonoli, 2012).

The situation has now become confused, with policymakers urging or imposing reforms with a confidence that is no longer so widely supported by experts and the evidence, and with a wide range of differently motivated policies claiming to operate on the supply side. One constructive outcome from the debates of the 1990s was the demonstration by several studies that not all kinds of labour security were incompatible with flexibility. Measures that, instead of protecting people in their existing posts, improved their employability and maintained their standard of living during periods of unemployment, were particularly favoured (see several chapters in Morel, Palier, and Palme, 2012). This produced the 'flexicurity' agenda, as discussed elsewhere in this volume.

Flexicurity policies emerged pragmatically, particularly in Denmark and the Netherlands, from attempts to resolve pressing problems, but they could easily be related to analyses of so-called new social risks, which were being developed around the same time by a number of labour-market and social policy specialists. This started by defining certain 'old' social risks—primarily unemployment, sickness, disability—which were deemed to be of declining relevance in the late twentieth and then early twenty-first centuries. Instead, the circumstances of modern life created a set of 'new' risks, prominent among them being those associated with: the entry of large numbers of women into paid work; the ageing of the population; the decline of unskilled industrial manual work; and the expansion of private services employment. Each of these indicated some possibilities for social policies that would expand labour force participation. In particular, authors placed emphasis on policies concerning childcare, pension reform, countering social exclusion, and increasing access to private care services (Bonoli, 2007; Taylor-Gooby, 2004).

The aspect of this general policy reorganisation that will be scrutinised here will not be the general array of policies that appeared under the 'new social risks' and flexicurity agendas, many of which have been highly valuable in improving employment opportunities and reducing barriers between labour-market insiders and outsiders. Rather, attention will concentrate on the claims that 'old' nineteenth-century and early twentieth-century risks had really been transcended. These claims form part of a larger set of arguments that contend that, with the demise of extreme poverty and the rougher kinds of manual work in the richer societies, there are no longer problems of 'class'. Much original social policy was concerned with 'class risks', designed to compensate manual workers for their lack of individual or family private property by enabling them to lay claim to collective resources. Propertied classes had security in that they could fall back on their wealth to help them through difficult times, or to assist family members finding less economic success than others. Advocates of the case that these class issues no longer existed could not contend that there were no longer major inequalities in property ownership, as they obviously continue. Their case was that, once the overall level of living in a society has risen, these inequalities do not matter. There is continuing debate over this contention, but our concern here will be concentrated, not on the material consequences of inequalities, but on those for power and decision-making capacity. We are therefore concerned with class in its Marxian meaning as signifying property relationships and their power implications, rather than the cultural and material aspects of those relationships that are usually seen to constitute class, particularly in Anglo-American intellectual traditions.

FROM INSECURITY TO UNCERTAINTY

For this task we need to move from the study of (in)security to that of (un)certainty. We may say that a person has a secure position (for our purposes in the labour market, but the term can be extended to many other areas of life) if there is a zero or very low probability that it will be lost and replaced by an inferior one. An important difference between job and employment security, so important to the flexicurity literature, is that in the former case a specific position is not lost at all; in the latter it may be lost but with a high probability of being replaced by one of at least equal quality.

Behind (in)security stands a larger concept, the absence of knowledge about one's situation, be it the labour market in the narrow sense or more generally about the economic parameters that affect one's life. This is the question of uncertainty. Its relationship to insecurity is complex. If one's position is uncertain, it is certainly insecure, but it is possible to be certain that one's position is insecure. However, that kind of certainty is only a certainty that a higher level of uncertainty exists, uncertainty about the likelihood that one's position will improve again. More generally, policies for social and labour-market security can be seen as strategies for helping people who have inadequate knowledge and resources to be self-sufficient in their encounter with uncertainty (i.e., most people).

A classical starting point for the study of economic uncertainty is the article by Knight (1921) that established a distinction between uncertainty and risk. If we can make probability calculations about the chances that an uncertain event will occur, we convert it into risk. In the economic field, probability calculations can be turned into money propositions. This simple point is fundamental to the entire financial sector of the economy and to concepts of insurance, investment, rates of interest, and share prices. Once prices can be placed on risks, people can invest in them, thereby sharing the initial risk widely and reducing the threat that it presents to either the original bearer of the risk or those to whom it has been sold. Uncertainty is never eliminated through this process, but it is shared, and therefore reduced, and can be compensated by agencies who, by taking on a wide range of risks, limit the impact on them of failure occurring in any one of their decisions to accept a share in a risk.

To engage in risk markets requires wealth and knowledge. A background of wealth is necessary if one's risk-worthiness, one's collateral, is to be accepted; it is also necessary, or at least strongly advisable, if one is going to indulge in risk trading. Knowledge is necessary, because the calculation of any but the simplest risks requires considerable information about threats to the risk and the chances that negative events will occur. Information of this kind is expensive, which serves as a further wealth-based barrier to entry into the risk market for those without a strong asset base.

There are therefore fundamental inequalities in the ability of persons to engage in risk markets, depending on their stock of individual (or family) assets. As we know, in all capitalist societies, wealth is far more unequally distributed than income, partly because it tends to remain in families for lengthy periods and does not face competition in the market as does human capital—the asset that produces income and its inequalities. Strangely, contemporary analysis of class inequalities concentrates on income and elements of lifestyle that are primarily determined by income and tends to ignore wealth. Although the distribution of wealth, like that of income and many other quantifiable attributes, forms a continuum, it is far easier than within income to distinguish among the following:

1. Those with large assets, great enough to protect their level of living against all but the most extreme shocks and to enable them to participate in risk markets likely to increase their assets further.
2. Those whose property is mainly limited to illiquid assets (primarily residential property) of which they could not divest themselves without major negative consequences for their standard of living, and perhaps small financial assets insufficient to protect them from any but very minor shocks.
3. Those with virtually no assets at all other than those they need for daily life.

The classic social policies that dealt with 'old' social risks assumed a population coming into the second and third categories, with the great majority being in the third, and therefore unable individually to adopt the solutions to uncertainty used by people in category 1. These solutions would include taking out major private insurance and investing wealth into ventures, which, although they carried some risk, were likely (these persons' expensively rewarded advisors could calculate) to bring in a good return, protecting and advancing the level of assets from generation to generation. Instead, the collectivity of the society as a whole (usually a nation-state) would provide this cover for the great majority of its members: income protection in the face of major definable risks to a person's economic situation, often using the insurance principle (sickness, disability, unemployment, survival past working age, the birth of children); social policy and often trade union action providing protection against or compensation for dismissal or redundancy; union action and sometimes public policy to try to protect the value of earnings.

These social policy tasks could be considered to have been performed and therefore no longer needed on either of two conditions:

i. If the labour-market risks no longer existed.
ii. If large numbers of persons entered category 2, with many becoming sufficiently wealthy to be included in category 1, leaving perhaps a minority of 3 needing special help.

But neither of these eventualities occurred. It might be argued that during the period of Keynesian demand management some of these risks were much reduced, fulfilling condition (i), but that period ended at precisely the moment when arguments about the need to tear down some of these protections started to develop. A globalising economy subject to rapid technological change and changes in the role and identity of different sectors is hardly one in which the importance of the old risks has declined. A far stronger case can be made out for the contrary position. It is not so much a decline of the 'old' risks that has produced powerful campaigns for the abolition of collective protections against them, but the very opposite: People are increasingly likely to need that protection now, and policymakers fear the costs of providing it.

As to (ii), although the very large rise in general affluence that took place during the second half of the twentieth century propelled large numbers of people from category 3 to 2, this did not mean that they were now indistinguishable from category 1 (i.e., able to confront serious labour market risk from their own accumulations of wealth).

The first period of the neoliberal regime (depending on the country concerned, from the late 1970s to the early 1990s) saw rising unemployment and stagnating wages in those countries that began to adopt the new approach, mainly the Anglo-American world (Lansley, 2011). (In most of continental Western Europe, far fewer labour-market changes were adopted; nor were reductions in social expenditure made.) Changes took place following the deregulation of capital markets and the development of sophisticated new financial techniques for risk sharing. These enabled many clearly category 2 people, and even some in category 3, to act as though they were in category 1, by taking mortgages representing eventually more than 100 per cent of the value of residential property in order to sustain their consumption standards. At a lower level, there was during the same period a massive expansion of opportunities for consumer debt through the growth of the credit card. These high-risk levels of credit were funded through the secondary markets (Crouch, 2009). By the time of the financial crash of 2008, a number of countries had levels of consumer debt that exceeded total disposable income. Debt is usually secured against assets, and, historically, only wealthy persons have carried high levels of debt (the poor may well have incurred debts that were, for them, crippling, but the actual sums involved were small). It was distinctive of these very high-debt countries in the early twenty-first century that people on relatively low incomes—the lower part of category 2—also incurred high levels of debt. The OECD first tried to collect data on this issue in 2006, although only a few countries had the necessary statistics available. These are shown in Table 2.1. It is notable that the countries with high debt among low-income people all achieved and maintained particularly high levels of employment, whether these countries were of the so-called liberal form (Ireland, UK, US) or 'flexicurity' cases (Denmark, Netherlands).

The financial markets that drove this system were eventually shown not to have been based on precise risk calculations as the economic models that supported them had contended (Fama, 1971, 1991), but on a volume of transactions so vast and rapid that no one ever actually calculated the risks involved, until the inevitable crisis broke. The effects of this crisis will

Table 2.1 Debt Burdens for Lower-Income Groups, Various Countries, mid-2000s

	Percentage with debt		Median debt as percentage of per capita income	
Percentiles of income distribution	< 20	21 to 40	< 20	21 to 40
Finland	29	40	34	96
Germany	17	29	430	430
Italy	9	19	44	57
Netherlands	31	42	208	542
Spain	16	38	93	107
Sweden	19	45	99	107
UK	31	49	38	30
US	52	70	24	54

Source: OECD (2006: 147–148).

continue for a lengthy period, as major adjustments have to be made. A good deal of consumption growth that took place from around the early 1990s to 2008 was fuelled by this expanded debt rather than through actual income gains. The adjustment may well therefore require taking consumer spending in Western countries back to where it would have been had it been powered by income growth unaided by unsustainable credit. Although there were a small number of casualties among the finance houses involved in these markets, the sector as a whole was deemed to be so important to some national economies (especially Iceland, Ireland, and the UK, to a lesser extent the US) that they would be protected from the decline that will affect incomes in the rest of their economies, making the burden born by the rest that much heavier. This will exacerbate still further the rise in wealth inequalities that took place around the advanced world during the 1990s and 2000s, a good deal of which can be explained by the growing earnings of the financial sector as well as the more general shift that has taken place in national income shares from labour to capital.

In retrospect we can see this period of debt-fuelled consumption (what I have called elsewhere privatised Keynesianism; see Crouch, 2009) as an attempt to make the argument that category 2 people had now joined category 1 in their capacity to deal privately with major financial risk come true. It failed, because its foundations were unstable. With that failure also collapses the idea that class is no longer important for social policy. Different levels of wealth holding continue to be fundamental in determining whether individuals can now face the 'old' social risks with their wealth and knowledge resources. The increasing inequality characteristic of the present period intensifies this problem. To the extent that there is a zero-sum game in financial markets, with wealth (and the knowledge on which it can call) enabling its holders to secure the best deals, those lacking in wealth will get the worst deals.

REAPPRAISING THE LABOUR-MARKET REFORM AGENDA

The neoliberal labour-market reform agenda can be re-examined in the light of this account of the class inequalities of coping with risk. Under the extreme form of the agenda, individuals become responsible for managing their own employment risks—including what training they will need to equip themselves for a changed occupational structure of the future. They cannot expect the state to equip them for labour-market searches or for equipping them with appropriate skills, because state policy is regarded by other parts of the neoliberal agenda as interfering with market efficiency and imposing high tax burdens as a result of its spending programmes. The state therefore shrinks as an agent for reducing uncertainty. But this does not mean that responsibility passes to employers, as under the neoliberal model they too have no duties towards assisting workers. In the ideal neoliberal labour market, there are no employees, only contractors of labour services. In line with this firms have increasingly outsourced their activities. They usually outsource to other firms rather than to individuals, and there have been important recent tendencies for large customer firms to squeeze ever tighter prices out of suppliers, making it difficult for these latter to pursue their own social policies. The measures of labour-market flexibility used by the OECD regard as evidence of inflexibility long average tenures of employees with one employer. This means that firm-specific knowledge and experience are entirely discounted, and firms who take no action to maintain and advance employees' skills in order to retain them are regarded with favour.

If neither the state nor employers have a responsibility to maintain the quality of the labour force, that task falls to individual workers. However, as we have seen, the great majority of workers lack the knowledge necessary to know how they should set about equipping themselves with the skills that will be needed in the future. From the perspective of the overall market, this is not a problem. Provided large enough numbers of workers all try different means of equipping themselves for the future labour market, some will succeed, and that may be all that employers need. The rest can be discarded and required to find work available to the relatively unskilled—which will exist provided wages are allowed to fall freely until the labour market clears. The same logic is routinely applied to entrepreneurs: many of them try ideas, most fail, but enough succeed to sustain a dynamic economy. Those who do succeed join those whose initial position of wealth exempted them from having to take risks in the first place.

And large numbers of those who succeed will do so because they are supported by the knowledge resources discussed above. The model is one that enhances inequalities as the gap between those who succeed and those who fail becomes wider and self-sustaining.

This pure neoliberal model is very rarely found in practice, but the official stance of the EU and the OECD, as well as the actual policy moves of many governments, is that labour-market 'reforms' should move in that direction. The obstinate survival of labour protection is usually attributed to the strength of popular veto groups, or the failure of democratic governments to stand up to vested labour interests, or perhaps the reality of social problems. Far less often acknowledged is the rational basis of resistance.

The refusal of the neoliberal approach to recognise the importance of the knowledge or information problem of ordinary workers leads it to generate a large amount of waste, directly in terms of workers' aptitudes and skills, and indirectly in inadequate demand in economies where workers feel so uncertain that they lack consumer confidence. More generally, the intensification of markets in any field necessarily creates externalities, of which this waste is an example. Some of these are accepted as less important than what is being achieved by the marketisation; to some extent market efficiency is simply a matter of abandoning certain objectives in favour of others. In some other cases, new markets develop to capture what had been an externality for the first market. In other cases again, however, an externality is judged sufficiently important for there to be a public policy response. The question then arises of where that cost is to be borne. In the classic public policy model, the state takes full care of externalities, taxing firms and individuals in order to fund the measures taken. In this way firms are able to keep the profits from their activities and pass the costs of the externalities they create on to other parts of the society. To the extent that corporate shareholders tend to be wealthier than the average citizen, classic public policy constitutes a shift in burden bearing from the wealthy to the average citizen. Partly for this reason, governments often seek to charge the producers of externalities for at least part of the cost of remedying the externality. This is the case with 'polluter pays' approaches to environmental regulation. In the labour-market field, it is the principle behind employers' contributions to social insurance funds. However, if firms are able completely to pass on such costs to customers (or in the case of labour-related charges to employees), the measures may remain regressive in their impact. Finally, firms may be induced in various ways to take their own action in relation to externalities, internalising them. This may result from their market needs (as is the case with company-level training provision and pension schemes) or from the need to achieve deals with trade unions and thereby win good employee relations.

There is therefore no simple formula that relates different interests to policy outcomes, and the contemporary neoliberal climate has generated a variety of responses. The scope for variety is initially established by the non-viability of the pure neoliberal paradigm, which proposes ignoring all externalities that are not remedied by markets themselves. It is generated further by differences in power relations between employers, employees and their representatives, and others in various different (normally national) contexts, and the availability to the various actors of different means of achieving compromises reflecting their power positions. The paradigm indicates that firms should neglect externalities, that governments should not have enough power to try to tackle them, and that in the labour-market burdens should fall on individual workers.

The original Danish flexicurity model enabled employers to shift burdens onto the state: Labour protection laws (which place the burden on employers) were reduced, and the burden of reducing uncertainty for workers placed on the social insurance system and therefore on to the general taxpayer—general taxation being used to relieve employers of part of their contributions to the system. In contrast, systems with strong labour protection laws, primarily in Southern Europe, throw the burden of reducing workers' uncertainty onto employers. This is paradoxical, as Denmark is an example of a society with a strong labour movement and a low level of inequality. Why did this political configuration produce a labour-market policy model that has removed a burden from corporations and thrown it onto the general taxpayer, whereas in Southern European countries with divided or weak labour movements and high levels of inequality the burden has been left with employers? Despite recent neoliberal shifts across wide areas of policy in Denmark (Campbell, Hall, and Pedersen, 2006), the country's social democratic legacy has given it a high level of public expenditure and redistributive taxation and a prominent role for government that has not been fundamentally challenged. The strengthening of corporate power could therefore here result in a transfer of externality management to the state (or rather to a body of taxpayers who were being taxed according to their ability to pay) rather than to a diminution of the state's power. The necessary openness of the Nordic economies has lent power to employers' arguments that they needed labour-market flexibility and help in bearing the costs of providing stable employment. The associated reduction in legal employment rights among Danish employees was made easier to accept by the fact that unions remained strong, not only at the national political centre, but also in individual workplaces, reassuring workers that their lack of rights would not easily lead to arbitrary or unreasonable dismissal. It is possible to hypothesise that the combination of strong union power and a redistributive tax system have helped create trust, which has made it easier for Danish workers and unions to accept both a relief of funding burdens for firms and increased labour-market flexibility.

The contrasting pattern in Southern Europe of high labour protection and low levels of unemployment compensation developed in a context of protected national champion firms, and a relatively small class of employed workers. A high proportion of the workforce was self-employed, worked in firms too small to be covered by legislation, or in the shadow economy.

Although large employers bore the burden of strong labour protection, they were in turn protected from external competition, and trade unions and labour inspectorates were often not strong enough to enforce the protection laws that existed. The protected part of the labour force was a minority, comprising in general two parts: manual workers in large firms, who might associate themselves with communist movements if not pacified, and public employees whose loyalty to the state needed to be guaranteed. Pensions, social insurance, and labour protection could be concentrated on these groups for political purposes and at relatively low cost.

Market liberalisation, including the EU single market programme, have fundamentally threatened this 'Southern' model. Firms became exposed to international competition and therefore began to object to bearing the burden of labour protection. The movement of rural populations into 'normal' employment imposed strains on social budgets in what remain low-tax regimes favouring the rich in highly skewed income distributions. These systems always protected insiders at the expense of excluded groups, but these latter used to be peasants who remained largely outside modern society. In their absence but in the continuing presence of externalising policies, a new group of excluded workers has developed: the young, immigrants, women, the old. These now form a large group of unemployed and workers in temporary posts without access to the extensive rights of the protected workers. This new compromise is not working. The wealthy evade taxation in what remain highly unequal societies; increasing demands are placed on social budgets because of the inadequate development of economies, which across many sectors have not developed post-protectionist comparative advantages. The large number of excluded place a further burden on social security budgets while being unable to generate much demand. There has been no development of positive-sum exchanges of the flexicurity kind. Instead, temporary workers bear the burdens of flexibility, producing segmented labour markets. Meanwhile, the industrial relations and political histories of these countries have produced a context of low trust (Muffels, 2010), in which unions and workers are likely to fight hard in defensive battles to maintain the achievements of the past. They suspect, perhaps correctly, that 'reforms' will bring only a worsening of employees' position without moves to a more constructive new social compromise.

LABOUR-MARKET CONFLICT IN NEOLIBERAL SOCIETIES

This discussion, based on a brief look at a few examples, suggests certain relationships among variables that might help in explaining the different labour-market approaches in different countries. Our central hypothesis is: *The more inequality there is in class power in the work situation, the less likely it will be that positive-sum compromises will be reached in the balance between flexibility and security.*

A wide range of variables could be chosen to represent the state of power inequalities among classes, but for this exploratory exercise we shall just consider two for which data can easily be found, and which are relevant to power in employment relations: the density of trade union membership as an indicator of the collective strength of employees in their relations with employers and the overall level of inequality in a society measured by the Gini coefficient. Unfortunately adequate data are not available to calculate inequality of wealth, the variable in which we are really interested. We therefore have to make do with data for the inequality of income. The flexicurity debate invites us to consider the dependent variables of different combinations of unemployment pay replacement levels (URL) and EPL. OECD statistics are available for both these data for its member states. There is some overlap between income inequality and unemployment compensation, in that the higher is unemployment compensation, the lower the overall level of inequality, if the unemployed constitute a relatively high proportion of the population. We should assume some time lag between the impact of any particular balance of class forces and an outcome in terms of policy outcomes. We shall therefore initially take statistics for union strength and inequality from the mid-1990s, the period by which point it is often assumed that major changes had begun to take place in most countries following the neoliberal turn. Figures for the dependent variables are for 2010, the most recently available at the time of writing. These take into account the initial effects of the Anglo-American banking crisis, but only the early effects of the European sovereign debt crisis.

Developing the initial hypothesis in more detail, initial reasoning based on the above anecdotal discussion would suggest:

1. Where labour's strength is high and inequality low, but where there have been no 'reform' initiatives, both forms of employee uncertainty reassurance will be strongly present.
2. Where labour's strength is low and inequality high, neither form of employee uncertainty reassurance will be present.
3. Where labour's strength is high and inequality low, and where there have been 'reform' initiatives, both forms of employee uncertainty reassurance will be present, but with more emphasis on URL than on EPL.
4. Where protectionist measures once protected favoured firms from international competition, labour's strength is low and inequality high, employers may assume a higher proportion of the burden of employee uncertainty reassurance, leading to higher EPL and lower URL.

The basic data are presented in Table 2.2. The number of cases is too low to permit sophisticated statistical manipulation. We shall therefore concentrate on inspection of countries' relative positions, and rank orderings are

Table 2.2   Basic Variables for Study of Labour Markets

Country	Union Density (%) (c. 1995)		Inequality* (Gini coefficient) (c. 1995)		EPL (c. 2010)		URL (c. 2010)	
	value	rank	value	rank	value	rank	value	rank
Austria	41.4	11	23.3	4	1.93	13	62	10=
Belgium	55.7	6	28.1	13	2.18	7	65	9
Czech Republic	43.5	10	25.1	7	1.96	10=	55	15
Denmark	77.0	3	20.1	1	1.50	18	75	1=
Estonia	32.3	14	34.8	21=	2.10	9	35	20
Finland	80.4	2	22.4	3	1.96	10=	70	6
France	8.8	23	28.0	12	3.05	2	61	12=
Germany	29.2	17	26.7	9	2.13	8	62	10=
Greece	31.3	15	32.2	18	2.73	4	23	22
Hungary	49.1	8	29.7	14	1.65	17	51	16
Ireland	52.3	7	32.1	17	1.11	20	75	1=
Italy	38.1	12	34.8	21=	1.89	15	9	23
Netherlands	25.7	18	29.8	15	1.95	12	73	3=
Norway	57.3	4	23.7	5	2.69	5	73	3=
Poland	30.8	16	31.8	16	1.90	14	48	17=
Portugal	25.4	19	34.2	22	3.15	1	61	12=
Slovakia	56.1	5	26.6	8	1.44	19	39	19
Slovenia	47.7	9	24.3	6	2.51	6	67	7=
Spain	16.3	21	27.8	11	2.98	3	48	17=
Sweden	86.6	1	21.6	2	1.87	16	67	7=
Switzerland	22.7	20	27.6	10	1.14	21	73	3=
UK	33.4	13	33.4	19	0.75	22	61	12=
US	14.3	22	35.1	23	0.21	23	32	21

* Post-tax and benefits income inequality, working age population (18–65) only.
Sources: Union density: Visser (2011); Gini coefficient: OECD; URL: Eurostat; EPL: OECD.

given in the table. In the case of the inequality measure the rank orderings are in reverse order (i.e., the most egalitarian have the highest rankings).

To ease discussion, we can group countries broadly into those with relatively 'very high' values (positions 1 to 5), 'high' (6–10), 'intermediate' (1–13), 'low' (14–18), and 'very low' (19–23). This gives us the distribution shown in Table 2.3 (with countries having very high or very low values on

Table 2.3   Countries Grouped for Independent Variables

A. General employee strength (high union strength and low inequality)	**Denmark, Finland, Sweden, Norway,** Slovakia, Slovenia, Czech Republic (intermediate union strength: Austria; indeterminate inequality: Belgium)
B. General employee weakness (low union strength and high inequality)	**US, Portugal,** Netherlands, Greece, Poland (intermediate union strength: Estonia, Italy, UK; intermediate inequality: France, Spain)
C. High union strength but high inequality	Hungary, Ireland
D. Low union strength but low inequality	Germany, Switzerland

both scores in bold type). The close association between our two indicators of the strength of employee interests is shown in the fact that only four countries lie outside the two main categories.

We now allocate the countries in a similar way according to the two dependent variables (Table 2.4). Countries are here indicated in bold if they occupy the 'very' positions conforming to their box. Countries with an intermediate position on one variable are seen as having contrasting positions (the intermediate position being counted as opposite to the one on which they held a high and low position. In fact, in all but one case (Austria) their high/low position was very high or very low.

Amalgamating the two groupings gives us the pattern shown in Table 2.5.

According to our hypotheses 1 and 3, countries that appear in A (labour strong in balance of class forces) should appear in either I or II, depending on whether they have experienced a labour-market reform process. This is confirmed for all our A cases except the Czech Republic and Slovakia, although only Denmark and Sweden (possibly Austria)

Table 2.4   Countries Grouped for Dependent Variables

I. General high protection (high EPL and high URL)	Norway, Belgium, Germany, Finland, Slovenia
II. High URL, low EPL	Denmark, Ireland, Sweden, Switzerland (intermediate EPL: NL) (Austria)
III. Low URL, high EPL	Greece, Czech Republic, Estonia, Spain (intermediate URL: France, Portugal)
IV. General low protection (low EPL and low URL)	USA, Slovakia, Italy, Hungary, Poland (intermediate URL: UK)

Table 2.5 Countries Grouped on Independent and Dependent Variables

	I	II	III	IV
A	Finland, Norway, Slovenia (Belgium)	Denmark, Sweden (Austria)	Czech Republic	Slovakia
B		(Netherlands)	Greece (Estonia, France, Portugal, Spain)	US, Italy, Poland (UK)
C		Ireland		Hungary
D	Germany	Switzerland		

conform to the flexicurity reform hypothesis. According to hypotheses 2 and 4, countries that appear in B (labour weak in balance of class forces) should appear in IV, unless there is evidence that firms benefited from protectionist regimes, when they should be in III. All our B cases except the ambiguous one of the Netherlands do appear in these boxes. As to this found in the 'protectionist' box BIII, France, Greece, Portugal, and Spain are all countries where there is strong evidence that, during the formative years of the social policy regime, industrial employers did indeed enjoy a compromise with the state of the kind suggested above. France had its noted regime of 'national champions' (Hayward, 1995), whereas the other three all had periods of dictatorship until the 1970s that kept them outside the full market economy. Estonia's position in this group cannot, however, be explained in this way. The other members of category B are to be found in IV, as in hypothesis 2. There is no evidence that employers experienced the protectionist social compromise in these cases.

Three of our four countries with mixed measures of labour strength are to be found in boxes I (Germany) or II (Ireland, Switzerland), suggesting that strength on one variable has been enough to secure class compromises. Hungary, however, does not fit that account.

It is notable that whereas the hypotheses suit Western European countries quite well, the Central and Eastern European states are found in very diverse positions. This is not surprising, for several reasons, but it means that the body of knowledge about the variables discussed in this chapter that has been developed for Western economies does not help us in accounting for what has been happening in Central and Eastern Europe. The old state socialist system was of course even more protectionist than anything practised in the Western capitalist dictatorships, and the entire approach to unemployment was different. Class relations were also completely different. The protectionist system was swept away after 1990 and an employing class emerged, although often a multinational one, but it is more complex to disentangle the extent to which the treatment of unemployment and

Table 2.6   Union Membership Decline

Country	Union Density (%)		Change 1995-2010	Country	Union Density (%)		Change 1995-2010
	c. 1995	c. 2010			c. 1995	c. 2010	
Austria	41.4	29.1	-12.3	Netherlands	25.7	21.0	-4.7
Belgium	55.7	51.9	-3.8	Norway	57.3	53.3	-4.0
Czech Republic	43.5	17.4	-26.1	Poland	30.8	15.0	-15.8
Denmark	77.0	68.8	-8.2	Portugal	25.4	19.3	-6.4
Estonia	32.3	6.7	-25.6	Slovakia	56.1	17.2	-34.9
Finland	80.4	67.5	-12.9	Slovenia	47.7	26.6	-21.1
France	8.8	7.6	-1.2	Spain	16.3	15.9	-0.4
Germany	29.2	18.8	-10.4	Sweden	86.6	68.8	-17.4
Greece	31.3	24.0	-7.3	Switzerland	22.7	17.8	-4.9
Hungary	49.1	16.8	-32.3	UK	33.4	27.4	-6.0
Ireland	52.3	36.6	-15.7	US	14.3	11.9	-2.4
Italy	38.1	35.1	-3.0				

Sources: As for Table 2.2.

employment protection evolved from the state socialist system or diverged sharply from it.

Keune (2007) has done this for the Czech Republic and Hungary, and Spieser (2009) for Poland. Both studies demonstrate a powerful drive for producing market economies where risk management is individualised, as a reaction against the state-socialist past. Both also describe systems of considerable political volatility, which shifts in, for example, the partisan character of governments producing more extensive but also more superficial changes than in countries with stronger path dependencies flowing from longer stable histories. Keune in particular also stresses the role of external agents—multinational firms and international agencies—rather than local elites in shaping institutions; especially relevant here is the often contradictory policies embodied in the EU's *acquis communautaire*. Keune, however, also presents evidence consistent with the role of class hypothesised here. A market-oriented capitalism had already taken root in Hungary before 1989, and this can explain some subsequent contrasts with the Czech case: for example, less collective bargaining, less concern with social policy, and a large informal sector. In Poland, Spieser shows, different interest coalitions were able to influence different areas of policy.

In the mid-1990s, when our measures of union strength were taken, union membership in CEE was inflated by continuation of old communist union membership lists. In the following years that membership collapsed. Table 2.6 shows the extent of decline in union membership in all countries covered. With the exception of Poland, where membership was already relatively low, the steepest declines are found in the Central and Eastern European countries. It is likely that Hungary and Slovakia 'really' belong with box BIV. Slovenia would seem to share Germany's ambiguous position. However, these allocations are still unsatisfactory, as the Czech Republic would seem to belong in the 'protectionist' box BIII for no obvious reason.

DOES IT ALL MATTER? WORKERS' SECURITY AND EMPLOYMENT

The central argument behind the debate over workers' security was that developed in the 1990s in the OECD, IMF, the European Commission, and a growing number of national governments, that high levels of security increased the level of unemployment. This view was later amended slightly by the EU in the light of the Danish flexicurity achievements. It is therefore relevant to see how the categories developed here relate to employment outcomes. Table 2.7 ranks our countries by the proportion of the 15- to 65-year-old population in employment during 2010, classified according to the categories of Tables 2.4 and 2.5. There is no evidence from the Table 2.7 data here that employee power has a negative effect in itself on employment performance, as would be suggested by neoliberal arguments. Five of the top ten positions are occupied by group A countries, four by group B.

The Table 2.7 data offer support for the flexicurity thesis, that a combination of strong unemployment support and relatively weak employment protection laws is associated with high levels of employment (column II). However, there are also strong performances from countries with 'unreconstructed' high EPL/high URL regimes (column I). Only Belgium has a weak employment performance among this group. It should be noted that Slovenia, the only AI case in Central and Eastern Europe, is also the highest–ranking Central and Eastern European country for employment. Contrary to the neoliberal thesis, poor employment performances are concentrated among countries with low levels of unemployment compensation, and it is difficult to decide whether overall the 'protectionist' model (III) performs worse than the preferred neoliberal position (IV). One cannot be highly confident about this conclusion as cause and effect here are complex; possibly countries with high unemployment find it difficult to sustain generous unemployment support. Nevertheless, these data give little support to the thesis that a primarily punitive approach to workers succeeds in reducing unemployment.

Table 2.7   Employment Levels by Tables 2.3 and 2.4 Categories

Table 2.3 categories				Table 2.4 categories			
A	B	C	D	I	II	III	IV
			CH (78.6)		CH		
NO (75.3)				NO			
	NL (74.7)				NL		
DK (73.4)					DK		
SE (72.7)					SE		
AT (71.7)					AT		
			DE (71.1)	DE			
	UK (69.5)						UK
FI (68.1)				FI			
	US (66.7)						US
SI (66.2)				SI			
	PT (65.6)					PT	
CZ (65.4)						CZ	
	FR (64.0)					FR	
BE (62.0)				BE			
	EE (61.0)					EE	
		IE (60.0)			IE		
	EL (59.6)					EL	
	PL (59.3)						PL
SK (58.8)							SK
	ES (58.6)					ES	
	IT (56.9)						IT
		HU (55.4)					HU

Figures in parentheses indicate percentage of working-age population (15–65) in paid employment (Source: OECD).

CONCLUSIONS

Most of the groupings of countries produced by these data are well known to comparative labour and social policy specialists: similar and usually performance among Nordic countries and, depending on the indicator, continental Western European countries north of the Alps and Pyrenees; similar and poor performances in Southern Europe and in Central and Eastern Europe. Research carried out before the financial crisis tends to show similar and strong performance among Anglophone countries, represented here by Ireland, the UK, and the US; these countries now offer a more mixed picture. The main novelty of the present chapter is to suggest a link between the policy and employment outcomes of these different patterns and the balance of class relations. The original tripartite division of social policy regimes proposed by Esping Andersen (liberal Anglophone, conservative 'continental', and social democratic Nordic) was also based on patterns of class relations, but those present during initial industrialisation. This chapter suggests that this approach can be continued into more recent historical periods. The identity of and balance of power between the relevant classes varies across societies and from time to time.

To take the analysis further, it is necessary to develop more extensive indicators of class power, including a better account of labour's collective strength than sheer union density. In several countries, unions occupy an institutionalised role or are organised in such a way that gives them more strength than implied by density alone. This is relevant to Austria, France, Germany, the Netherlands, and Spain in particular. The identity of parties in governments, and their relations to different classes, provides a further source of variables. Further study should also examine moments of important change in independent and dependent variables. For example, at different moments during the past thirty years major shifts (detrimental to labour interests) have taken place in the balance of class forces in Austria, Denmark, Germany, Sweden, and the UK. These seem also to have been associated with changes in labour policies. Have they also been associated with changes in outcomes, and could these accounts be extended to other cases? The accounts of Keune (2007) and Spieser (2009) suggest that they certainly help our understanding of Central and Eastern European countries. There is, therefore, an attractive research programme here that could deepen our understanding of why certain institutions appear in some countries and not others.

ACKNOWLEDGEMENTS

This paper has benefited from the work of my colleagues in European Union Framework Programme 7 project 'The Governance of Uncertainty and Sustainability: Tensions and Opportunities' (GUSTO) (grant no. 225301), though they are not responsible for nor necessarily agree with its contents.

BIBLIOGRAPHY

Bonoli, Giuliano. "Active Labour Market Policy and Social Investment: A Changing Relationship." In *Towards a Social Investment State?*, edited by Nathalie Morel, Bruno Palier, and Joakim Palme, 181–204. Bristol: Policy Press, 2012.
Bonoli, Giuliano. "Time Matters: Postindustrialization, New Social Risks, and Welfare State Adaptation in Advanced Industrial Democracies." *Comparative Political Studies* 40 (2007): 495–520.

Campbell, John L., John A. Hall, and Ove K. Pedersen, eds. *National Identity and the Varieties of Capitalism: The Danish Experience*. Montreal: McGill-Queen's University Press, 2006.

Crouch, Colin. "Privatised Keynesianism: An Unacknowledged Policy Regime." *British Journal of Politics and International Relations* 11 (2009): 382–399.

Fama, Eugene. "Efficient Capital Markets: II." *Journal of Finance* 46 (1991): 1575–1617.

Fama, Eugene. "Risk, Return and Equilibrium." *Journal of Political Economy* 79 (1971): 30–55.

Hayward, Jack, ed. *Industrial Enterprise and European Integration: From National to International Champions*. Oxford: Oxford University Press, 1995.

Keune, Maarten. "Creating Capitalist Labour Markets: A Comparative–Institutionalist Analysis of Labour Market Reform in the Czech Republic and Hungary, 1989–2002." PhD diss., European University Institute, 2007.

Knight, F.H. (1921), *Risk, uncertainty and profit* New York

Lansley, Stewart. *The Cost of Inequality*. London: Gibson Square, 2011.

Morel, Nathalie, Bruno Palier, and Joakim Palme, eds. *Towards a Social Investment State?* Bristol: Policy Press, 2012.

Muffels, Ruud. "The Governance of Sustainable Security: The Impact of Institutions and Values on Labour Market Transitions." Working paper. FP7 Project GUSTO, 2010.

OECD. *The Jobs Study*. Paris: OECD, 1994.

OECD. *Growing Unequal*. Paris: OECD, 2008.

OECD. *OECD Economic Outlook*. Paris: OECD, 2006.

Spieser, Catherine. "Institutionalising Market Society in Times of Systemic Change: The Construction and Reform of Social and Labour Market Policies in Poland in a Comparative Perspective (1989–2004)." PhD diss., European University Institute, 2009.

Taylor-Gooby, Peter, ed. *New Risks, New Welfare: The Transformation of the European Welfare State*. Oxford: Oxford University Press, 2004.

Visser, Jelle. *Data Base on Institutional Characteristics of Trade Unions, Wage Setting, State Intervention and Social Pacts, 1960–2010 (ICTWSS) Version 3.0*. Amsterdam: Amsterdam Institute for Advanced Labour Studies, 2011.

3 From Flexicurity to Social Employment Regimes

Carlos Prieto

> The critical theory of capitalism is the expression of an alternative subject to capitalism. Insofar as that subject does not exist, the critical theory is a mere utopia. (Bilbao, 1993: 47)

INTRODUCTION

The issue of "flexicurity" was placed on the political agenda of the EU member states by the European Commission some years ago, particularly with its communication to the European Parliament of June 2007. Since then there have been a great many papers, documents, books, and studies of all kinds on the topic; so many indeed that it might seem surprising that there is anything left to say that could be new or better than what has already been said by (some) others. For instance there are the papers on the changes in the European social model published by Serrano (2007); the analysis by Méda (2009) of the contrast between the social model of employment that prevailed in the 1950s and 1960s, in which protection was at the very core of employment, and the flexicurity model, in which employment and protection have become antonyms and protection is considered likely to crush and eventually kill employment; the analysis of the troubled relationship between flexicurity and gender relations by Jepsen (2008); the critical analysis by Jorgensen (2009) of the changes over time in the way in which flexicurity has been dealt with in Denmark (the country that is almost always held up as a benchmark); the analysis of the link between flexicurity and transitional labour markets (TLMs) by Schmid (2009); and so on. Here, I look at flexicurity exclusively from the perspective closest to my own field, which I hope will not prove uninteresting, i.e., its potential relationship with 'quality of employment', considered and analysed on the basis of the situation in Spain, somewhat along the lines taken by Jorgensen (2009) in his splendid paper on the changes over time in the Danish model.[1]

The link between quality of employment and flexicurity is clearly a core issue in the debate. Indeed, it is referred to in the title of the communication by the European Commission to the European Parliament mentioned above: "Towards common principles of flexicurity: *more and better* jobs through flexibility and security" (my italics). The Commission is calling on EU member states to develop employment policies based on flexicurity precisely with a view to achieving the objective proclaimed by the European

Council in Lisbon in 2000 of creating "more and better jobs". Here I take that idea as a basis and seek to show and argue that there is a link between the quality (good, bad, or indifferent) of employment and the social conditions and public regulations that produce it, taking Spain as a case in point.[2] Rather than studying and analysing flexicurity itself, it focuses on the dimensions which constitute flexicurity (e.g., internal and external flexibilisation of employment, qualification practices, ascending and descending mobility, and wage adjustments). The peculiarity of this approach lies in the fact that all elements are regarded and analysed in terms of quality and decency of work. They are placed in a framework of meaning which, besides the public socioeconomic employment policies, includes other relational practices, such as the productive model and power resources that are mobilised in industrial relations. This chapter starts by looking at the basic characteristics of quality (and decency) of employment in Spain and then goes on to examine the web of economic, social, and political practices and conditions through which those characteristics can be understood. Public policies regulating employment—which must necessarily contain a regulatory combination of job flexibility and security—are only a part of that web and will not be effective without the other parts. The concept of 'social employment regime' will be used to argue this point. Finally, some brief thoughts will be presented about the link between quality of employment, flexicurity, and social employment regimes.

SEGMENTS OF QUALITY/DECENCY OF EMPLOYMENT: A CONFIGURATION WHICH IS BOTH DUAL AND HIGHLY VULNERABLE

Any analysis of the quality-based segments into which the labour market is broken down must define—or at least assume—just what 'quality' means. This is not the place for a detailed analysis of this issue (see Prieto, 2009: chap. 2), but I maintain that (a) any definition of quality of employment is a value judgement and as such is variable and subjective (though it may be collectively subjective); (b) quality of employment can initially be defined/assessed in terms of 'decency' (or 'due quality') as the term is used by the ILO, leading to a distinction between 'decent jobs', i.e., those in which the social rights of workers are respected, particularly as regards remuneration and working hours, and 'precarious jobs', where they are not; and (c) once this initial definition is established, quality can be defined on a second level on the basis of the extent to which the properties that define decency are fulfilled: decent employment can have different quality levels.

The breakdown into segments shown here for quality of employment in Spain is based on data from the ECV ("Living Conditions Survey") for 2006.[3] An analysis of clustered data from the ECV enables the following conclusions to be drawn: overall employment can be grouped into two major segments on the basis of the two features that best characterise quality and/or decency of work: its degree of stability (job security) and its level of remuneration. [4] The first segment is 'precarious work' and the second is 'decent work'. The difference between the two is that in the former the standard defined as socially 'fair' or 'decent' (as the term is used by the ILO), is not met, whereas in the latter it is. This latter segment can be broken down into two distinct sub-segments which, following other authors, I refer to as 'central' and 'higher'. More specifically, these three segments are as follows[5]:

- *Precarious*: This segment comprises all the jobs whose quality is below the level considered as socially 'decent'. These jobs are characterised by their lack of security and/or low wages. Twenty-seven per cent of wage-earners workers fall into this segment. Within the segment two strictly precarious clusters (i.e., below the standard of decent employment seen by society as a right) can be distinguished: jobs that pay less than the legal minimum wage (4.5 per cent of all waged work) and jobs that last less than four months (6 per cent), with the consequent reduction in annual wage income.
- *Central*: This segment is characterised by respect for the social standards of employment, and features relatively high stability (duration) of employment and 'decent' (though still low: see below) average wages. Forty-one per cent of all waged jobs fall into this segment.
- *Higher*: This segment is characterised by greater job security and relatively high wages. It accounts for 32 per cent of total waged work. Within this segment there is a group of especially privileged workers comprising 8 per cent of the total whose wages are eight times higher than those of the least favoured precarious group.

By breaking down employment by segments, information not apparent from previous analyses of the Spanish labour market is revealed. Many authors have studied and pointed out segmentation of employment along these or similar lines, but the data from the ECV on which the present study is based also reveal two less frequently discussed features:

- *The wages of most wage-earners are moderate to say the least.* This applies not only to holders of precarious jobs, but also to those in the central segment. Sixty-eight per cent of Spanish wage-earners earn on average less than €1,100 per month. This situation is so widespread that a name has been coined for it in Spain: *mileurismo* (literally "thousand euro-ism"). These data are deduced from the ECV, but are also confirmed by other sources. Comparatively, these are among the lowest wages in the EU-15 (Table 3.1), at around 30 per cent below average.
- *Widespread job fragility (or vulnerability) in a context of high job turnover.* Between 2004 and 2006 no less than 60 per cent of the

Table 3.1   Average Annual Wages in PPP in Some European Countries (Euros p.a., 2005)

Germany	UK	Denmark	Netherlands	Sweden	France	Italy	Spain	Portugal
36,378	35,987	34,396	33,269	27,753	25,067	23308	20,672	18,221

Source: Eurostat and own work.

wage-earners in the precarious segment, 38 per cent of those in the central segment, and 27 per cent of those in the higher segment changed their employment situations. But still more significant than job turnover *per se* is the high percentage of downward mobility, in many cases towards precariousness or unemployment. According to the ECV for 2006, downward mobility affected 22 per cent of central segment workers (6 per cent lost their jobs, 16 per cent dropped into the precarious segment), whereas only 13 per cent moved up, and a startling 26 per cent of higher-segment employees (20 per cent dropped into the central segment and 6 per cent dropped into the precarious segment or lost their jobs). This widespread vulnerability becomes easier to understand when it is set against a context in which almost half of all wage-earners have been unemployed or have worked under short-term contracts (with the same individuals frequently having experienced both situations) since the early 1990s (Prieto, 2009: 238). Thus, there is an ever-present threat of a worsening of employment conditions, even to the extent of dropping into precarious work, even in the most highly favoured segments. Spain suffers from "weak employment" (Alonso, 2001).

This conclusion is drawn from the 2006 survey, which was conducted when employment growth was at its highest in the previous stage of the cycle, so it is logical to assume that these negative features can only have been exacerbated as the country has slipped into the current downward stage.

There are two main reasons why employment in Spain is configured in this way. The first can be called the 'regulationist' explanation. The argument goes like this. Employment in Spain is segmented and fragile mainly because the regulations in force are overprotective towards open-ended jobs and underprotective towards short-term contracts, and there is a need to introduce a new regulatory combination of job flexibility and security (the benchmark for which is the Danish system of 'flexicurity'—or at least its media image). This is the predominant school of thought, and it is based on neoliberal economic orthodoxy as expressed by, among others, the "Manifesto of the 100 Economists", the CEOE (Spanish Employers' Association), and the "Partido Popular" ("People's Party"—Spanish conservative party).

The second explanation, which can be described as 'productivist', is defended above all by the trade unions, especially CCOO and UGT. Its argument is that the segmentation and poor quality of employment in Spain are explained by the model of production and economic growth. A document on the matter produced by CCOO in 2009 states that in Spain "a close relationship has emerged between the tendency for growth to be concentrated in activities with low levels of innovation and productivity, the creation of poor-quality jobs and the segmentation of the labour market" (Fundación 1° de Mayo-CCOO, 2009). Neither explanation seems to be sufficiently comprehensive in itself. I would like to suggest a further explanation that takes them both into account, but which regards them as limited and integrates them into a more comprehensive, more complex, approach. My proposal is centred on the concept of the 'social employment regime'.

THE CONCEPT OF THE SOCIAL EMPLOYMENT REGIME

I use the concept of the 'social employment regime' because, as defined here, it obliges analysts to take into account not only public labour regulation policies and models of production and growth, but also the various fields of social practice from whose interaction and articulation one or other configuration of the quality of employment in a country at a specific moment in history emerges.[6] Each of those fields has its own logic and its

Figure 3.1   Social regime of employment.

own relative autonomy, but none of them is independent of or understandable without the others.

A social employment regime is a set of formal and informal principles, regulations, and procedures and political, social, and economic practices that establish guidelines in reference to the asymmetry of wage relationships that regulate the working, employment, and living conditions of workers and the job turnover and sociodemographic distribution of the population in a given society. This somewhat complex definition is easier to understand in graphic form (Figure 3.1).

As can be seen in the figure, a social employment regime comprises the interactive articulation of various sets of social practices, the purpose and result of which is to establish a certain social order in employment. Specifically, those sets are as follows:

- Public economic and social policies that directly or indirectly affect employment, its configuration and its 'decency' or 'quality'. These include regulatory and social policies directly aimed at promoting and protecting employment in general—and within that field a combination of flexibility and security policies—but also economic and social policies that affect it indirectly (e.g., family and education policies).
- The model of organisation of goods and services production, including the makeup of the fabric of production (branches of activity), the model of organisation of work, and technology level (productivity) and relations between firms (networking and subcontracting).
- Labour relations based on social agreements and collective bargaining, in which the power of trade unions has a core role to play.
- The tiers of the social hierarchy that operate in those areas of society that lie outside work and affect the job turnover in the population (family and gender relationships, relations between locals and migrants, etc.).
- The web of social norms concerned with employment that express and distil the 'spirit' (Weber) of social practices in the said fields and that underlie and in themselves create a particular configuration of social order.
- Corporate employment and labour policies (conditioned by the context of the sets of social practices indicated above). These appear at the point where the above sets converge, because it is at company level that employment practices take on their final form.

It is from the interactive conjunction of all these fields of social practices that one breakdown or another into segments of quality of employment emerges. In the case of Spain there is an imperfect dual configuration, with low wages and widespread job fragility, because Spain has a dualising social employment regime that is inclusive only within certain limits and provides scant social protection. This is so not just because public labour policies (the "Manifesto of the 100") or the model of production and growth take this form but because of the action and interaction of *all* the fields of practices listed above. I would now like to show how each of these sets of social practices is connected to the configuration of the quality of employment, and then give a few thoughts on the situation as a whole. The network of social norms on employment is left out not because it is unimportant but because including it would make the exposition overlong.

SPAIN'S SOCIAL EMPLOYMENT REGIME IN LEGISLATION

Relationship between Public Economic and Social Policies Affecting Employment and the Breakdown of Employment into Segments

Of all the public policies that affect employment directly or indirectly, none has received more attention or sparked more research in Spain than employment regulation policy. Public regulation of employment has been through four different stages in the past few decades. The first ran from the advent of the transition to democracy (the 1976 Labour Relations Act [*Ley de Relaciones Laborales*]) to the major reform of the Workers' Statute [*Estatuto de los Trabajadores*]) in 1984, which established that only open-ended, full-time employment contracts were worthy of recognition in a 'social and democratic state' (as Spain was described in the constitution enacted in 1978). This policy sought to achieve "full employment with good jobs" (Miguélez and Prieto, 2008). Stage two ran from 1984 to 1994, when fixed-term contracts and part-time work became the norm. The policy objective of this period was to achieve "maximum employment in jobs of any kind". Stage three followed, in which all the existing forms remained in widespread use, but the public authorities sought to reduce the prevalence of short-term contracts. Stage four began in 2010—with the crisis in full swing, massive destruction of jobs, and rocketing unemployment—and has been marked by further measures that have increased the power of employers and made jobs still more fragile.

The fact that forms of contract considered as non-standard in the wording of the initial Workers' Statute (dating from 1980) became the norm did not in itself make employment in Spain so fragile, but it did clear the way for firms to resort to every possible type and combination of types of contract in pursuit of their objectives of differential turnover of the labour force (see below) and actually legitimised their doing so. It also contributed to the segmentation of employment that can now be observed. Indeed, the most precarious employment conditions (lack of security, low wages, higher accident rates, etc.) are generally found among 'short-term' jobs (Miguélez and Prieto, 2008). On the other hand, the general public system of social protection in no way offsets the weaknesses that appear in employment *per se*. It offers universal coverage, but the level of protection provided is low

Table 3.2   Social Spending as a Percentage of GDP in Some European Countries, 2005

Spain	Euro Zone	Denmark	Sweden	Germany	France	UK
20.8	27.8	30.1	32.0	29.4	31.5	26.8

Source: European Commission (2010).

(Rodríguez Cabrero, 2008); the percentage of GDP earmarked for social spending is much lower than in those EU member states usually cited as benchmarks (Table 3.2).

Of course, official employment regulation policies are not the only factor that influences the configuration and quality of employment, but they have a more direct influence and have been more widely investigated than any other.

The Links between the Organisation of Goods and Services Production and the Segments into which Employment is Broken Down

Numerous authors have investigated the links between the way in which production is organised (model of production, breakdown of activities by braches, and relations between companies through networks and subcontracting), on the one hand, and the type of employment that results, on the other (e.g., Pitxer i Campos and Sánchez Velasco, 2008). A paper by Rocha Sánchez, Aragón Medina, and Cruces Aguilera (2008) dealing expressly with this issue reveals how the generally low quality of employment in Spain is linked to the country's basic organisation of goods and services production:

• Highly labour-intensive activities such as construction and catering have much more weight in the fabric of production in Spain than on average in Europe.
• Levels of technology and productivity are much lower than in the core European countries.
• Spain has a great many very small firms and self-employed persons, whose relationship with medium and large-size firms tends to be peripheral and frequently involves them working for the latter as dependent workers or subcontractors (see also Castillo, 2005).

These three aspects of the way in which goods and services production are organised are clearly associated with the segmentation of employment noted above. It is the most labour-intensive activities, the firms with the lowest levels of technology and the peripheral and dependent firms (which, usually, are also the smallest) that account for the bulk of the low-

Table 3.3   Employment Segments Broken Down by Sectors of Activity and Size of Firms

SEGMENT	Wage-earners as % of total	Size of firms with relatively highest presence	Main sectors of activity
PRECARIOUS	27	1–5 employees.	Catering, retail and repair services, other social and domestic services
CENTRAL	41	1–19 employees	Industry, construction, retail and repair services
HIGHER	32	50 or more employees	Public administration, education, financial intermediation

Source: Prieto (2009: 222).

quality jobs. Table 3.3 shows that precarious jobs tend to be concentrated in smaller companies and in the activities where technological development is at its lowest. By contrast, jobs in the higher segment tend to be located at larger companies and in areas where the levels of technology and use of knowledge are higher.

These links in the production of goods and services between the size of organisations and the quality of employment are found to some extent in all countries. What is different about Spain is how prevalent those features of the organisation of production that weaken the quality of employment are. By way of illustration, the proportion of workers employed by micro-companies (those with less than ten employees) and the proportion of self-employed workers (who are not only the smallest production units, but also usually the most heavily dependent on core producers) are considerably higher in Spain than in the most highly industrialised benchmark countries in Europe (Table 3.4).

Table 3.4   Wage-Earners Employed by Firms with Less Than Ten Employees as a Percentage of Total Wage-Earners and Self-Employed Workers as a Percentage of Total Job-Holders, 2005

	Spain	Denmark	Sweden	Germany	France	UK
% wage-earners	38.6	20.1	24.9	18.9	23.9	21.4
% self-employed	14.6	6.3	5.3	11.2	8.9	12.8

Source: Eurostat and own work.

The Links between Labour Relations (Trade Union Power) and the Segments into which Quality of Employment Is Broken Down

The situation in Spain as regards labour relations and the trade union power that characterises them is ambiguous. On the one hand, the country's trade unions are relatively strong and influential in labour relations at supra-company and inter-confederation levels. This is evidenced by the consensus-based bargaining that has predominated in the recent history of labour relations and social dialogue (except in the period of strained relations between government and unions from 1987 to 1996, when reforms that stripped wage-earners of a great deal of social protection were being implemented). It can also be seen in the widespread support enjoyed by the four general strikes called by the main trade unions—the first in 1988 and the latest in 2002—in response to four government plans for labour reforms that reduced social protection. But this relative strength at the supra-company level is not echoed in individual workplaces: trade unions in Spain have some degree of effective power and influence in medium and large-size firms, but little or none in smaller ones. A breakdown of trade union membership according to the size of companies (Table 3.5) clearly illustrates this. The overall figure of 19.5 per cent is low in itself, but at firms with less than ten employees, membership stands at just 5 per cent (Pitzer i Campos and Sánchez, 2008). A strong union presence in the workplace (medium and large firms) makes for greater job stability and can pressure firms into fulfilling labour-related commitments entered into. No such pressure is exerted in the small and very small firms which make up the majority of workplaces. This weakness of trade unions in workplaces is also conducive to a high incidence of breaches of collective bargaining agreements by Spanish firms, especially as regards those clauses concerned with working hours and remuneration (Escudero, 2004).

Moreover, Spanish trade unions have tended to press in collective bargaining processes for wage increases that seldom, in themselves, result in real increases in the purchasing power of wage-earners. As a result of the so-called Moncloa Agreements (*Pactos de la Moncloa*) of 1977, since 1978 they have tended to call for wage increases in line with expected annual inflation (as forecast by the government), which have almost always proved to be lower than actual inflation. This approach by unions has helped to create and above all maintain the low wage levels characteristic of the Spanish labour market. According to calculations by Pitzer i Campos and Sánchez Velasco (2008: 102), real remuneration per job-holder in Spain fell by 1.7 per cent between 1995 and 2005 (the same calculations showed a rise of 11.6 per cent in the EU-15).

The scant power of trade unions in Spain is therefore an essential component of the country's social employment regime and a factor in understanding the resulting low quality of employment and the segments into which it is broken down.

Table 3.5   Trade Union Membership Rates and Proportion of Employees
on Fixed-Term Contracts Broken Down by Size of Firms

	1–10 employees	11–50	51–250	> 250	Total
% union members	6.9	13.2	20.5	30.5	19.5
% fixed-term contracts	36.1	28.9	21.7		32.1

Source: (a) Pitxer i Campos and Sánchez Velasco (2008) for union membership; (b) Active
Population Survey (EPA) for second quarter of 2006 and own work for fixed-term contracts.

Corporate Working and Employment Policies and the Breakdown by Segments

A highly flexible body of labour and employment regulations, goods and
services production with low levels of technology, low productivity and
broken into many segments and hierarchical tiers, and, finally, trade unions
with little real power combine to give employers a framework in which
they have a great deal of power and freedom to implement whatever labour
practices best suit their own interests, as opposed to the interests of their
wage-earning employees. That power is amplified by the job fragility suffered by wage-earners, caused by the combination of high unemployment
and prevalence of short-term contracts that has characterised the Spanish labour market consistently since the early 1990s (Prieto, 2009: 238). I
believe that Spanish firms exercise this power mainly through two labour-
market management practices that can be seen as real strategic options for
mobilising production[7]: the widespread use of short-term contracts and the
placement of most workers in job categories with low qualification requirements—or at least with requirements lower than the professional qualifications that they actually hold. This is in line with the clear predominance
of low-skilled work in the form in which labour is organised (Lorenz and
Valeyre, 2004).

In this context short-term contracts should not be seen in their usual
role of indicators of job precariousness *per se*, but rather as a corporate
strategy aimed at giving firms as much control as possible over their workforces (low wages, longer working hours, availability, turnover, etc.) that
reaches its full effect in terms of mobilisation of production when it is combined with open-ended contracts. The proportion of fixed-term contracts
in Spain is far higher than the European average (Table 3.6).

There is support for the idea put forward by a major school of thought
among French-speaking specialists in the sociology of labour that professional qualifications (and their translation into job categories) are much
more than just a way of recognising an order of objectively determinable
skills (see Alaluf, 1986; Stroobants, 1993: chap. 3). Inherent in professional
qualifications there is a fundamental connotation of social classification

Table 3.6 Proportion of Fixed-Term Contracts in Spain and Other EU Countries, 2008

Spain	EU-15	UK	Germany	France	Denmark	Sweden
29.3	14.4	5.4	14.7	14.2	8.4	16.1

Source: European Commission (2010).

of jobs and the workers who do them, and therefore a value judgement—which is disputed, at least in the field of labour relations—on both, according to which some jobs and some workers are worth more than others and are ordered on a hierarchical scale of recognition (and remuneration in the form of wages) (Prieto, 2009). When firms use these connotations, they take into account the formally recognised skills of workers (e.g., diplomas), but this is in no way translated into immediate recognition of those skills in the hierarchy of qualifications. Evidence of this in Spain can be found in the widespread over-qualification of Spanish job-holders and the resulting fact that over 20 per cent of university degree holders with jobs are working in job categories for which higher education qualifications are not formally required (CES, 2009: 219). Firms use this classification as a way of giving 'objective' meaning to and legitimising their specific employment practices. It thus seems—or ends up seeming—logical and normal for there to be a correspondence between the level of professional qualifications and the level of quality of employment. Defining a job as 'unskilled' or 'low-quality' is tantamount to passing a negative value judgement on it, and the opposite is true for jobs described as 'skilled' and 'high-quality' (stable and well paid) (Prieto, 2009: 225).

This modus operandi on the part of firms shows up in two ways: first in the form in which work is organised at production plants, and second in the distribution by job categories of workers within that organisation. Spain is characterised in the first case by the predominance of low-qualification (Taylorist or 'lean production') forms of organisation (Table 3.7), and in the second by a relative predominance of workers allocated to low-level job categories (Table 3.8).[8] It is especially interesting for the problem under consideration here to observe the contrast between the high proportions of wage-earners in Denmark and Sweden who work in 'cognitive' organisations (60 and 52 per cent, respectively) and the figure of just 20 per cent in Spain.

Both the type of employment contract used and way in which work and workers are qualified/classified contribute to the creation in society of a type of employment that is weak in overall terms, and to segmentation based on levels of remuneration and the duration of employment. These two criteria are used to analyse and define the configuration by segments of the quality of employment in Table 3.9.

Table 3.7   Forms of Organisation of Work in Some European Countries
(Percentage of Wage-Earners in Each Country Employed in Each
Type of Organisation of Work)

	1. "Cognitive" organisations	*2. Lean production organisations*	*3. Taylorist organisations*	*2+3*	*4. Organisations with simple structures*
Spain	20.1	38.8	18.5	57.3	22.5
Germany	44.3	19.6	14.3	33.9	21.9
Denmark	60.0	21.9	6.8	28.7	11.3
France	38.0	33.3	11.1	44.4	17.7
UK	34.8	40.6	10.9	51.5	13.7
Sweden	52.6	18.5	7.1	25.6	21.7

Source: Lorenz and Valeyre (2004: 20).

Table 3.8   Percentage of Job-Holders Employed in Some Job Groups in Spain and
EU-15, 2006

Job group	Spain	EU-15	Difference
High-grade specialists and technicians	12.5	13.7	-1.2
Supporting specialists and technicians	11.5	16.9	-5.4
Unskilled manual workers	14.7	9.9	+4.6

Source: Pitxer i Campos and Sánchez Velasco (2008: 96).

Table 3.9   Employment Segments per Proportion of Fixed-Term Contracts and
Qualification Levels

SEGMENT	Wage-earners as % of total	Fixed-term contracts as % of total in each segment	Main job qualification types and levels
PRECARIOUS	27	64	Unskilled and skilled service workers
CENTRAL	41	28	Skilled industrial workers and skilled service workers
HIGHER	32	10	Managers, technicians, and clerical staff

Source: Prieto (2009: 226).

An Employment Regime Whose Various Components
Work in the Same Direction and Interact

In view of the overall relationship between the breakdown by segments of quality and decency of employment, on the one hand, and on the other hand the web formed by flexible labour regulations, a low-technology, low-productivity based (but highly hierarchical) model and fabric of production, collective labour relations in which trade unions have little power (in the actual workplace), corporate labour management policies characterised by frequent recourse to short-term contracts, organisations that underrate the professional skills of their employees, considerable intensification of work, and, finally, relatively low wages, it can be concluded that this social structure has a high degree of internal consistency. The current breakdown by segments of employment in Spain, with its characteristic imperfect duality, its relatively low wages and its high levels of vulnerability is the result of:

- An institutional framework that offers firms the possibility of managing their workforces with great numerical flexibility
- A form of organisation of production characterised by the prevalence of sectors with very low productivity (domestic service, hospitality industry, construction) and very small companies that often work as subcontractors
- Labour relations in which there is little active presence of trade unions in the workplace, which in turn gives companies great power and autonomy in labour-related decision making
- Strategic options available to companies for job turnover, which result in high proportions of short-term contracts and relatively low average professional qualification levels

The current breakdown into segments of employment in Spain can thus be put down to a combination of these four sets of practices. Each has its own direct influence on the configuration of the quality of employment but also interacts with the other three: None of them is fully independent of the others. It is the cluster of all four sets of practices that is referred to here as the 'social employment regime'. This conclusion is reached after an analysis of the characteristic features of employment in Spain and the form of production, using the concept of 'social employment regime'.

This regime is specific to Spain, and seems clearly distinct from those in place in the other European countries which are generally used as benchmarks for comparison. An overall comparison of the indicators of socioeconomic conditions affecting the configuration of employment in Spain and in the EU-15 shows just how distinctive the case of Spain is (Table 3.10). The prevalence of traditional production activities in Spain compared to more modern activities in the EU-15, the smaller size of workplaces in Spain, a proportion of short-term contracts more than twice as high as for

Table 3.10 Socioeconomic Factors Conditioning the Segmentation of Quality of Employment in Spain and the EU-15

		Spain	EU-15
Production sectors with highest relative weight		Construction, hospitality, domestic service	Financial activities, education, health
% of job-holders per size of firm	1–19 employees	49	40
	50 or more	37	49
% of wage-earners with fixed-term contracts		32	15
% of wage-earners per qualification level	Unskilled	18	11
	Managers and technicians	28	37
% of trade union membership		19.5	35

Source: own work based on EUROSTAT (data for 2005) for the first four rows; Beneyto (2008) and own work (Prieto, 2009: 227) for trade union membership.

the EU-15, a distribution of professional qualifications that includes more unskilled workers and less highly skilled workers, and considerably lower rates of trade union membership denote an employment regime in Spain with low levels of inclusiveness. This in turn is responsible for a breakdown into segments in terms of decency and quality of employment that is dual in nature, with insecure jobs and relatively low wages.

The Web of Social Hierarchies outside Work as Part of the Social Employment Regime

Although my approach so far in establishing links between the cluster of social practices that make up a social employment regime and the breakdown by segments of quality of employment may seem to include all the sets of practices that have a significant, relevant influence on that quality, I believe that a further group of social practices should be added that does not actually lie within the social area of the labour market *per se*. The relevant concept appears in Figure 3.1: those areas of the social hierarchy that operate outside work and affect the economic mobility of the population, e.g., family and gender relationships, relations between Spanish nationals and immigrants, etc.

There are three main non-labour-related attributes that regularly produce hierarchical social classifications in life in our societies ('social classes' at the extreme)[9]: gender, education level, and provenance. The hierarchical structuring that results from these attributes (man/woman, Spanish national/immigrant, different education levels) to some extent (indeed, to

Table 3.11   Employment Segments per Hierarchical Tier for Types of Job-Holders

SEGMENT	% breakdown by gender		Avg. age	% of non-EU immigrants	Predominant education level
	Men	Women			
PRECARIOUS	37	63	38/35	11	Primary and lower secondary
CENTRAL	59	41	38	9	Primary, lower, and upper secondary
HIGHER	70	30	43	2	Higher education

Source: own work based on data from the 2006 Living Conditions Survey (Spanish National Statistics Office).

a very large extent) gives an air of legitimacy to corporate practices of discrimination in employment, and thus helps to exacerbate differences: Placing a young, university-educated Spanish man in a poorly paid, unskilled job may be seen as scandalous, but placing a young female immigrant in such a job is not. In turn, the hierarchical structure of employment has a performative effect on the social hierarchy: A poorly paid immigrant is even more of an immigrant.

If this argument (which needs to be developed much more extensively) is applied to the groups and segments of quality of employment determined via statistical analysis, the logical conclusion is that women, less educated individuals, and immigrants taken on by firms may be expected to make up most of the precarious work segment, whereas the higher segment should comprise mainly adult men of Spanish provenance with relatively high education levels. And that is precisely what Table 3.11 shows: women, immigrants, and less educated workers (hierarchical structuring by age is less evident in the survey data) not only occupy second-order positions in society as compared to their 'opposites' (men, Spanish nationals, and the highly educated), but also, as a result, are assigned to lower-quality, less decent segments of employment.

This perverse parallelism between the breakdown by segments of employment and the hierarchical structure and distinctions between social classes (outside work) in Spanish society shows that the issue is not merely one of an ordinal scale of types of employment and types of population group. There are direct parallels between them. To paraphrase Gallie (2007), one could say that those jobs which are relatively good are so at the expense of bad ones, and the (relatively) good living conditions enjoyed by some (males, Spanish nationals, the highly educated, etc.) are so at the expense of poor conditions suffered by others (women, immigrants, the uneducated, etc.).

Table 3.12 Proportion of Job-Holders Aged 15–64 per Country and Gender, 2008

	Spain	France	Germany	UK	Denmark	Sweden	EU-15
Overall	64.3	65.2	70.7	78.5	78.1	74.3	67.3
Men	73.5	69.8	75.9	77.3	81.9	76.7	74.2
Women	54.9	60.7	65.4	65.8	74.3	71.8	60.4

Source: European Commission (2010).

As long as these social hierarchical structures are maintained outside work, it will seem reasonable and legitimate to segment employment and assign lower-class jobs to lower-class population groups; the point may even be reached where low-class jobs are created specifically for them (as evidenced by the case of immigrants). And the greater the degree of hierarchical structuring, the more effectively legitimised firms will feel in applying their discriminatory policies.

To highlight this, consider the case of women and men and asymmetrical gender relations. The position of women is clearly unfavourable relative to men in the labour market, whatever dimension is considered. This imbalance is more accentuated in Spain than in benchmark countries elsewhere in Europe: See the differences in the proportions of job-holders by gender summarised in Table 3.12.

The clear differences observable in the social sphere of employment can be understood by comparing them to the asymmetrical relations between men and women outside work, as exemplified in practice by the time that each gender devotes to domestic work and work outside the home (Table 3.13). Spain has the biggest gap between men and women of any of the countries considered. On average women spend 198 minutes more per day

Table 3.13 Average Number of Minutes per Day Spent by Men and Women on Work outside and inside the Home in Some European Countries; Population Aged 20–74, 2000

	WOMEN			MEN		
COUNTRY	Outside the home	Inside the home	Total	Outside the home	Inside the home	Total
Spain	126	295	421	261	97	358
France	137	270	407	228	142	370
UK	144	255	399	250	138	389
Sweden	173	222	396	251	149	401

Source: Eurostat (2001). Data compiled by Henau and Puech (2008: 17).

on domestic work than men. At the other end of the scale, in Sweden the difference is seventy-three minutes, almost three times less. It does not seem possible to understand the differences (and possible discrimination) in quality of employment between men and women in Spain without taking into account the differences in their positions outside work. And if that is the case, then it must be concluded that the web of social hierarchies outside work forms part of the social employment regime.

SOME (PROVISIONAL) CONCLUSIONS THAT PROMPT A RETHINKING OF THE SIGNIFICANCE OF THE ISSUE OF FLEXICURITY

New light is thus shed on the matter of flexicurity. Public regulations concerning conditions of employment (and unemployment) in Spain provide an institutional basis for the weakness and duality that characterise employment in the country. But if the theory and the analysis put forward here are correct, then this type of employment is also the result of other public policies and, above all, a further four sets of social practices: the way in which goods and services production is organised, labour relations (trade union power), the hierarchical relations that exist in society outside work, and, within that framework, the strategic options open to firms for managing their workforces. In other words, it is the product and result of a social employment regime as a whole, with all its components in action. Jorgensen (2009) analyses employment in Denmark in a similar way, although he does not use exactly the same concept. He finds—as I do for the case of Spain—that Danish employment and education policies have given rise to a discourse of flexicurity that can only be understood in the context of "some basic policy traits" on which it is built and with which it is associated (Jorgensen, 2009: 4).

If this is how the existing configuration of quality of employment is produced and reproduced, then it is unlikely to be changed merely by changing labour-market regulations. 'Strong' (high-quality or at the very least decent) employment, be it via recourse to job stabilisation and social protection policies inspired by Keynesian theories or via Danish-style flexicurity employment policies, is unthinkable in the framework of a production structure made up largely of small, dependent companies with little capacity for innovation, toothless trade unions, and corporate workforce management strategies that have scant regard for corporate social responsibility. Whatever regulation option is adopted—and flexicurity is one of the possibilities—with the objective of achieving first decent employment for all and then a generalised improvement in quality, it will only be effective if it is implemented in the context of a competitive structure of goods and services production that is not dominated by small, dependent companies, that has powerful trade unions, where there are balanced relations between the groups that make up the social order outside work and, finally, that has corporate labour force management strategies with high levels of corporate social responsibility towards employees. The objective of decent, quality employment calls for suitable employment policies, but adjusting the other sets of social practices with which they interact is just as essential to that objective as are employment policies themselves. Indeed, the importance of public regulations is relativised by the extent to which those sets of practices work towards producing decent, quality employment.

In conclusion, I would like to bring up an epistemological proposal that is relevant to this case. My intention here is to offer an alternative to the hegemonic orthodoxy of flexicurity that seeks to bring about effective improvement in the quality of employment. As Serrano claims, and as is confirmed in her chapter with Keune in this volume, we find ourselves in the midst of a battle of 'scientific' ideas that seek to define, identify, and analyse the social reality of employment. However, scientific alternatives in social issues can only attain their 'political' objectives if there is a social subject on which they can be supported. In the words of Andrés Bilbao, "The critical theory of the hegemonic concept of quality of employment is the expression of an alternative subject to the European neo-liberal order. Insofar as that subject does not exist, such a critical theory is a mere utopia" (1993: 4). It is not up to me to determine whether such a subject exists, but merely to assert that it is necessary.

NOTES

1. The *Revue de l'IRES* has published a special issue on the topic: *Revue de l'IRES* 63(4) (2009): *Flexicurité, sécurisation des parcours professionnels et protection sociale.*
2. A slightly different, somewhat shorter, version of this text was published in the 2009 CCOO Yearbook under the title *Crisis, reforma laboral, modelo productivo y régimen de empleo* (Crisis, Employment Reform, Production Model and Employment Regime).
3. An analysis of clustered data based on the ECV for 2010, with the 20 per cent unemployment level prevailing at the time of the survey, would of course give different results from that of 2006 in quantitative terms, but not in the structural terms which are of interest here.
4. This analysis was drawn up in the course of research into quality of employment led by myself with funding from the Ministry of Labour and Immigration in which M. Arnal, M. Caprile, and J. Podgorny also took part. A report on this research was published by the ministry itself (Prieto, 2009).
5. As mentioned, many research projects have analysed the segmentation of the labour and employment market in Spain. The paper by the economist Recio (1997) can be considered practically as a classic. More recently Alós Moner (2007, 2008) produced an in-depth reflection intended as a rethinking of the entire topic. This last author increases the number of segments to six: independent primary, integrated primary, traditional primary, uncertain secondary, certain secondary, and weak secondary. But the list of authors who support the idea of segments is much longer.

6. The concept of the social employment regime—or just 'employment regime'—is relatively frequent in social research. The particular meaning of the concept as defined and used here is my own, but is inspired above all by the work of Gallie (2007).
7. For more information on strategic options for businesses, see Kochan, Katz, and McKersie (1987).
8. On this matter, as on definitions of forms of organisation of work, we follow the research of Lorenz and Valeyre (2004).
9. On this point, see Prieto (2009: 228ff.).

BIBLIOGRAPHY

Alaluf, Mateo. *Le Temps du labeur. Formation, emploi et qualification en sociologie du travail.* Brussels: Université de Bruxelles, 1986.
Alonso, Luis Enrique. *Trabajo y posmodernidad. El empleo débil.* Madrid: Fundamentos, 2001.
Alós Moner, Ramón. "Mercat, clase i persona en les relacions laborals. Entre la individualitat i l'acció collectiva." PhD thesis, Universidad Autónoma de Barcelona, 2007.
Alós Moner, Ramón. "Segmentación de los mercados de trabajo y relaciones laborales. El sindicalismo ante la acción colectiva." *Cuadernos de Relaciones Laborales* 26(1) (2008): 123–146.
Beneyto, Pere J. (2008). "El sindicalismo español en perspectiva europea: de la anomalía a la convergencia." *Cuadernos de Relaciones Laborales* 26(1) (2008): 57–88.
Bilbao, Andrés. *Obreros y ciudadanos.* Madrid: Trotta, 1993.
Castillo, Juan José, ed. *El trabajo recobrado.* Buenos Aires: Miño Dávila, 2005.
CES, *Memoria sobre la situación socioeconómica y laboral.* Madrid: Consejo Económico y Social, 2009.
Consejo Económico y Social. *Memoria sobre la situación socioeconómica y laboral. España 2009.* Madrid: Consejo Económico y Social, 2010.
Escudero, Ricardo, ed. *La negociación colectiva en España: una visión cualitativa.* Madrid: CCOO, Titant lo Blanc, 2004.
European Commission. *Employment in Europe 2009.* Brussels: European Commission, 2010.
Eurostat. *Harmonised European Time Use Surveys 2000.* Brussels: European Commission, 2001.
Fundación 1º de Mayo-CCOO. *Reflexiones y propuestas para el cambio de modelo productivo en España.* Madrid: Fundación 1º de Mayo, Mimeo, 2009.
Gallie, Duncan, ed. *Employment Regimes and the Quality of Work.* Oxford: Oxford University Press, 2007.
Henau (de) Jérôme and Puech, Isabelle. "O tempo de trabalho de homens e de mulheres na Europa." In *Mercado deTrabalho et Gênero. Comparações internationais,* edited by A. de Oliveira Costa, B. Sorj, C. Bruschini, and E. Hirata, 207–226. Rio de Janeiro: FGV Editora, 2008.
Jepsen, Maria. "Quand la dimension du genre entrera-t-elle réellement en jeu?" *Travail, Genre et Sociétés* 19 (2008): 163–169.
Jorgensen, Henning. "From a Beautiful Swan to an Ugly Duckling: Changes in Danish Activation Policies since 2003." Paper presented at the ASPEN/ETUI activation conference, Brno, 20–21 March 2009.
Kochan, Thomas, Katz Harry, and Robert McKersie. *The Transformation of American Industrial Relations.* New York: Basic Books, 1987.

Lorenz, Ernest and Antoine Valeyre. *Les formes d'organisation du travail dans les pays de l'Union Européenne.* Paris: Centre Etudes de l'Emploi, Document de travail n° 32, 2004.

Méda, Dominique. "Flexicurité: quel équilibre entre flexibilité et sécurité?" *Droit Social* 7(8) (2009): 763–776.

Miguélez, Fausto and Carlos Prieto. "L'autre côté de la croissance de 'emploi: une précarité qui se perpétue." *Travail et Emploi* 115 (2008): 45–57.

Pitxer i Campos, Joseph and Amat Sánchez Velasco. "Estrategia sindicales y modelo económico Español." *Cuadernos de Relaciones Laborales* 26(1) (2008): 89–122.

Prieto, Carlos, ed. *La calidad del empleo en España: una aproximación teórica y empírica.* Madrid: Ministerio de Trabajo e Inmigración, 2009.

Recio, Albert. *Trabajo, personas, mercados.* Madrid: FUHEM e ICARIA, 1997.

Rocha Sánchez, Fernando, Jorge Aragón Medina, and Jesús Cruces Aguilera. *Cambios productivos y empleo en España.* Madrid: Ministerio de Trabajo e Inmigración, 2008.

Rodríguez Cabrero, Gregorio. "L'État-providence espagnol: pérennité, transformations et défis." *Travail et Emploi* 115 (2008): 95–109.

Schmid, Gunter. "Theory of Transitional Labour Markets and "Flexicurity": Lessons for Transition and Developing Countries." Paper presented to the European Training Foundation (ETF), Turin, 14 May 2009.

Serrano, Amparo. "Reshaping Welfare States: Activation Regimes in Europe." In *Reshaping Welfare States: Activation Regimes*, edited by Amparo Serrano and Lars Magnusson, 11–35. Brussels: Peter Lang, 2007.

Serrano, Amparo, Alba Artiaga, Carlos Fernández, Paz Martín, and José Francisco Tovar. *Protección y flexiguridad. La modernización de los servicios públicos de empleo.* Research Report, 2009.

Silvera, Rachel. "Flexicurité et genre, un angle mort." *Travail, Genre et Sociétés* 19 (2008): 151–153.

Stroobants, Marcelle. *Sociologie du travail.* Paris: Edits. Nathan, 1993.

4 Inequality as a Central Component in the Redefinition of Security
The Case of Gender

Maria Jepsen

INTRODUCTION

Over the past couple of decades, a host of concepts dealing with social policy and labour-market reforms have emerged: transitional labour markets (TLMs) (cf. Schmid, this volume); capabilities (cf. Salais, this volume); social investment (e.g., Hemerijck, 2012); and flexicurity, to name some of the most frequently cited. Although the concepts differ somewhat in nature, insofar as they take their inspiration from different approaches to the question of what a labour market should look like and how the population can best be empowered and/or protected, they do share certain common features, and all of them, notably, represent counterproposals to the market-based paradigm of complete deregulation of labour markets and retrenchment of the welfare state. Common to these concepts is also their concern with the failure of the current configuration of labour-market regulation and social policies to manage the ever-changing nature of the labour market and to deal with the growing inequality in society. Most concepts build their arguments for the need for change on three main developments: the changing configuration of demographics, globalisation, and technological change. Their proposed solutions vary strongly, however, ranging from concepts built on protection to others based on investment and, yet again, others that argue in favour of re-commodification (Bonoli, 2009). The manner in which they incorporate the issue of inequality also varies strongly; yet in all cases it is stated that one of the aims is to increase gender equality.

This is a straightforward claim which, simple as it may at first appear, does however require that the policy concepts should be able to encompass, mitigate, and correct long-standing inequalities in the labour market and society at large. Although the past thirty years of gender-equality awareness and corrective policies have, to some extent, improved equality between women and men, important forms of inequality between the sexes are still present and progress towards closing the gaps is slow (CEC, 2012b). The main issues to be tackled by social and labour-market policies pertain to women's weaker link with the labour market and the unequal distribution of unpaid work.

Broadly speaking, there are six issues that justify a gendered approach to social and labour-market policies:

1. Women make up the greater part of employees in atypical employ-ment accompanied by broken career paths.
2. This results in relationships with the welfare state that are more com-plicated than those of men.
3. Women are unpaid providers of welfare.
4. They are segregated into certain segments of the labour market.
5. They continue to be discriminated against, mostly due to their (poten-tial) role as mother and carer.
6. They still tend to be regarded as second earners, and hence not in need of financial independence.

This chapter sets out to explore how gender equality is understood in the currently politically most important concept of labour-market reform, namely, flexicurity. It argues that, whereas increasing gender equality is claimed as an aim of the concept, there exist few, if any, concrete policy proposals to back up this claim and that, furthermore, given the way in which the concept tends to be constructed, flexicurity strategies could very well turn out in fact to have precisely the opposite effect.

The chapter is structured as follows: The following section will briefly present the literature on flexicurity and gender; the next will empirically explore the link between gender equality and flexicurity; and the final sec-tion will discuss the implications of the flexicurity nexus for a redefinition of security, as well as of flexibility, and will conclude.

FLEXICURITY AND GENDER: A LOOK AT THE LITERATURE AND THE POLICY DOCUMENTS

There can be no doubt that *flexicurity* is nowadays one of the most fre-quently used terms in Europe in the discussion of labour-market reforms. This concept has risen high on the policy agenda on the European level and has come to occupy a foremost place in the academic literature with almost unprecedented speed and intensity. Although this rise on the political agenda has been accompanied by some controversy, there does seem to be a degree of consensus, among certain actors at least, that flexicurity is indeed a useful concept around which to shape the debate on labour-market reforms (Keune and Serrano, this volume; Keune and Jepsen, 2007), despite the fact—or maybe because of the fact—that dif-ferent actors (political as well as academic) do not define and perceive the concept in the same way. There exists, in fact, no clear definition of flexicurity, although the documents that have come out of the European Commission's DG Employment and Social Affairs in the past few years have certainly been aimed at making the concept more concrete and at translating it into concrete policy reforms. In short, flexicurity is cur-rently one of the key concepts used in the discussion of labour markets, both in the policy arena and in academic research.

Despite the constantly growing literature and policy debate on flexicurity since the beginning of the 2000s, there are actually relatively few articles dealing with the gendered aspect of flexicurity (for a review, see Lewis and Plomien, 2009). This seems astonishing, given that men and women start out from different positions, that the power balances are skewed, and that, in general, the implications of labour-market reforms for men and women are rather different (Lewis, 2009; Crompton, 2006). At present, the failure to take these facts into consideration is creating a situation in which it is likely that women will remain confined to their current status, namely, the adjustment factor of the labour market. The following section will provide a brief analysis of the conception of gender equality and flexicurity as put forward by the European Commission, as well as a brief overview of the literature that has dealt with the issue.

The European Commission

A careful gendered analysis of the main documents that have shaped the European Union's flexicurity approach and policy (CEC, 2006, 2007a, 2007b, 2007c, 2012a, 2012c) serves to reveal the inadequate consideration paid to the gendered implications of labour-market and social policy reforms. Whereas it cannot be stated that gender is not taken into consideration at all, it is possible to question the way that this aspect is dealt with, a criticism that will be discussed briefly below. In all documents women are mentioned as one of the groups at risk of marginalisation or as representing a category of the population at risk of discrimination, alongside youth, older persons, and non-Europeans. That all the latter groups are in fact constituted of both men and women, and that each group has its particular issues that need to be dealt with, are aspects that seem to be regarded as less relevant. This does not mean that there is no direct emphasis on the fact that the issues and impact of labour-market policies on men and women are not the same; the fact remains, however, that core aspects of gender inequality are not taken into account.

On an overall basis, there does seem to be a commitment to ensuring that flexicurity measures should be to the benefit of both men's and women's situations on the labour market, although the wording, nature and extent of the commitment vary. One of the first more widely distributed documents on flexicurity to have come out of the European Commission, namely, the annual report *Employment in Europe 2006* (CEC, 2006), has the least emphasis on the gender dimension. In this document there is a very strong emphasis on reforming unemployment benefits and the employment protection legislation (EPL). There seems to be no concern regarding the facts that less women have access to unemployment benefits than men, that when women do receive unemployment benefits they receive on average less, and that this is due to their initial labour-market situation characterised by more interruptions and less hours worked per day, week, month, or year (OECD, 2010; Leschke, 2007). Hence restrictions on unemployment benefits are bound to have differing impacts on women and on men. Furthermore, in CEC (2006) the lower employment rate of women is partly explained by the EPL; the conclusion thus put forward is that strict EPL is detrimental to women's integration on the labour market, so that easing the restrictions would facilitate women's access to employment. This argument is reiterated in the communication from the European Commission *Towards Common Principles of Flexicurity* (CEC, 2007a). On page 10 of this document, the point that "flexicurity should support gender equality by promoting equal access to quality employment" is put forward, and it is also emphasised that flexicurity should offer possibilities to combine work and family life, including the provision of childcare. It remains an open question, however, whether the policy proposals put forward will ensure this outcome, for the emphasis is very strongly on external numerical flexibility and the upgrading and maintenance of the skills needed to manage this flexibility. In the report from the European expert group on flexicurity, *Flexicurity Pathways. Turning Hurdles into Stepping Stones* (CEC, 2007b), the gendered aspect of flexicurity is explicitly highlighted as a key issue needing to be addressed. There is an acknowledgment in this document that gender gaps remain wide, and that there is a genuine need to commit to the European Pact for Gender Equality (Council of the European Union, 2006).[1] The accent is placed on the need to enable women and men to combine work with care and on the fact that achievement of this aim should contribute to equal opportunities and gender equality. The report goes on to offer a number of pointers as to how this is to be achieved. There is a reference to the fact that pension schemes should not be organised in accordance with the pro rata principle as this would be to the detriment of part-time workers (read women) and work-life incentives (again read women) (CEC, 2007b: 28), and also to the fact that there is a need for some countries to develop working time flexibility and part-time jobs with equal treatment at all job levels, to tackle the pay gap and to provide the necessary means for parents to combine work with care. The seemingly genuine commitment of the expert group to tackling the gender gaps, however, starts to appear slightly suspect in that an identical paragraph on women—stating that improvements are needed with regard to measures facilitating combining care and work, and that women need help in meeting the flexibility demands at the higher levels of the labour market—is to be found in three different places in the document (CEC, 2007b : 24, 26, 29). This repetition appears to betray a 'paste-and-copy' approach to the subject without any further reflection having been given to the question of what particular measures should address the different problems arising in relation to gender equality.

In more recent documents from the European Commission on the subject, there has been a tendency to even further reduce the gendered perspective of flexicurity. Whereas the communication from the European Commission on *Towards a Job-Rich Recovery* (CEC, 2012c) points to the need to achieve equal pay for men and women, adequate childcare, the elimination of discrimination and tax-benefit disincentives for female participation in the labour market, and optimisation of the duration of both maternity and parental leave (CEC, 2012c: 10), the supporting document to the communication addressing flexicurity (CEC, 2012a) displays a flagrant failure to take this dimension into account. In CEC (2012a) the brief overview of welfare state and labour-market challenges across the European Union addresses gender inequalities as representing a challenge in the Southern European countries alone and even there only with respect to the different types of employment contract. The document acknowledges that flexicurity should contribute to gender equality, but then goes on to qualify this need as being the ability to better combine work and family. This is a clear step backwards from previous European Commission documents on the issue, as the multidimensional aspect of gender equality is neglected and the issue is treated as being merely a question of work–life balance, thereby neglecting the unequal distribution of paid and unpaid work and the consequences of this unequal distribution.

It thus becomes quite clear from an examination of these documents emanating from the European level that the gender aspect and gender equality are hardly perceived as constituting an important issue in this context. When the issue *is* put forward, it is with the aim of ensuring that women have access to employment and that they can combine work and care. Although this is indeed an important issue, it is far from being the *most* important one. What is most important is to ensure that women are not discriminated against, either directly or indirectly, that they acquire financial independence, and are not maintained in their current situation. There are very few concrete proposals on how to change the currently persisting imbalance and to ensure that women have equal access to quality employment. The point to be stressed in relation to the above is that when there is an emphasis on improving the situation of women on the labour market, its sole purpose is to enable women to combine work and care; in other words, the view implicitly expressed here is that the meaning of *quality* employment for women is employment that offers them the possibility of combining work and care.

In conclusion, a careful analysis of policy documents coming out of the European Commission leads to the conclusion that any commitment to gender equality seems to be no more than lip service, in the sense that the perception of gender equality is that it has been adequately achieved once women have been integrated into the labour market. This furthermore entails the outcome that quality employment for women seems to be reduced to the creation of jobs that enable women to combine work and family life, including the provision of childcare (Jepsen, 2008; Lewis, 2009). This problem has been explicitly recognised by the European Commission, which, in July 2007, in its manual for the gender mainstreaming of employment policies, included a section on the gender mainstreaming of flexicurity (CEC, 2008). The main problem lies in the fact that gender mainstreaming is marginalised and rarely carried out in a systematic and coherent manner (Rubery et al., 2006; Platenga, Remery, and Rubery, 2007).

The Research-Based Literature on Gender and Flexicurity

The few research-based articles that explore the gendered impact of flexicurity policy strategies seem to converge on the conclusion that flexicurity, as it is set out in the European Commission documents and described in the academic literature, is far from representing a guarantee to the promotion of gender equality.

The articles emphasise the lack of clarity surrounding the impact of flexicurity on income security and labour-market segregation, which are some of the more problematic issues with regard to the achievement of gender equality.

Lewis and Plomien (2009) explore the meaning of internal and external flexibility, as well as of employment-based security, and their differing implications for men and women. Their analysis concludes that women are already more present in 'flexible' work than men, but that the security side of flexicurity is insufficient to compensate for the income insecurity and labour-market segregation arising from this situation. The main reason for this shortcoming is that the security side fails to deal adequately with the unequal distribution of unpaid work between men and women.

Löfström (2009) focuses on a broader examination of gender equality, beyond the sole issue of flexicurity, but her conclusions with regard to the potential impact of flexicurity on gender emphasise that:

> Women's responsibility for the home and children not only affects their security of employment, it also compromises their inclusion in workplace flexibility strategies involving working hours and on-the-job training, with all that this implies for their career prospects and employability. Childcare and family policy issues are therefore of crucial importance if flexicurity is to contribute to greater gender equality and establish the balance between production and reproduction needed in many countries today. (2009: 39)

Hansen (2007) is one of the very few authors to have assessed the Danish 'golden triangle' from a gendered perspective. She argues that what political and academic observers alike tend to miss, and which is absolutely vital for interpreting the Danish model, is the broad range of public care services that provide quality employment for women, alongside the individualised taxation and social protection system, features which enable women to navigate on the labour market on an equal footing with men. She calls for a renaming of the Danish model, from flexicurity to flexicarity. Fredman (2004), on the other hand, states that women in the UK are far from having achieved flexicurity, despite the framework of social rights that has been built up since the 1970s and which protects non-standard workers to a certain extent, because women remain in a precarious labour-market situation, finding themselves all too often in situations that are beyond the bounds of legislation. The main reason for this chronic precarity, despite the introduction of some security, is the absence of guarantees that individuals who navigate between paid and unpaid work can do so without incurring too high a cost. This situation is compounded by the long-hours culture in the UK and the lack of affordable childcare, which leaves women—especially low-income earners—with no choice but to reduce their working hours or, in the case of middle-income women, to leave the labour market completely. Fredman concludes that it is only when the losses that result from transiting between paid and unpaid work can be eliminated that men will start taking their share of the responsibility for unpaid work. She concludes also that this reality remains very far away.

Jepsen (2005, 2006, 2007, 2008) extensively examines the link between gender equality and different elements of the flexibility—security nexus. She argues that, as flexicurity is currently conceptualised and proposed as a policy strategy, there is little doubt that it can have a rather negative impact on gender equality, which makes the flexicurity approach worrying from a gender perspective insofar as it obstructs options for ensuring an evolution in gender role models and their definition. However, she also argues that, by expanding the flexicurity approach to take into account the gender perspective and break the existing gender divide, it could become possible to establish the conditions for a new work culture that would not only engage women in paid work, but would also legitimise and normalise men in unpaid work, as well as emphasise the need for quality employment for all.

Her analysis demonstrates that there seems to be a potential for the flexicurity approach to improve the situation for employees as well as employers, because various types of contracts and working time arrangements could become more secure; this approach can give momentum to extending and reinforcing rights to paid leave, to LLL (Life Long Learning strategies), while also providing incentives to make transitions between different working time regimes, as well as between paid and unpaid work, smoother and less costly to the individual undertaking the transition. The main problem lies, however, in the fact that the flexicurity approach does not deal with the problem of financial independence that is linked to working few hours a week or a year, or with the related problems that occur in the social protection system where benefits are becoming increasingly individualised. Nor does this approach deal with the problem of persisting gender-segregated labour markets as it tends to reinforce the current gender roles rather than to propose new ones. In essence, flexicurity simply does not enter into discussion of who bears the long-term risks associated with time taken out of work, childcare, fixed-terms contracts, etc. And as long as these elements are excluded from consideration, doubts will remain as to whether flexicurity does actually promote gender equality and, furthermore, offer a route to providing quality employment for men and women.

The above analyses are brought together and combined in Knijn and Smit (2009), who argue that the three current paradigms used to discuss and frame labour and welfare state reforms—namely, the social investment approach, the TLM model (including flexicurity) and the individual life-course model—all tend to be used as foundations and building blocks for constructing work–life balance policies across the European Union. However, in their efforts to move forward in this direction, member states have subordinated the gender-equality agenda to the creation of competitive economies, such that equal-opportunity and work-family policies have been adjusted for the sole purpose of promoting higher employment rates, while the aspect of ensuring gender equality has been very much neglected.

LINKING THE FLEXICURITY POLICY STRATEGY TO GENDER EQUALITY

Flexicurity, as promoted in the European Commission communication (CEC, 2007c), emphasises four main components, listed below :

1. *Flexible and reliable contractual arrangements* (from the perspective of the employer and the employee, of "insiders" and "outsiders") through modern labour laws, collective agreements and work organisation;
2. *Comprehensive lifelong learning (LLL) strategies* to ensure the continual adaptability and employability of workers, particularly the most vulnerable;
3. *Effective active labour market policies (ALMP)* that help people cope with rapid change, reduce unemployment spells and ease transitions to new jobs;
4. *Modern social security systems* that provide adequate income support, encourage employment and facilitate labour market mobility. This includes broad coverage of social protection provisions (unemployment benefits, pensions and healthcare) that help people combine work with private and family responsibilities such as childcare.

These four components can be implemented by using eight common principles as guidelines (Council of the European Union, 2007). Gender equality is referred to, in particular, in common principle number 6, which states that:

flexicurity should support gender equality, by promoting equal access to quality employment for women and men and offering measures to reconcile work, family and private life.

As already mentioned in the first section, this statement is not supported by any concrete policy proposals other than that mentioned in the four components of flexicurity listed above, thereby implying that a rigorous implementation of the four components will lead to gender equality. This section sets out to test the truth of this claim by examining whether there is a correlation between any of the four components of flexicurity and gender equality. It will do this by correlating the European Gender-Equality Index (EUGEI) (Platenga et al., 2009) with variables representative of the four components.

The EUGEI is based on the universal caregiver model (Fraser, 1997) and is composed of four dimensions, namely, the equal sharing of paid work, of money, of decision-making power, and of time, with each of the dimensions covering two sub-dimensions. The different dimensions of the index can be found in Annex 4.1. These indices are influenced not only by labour-market developments, but also by the institutional settings and policies that support the labour market, such as the welfare state provisions. Hence the four components of the flexicurity strategy as defined in CEC (2007a) will be assessed as to their gender-equality-enhancing ability by using the EUGEI.[2]

The first component of the flexicurity strategy concentrates on flexible and reliable contracts. Whereas this can interpreted in a host of manners, the policy papers and discourses tend to concentrate on the importance and design of the EPL (see Keune and Jepsen, 2007; CEC, 2007a, 2012a). For this reason, we will measure the first component using the OECD EPL indicator. The second component emphasises the importance of LLL in providing security; we measure this component by the proportion of GDP spent on LLL. Likewise, because ALMP is put forward as a means of providing employment security; this third component of flexicurity will be measured by the percentage of GDP spent on ALMP. The fourth component emphasises income security and childcare, and the percentage of GDP spent on unemployment benefits and percentage of children covered by childcare will therefore represent the last component. We will not test the link between other work–life balance policies and gender equality, as this has already been extensively analysed as reported in the first section.

This empirical part is based on correlations at a fixed point in time. Hence whereas the correlations can provide us with an idea of how two variables, or rather in this case indices, are correlated, they do not tell us anything about causality. The correlations are carried out for the EU-25 countries (Austria, Belgium, Cyprus, Czech Republic, Denmark, Estonia, Finland, France, Germany, Greece, Hungary, Ireland, Italy, Latvia, Lithuania, Luxembourg, Malta, Netherlands, Poland, Portugal, Slovak Republic, Slovenia, Spain, Sweden, United Kingdom), except for the correlations using OECD data on EPL, unemployment benefit, and ALMP spending as a percentage of GDP, where data are available for only a sub-set of the EU-25.

EPL and Gender Equality

One of the most debated labour-market institutions, the EPL, has been extensively researched, theoretically as well as empirically, in order to assess its impact on the overall employment and unemployment rate. Although the empirical literature cannot conclude that the EPL affects the overall rates, there seems to be some evidence that it can impact on the structure of the labour market (IILS, 2012). In CEC (2006) the authors seem to conclude that a high EPL impacts negatively on the female employment rate and hence has a detrimental effect on gender equality. However, as Figure 4.1 displays, there seems to be no correlation between the measure of the

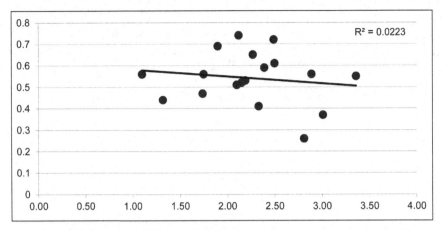

Figure 4.1 Correlation between EPL and EUGEI, 2005.
Source: Author's computation based on OECD (2005) and Platenga et al. (2009).

overall strictness of EPL and the EUGEI. Nor do correlations between the sub-indices of the EPL (regular employment and temporary employment), not shown, display any correlation, thereby seemingly corroborating the lack of any strong correlation between EPL and gender equality. In other words, easing, reconfiguring, or restricting EPL does not seem to imply that gender equality will either improve or deteriorate (this will be discussed more extensively below). These observations serve to call into question the strong emphasis placed on easing EPL as a means of improving gender equality (CEC, 2007a, 2012a) by increasing female employment rates.

Countries: Austria, Belgium, Czech Republic, Denmark, Finland, France, Germany, Greece, Hungary, Ireland, Italy, Luxembourg, Netherlands, Poland, Portugal, Slovak Republic, Spain, Sweden, United Kingdom.

LLL and Gender Equality

LLL has long been promoted as a tool and process to enhance and strengthen the adaptability and employability of employees in an ever-changing labour market. Hence in a flexicurity policy strategy, LLL can be regarded as enhancing both flexibility and security insofar as it enables employees to become more flexible and thereby provides them with the security of being able to adapt and be employable. Whereas this strict causality can be discussed, there seems to be little doubt that LLL tends to benefit those that already have a higher level of formal education and a firm foot in the labour market, while failing to benefit those most in need of LLL, i.e., the more vulnerable groups on the labour market, such as older workers, youth, fixed-term contracts, and part-time workers (Holford et al., 2009).

Hence it is no surprise to see the weak correlation between the percentage of working age population participating in any form of LLL and the EUGEI (Figure 4.2).[3]

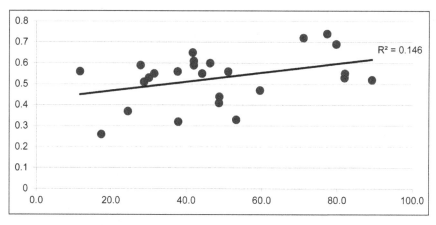

Figure 4.2 Correlation between participation in any LLL and EUGEI, 2005.
Source: Eurostat, labour force survey and Platenga et al. (2009).
Countries: Austria, Belgium, Cyprus, Czech Republic, Denmark, Estonia, Finland, France, Germany, Greece, Hungary, Ireland, Italy, Latvia, Lithuania, Luxembourg, Malta, Netherlands, Poland, Portugal, Slovak Republic, Slovenia, Spain, Sweden, United Kingdom.

Research focused on gender and LLL tends to emphasise three issues: firstly, that women outnumber men in higher-level formal education; secondly, that women could potentially benefit from a stronger focus on LLL as it would empower women seeking to (re-)enter the labour market after a spell of (un)paid leave. The third issue often raised is, however, that the higher-level educational attainment and rather equal participation in LLL does not necessarily translate into better labour-market outcomes. This lack of translation can be explained by the lack of supporting social welfare policies (Holford et al., 2009) required to enable women to participate in the labour market, as well as by the potential limiting factor of LLL insofar as it actually tends to accommodate and reinforce gender segregation along the lines of occupation and sectors (Rubery et al., 2006).

In other words, enhancing and extending opportunities for LLL will not automatically improve gender equality, even though this form of education does undoubtedly represent the potential for offering improved opportunities for learning.

ALMP and Gender Equality

Much along the same lines of thinking, ALMP are aimed at providing support to the unemployed, at helping them to achieve rapid change, and easing their labour-market transitions. In theory, ALMP can lower structural unemployment in two ways: by promoting more efficient matching between job-seekers and vacancies and by bringing discouraged and

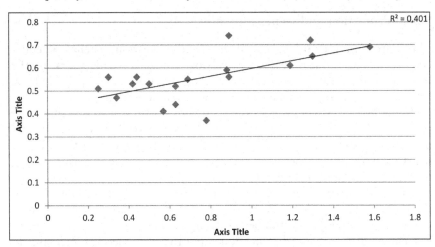

Figure 4.3   Correlation between % of GDP spent on ALMP and EUGEI, 2005.
Source: OECD (2006) and Platenga et al (2009).
Countries: Austria, Belgium, Czech Republic, Denmark, Finland, France, Germany, Greece, Hungary, Ireland, Italy, Luxembourg, Netherlands, Poland, Portugal, Slovak Republic, Spain, Sweden, United Kingdom.

socially excluded workers back into the labour market (Dar and Tzannatos, 1999), thereby representing an opportunity to integrate or reintegrate women who have been regarded as inactive or are returning from periods of providing unpaid care.

Evaluations of ALMP programmes show very different outcomes in terms of getting the unemployed into employment, as well in terms of their impact on wages. Although the results are inconclusive, there does appear to be a convergence around the conclusion that, whereas there might, in the short term, be some positive impacts, in the long term this is much more difficult to obtain (Dar and Tzannatos, 1999; OECD, 2005). Furthermore, there seems to be a difference regarding the types of programme that have a positive impact for men and those that prove of benefit to women (Leschke and Jepsen, 2011; Rubery et al., 2006).

Figure 4.3 seems to indicate that there is a positive correlation between spending on ALMP and gender equality. This would in turn imply that adequate financing of ALMPs could contribute to gender equality, as operationalised by the EUGEI, by reducing gender gaps. There is also the risk, however, that ALMPs may reinforce the lines of segregation where the allocation of places provided by the ALMPs serves to reinforce gender stereotypes or divisions on the labour market (Rubery et al., 2006). Whereas this risk is compounded by the segregation with regard to time and type of ALMP allocated to men and women, women do seem to have better access to ALMPs where the schemes are encompassing and generous (Leschke and Jepsen, 2011).

Social Protection and Gender Equality

The contribution, or otherwise, of the social protection systems to gender equality has been researched extensively over the past twenty years (see the reports from the EGGE network for a good overview, downloadable from http://ec.europa.eu/justice/gender-equality/document/index_en.htm).

To analyse all components of the social protection system and their contributions to gender equality is beyond the scope of this article. We will instead focus on two elements of social protection that seem to be at the heart of many policy documents and research articles (see above), namely, unemployment benefits and childcare.

One of the main challenges for unemployment benefits is to ensure that job-seekers are provided with an adequate income, thereby enabling them to search for employment and benefit from income security. In this respect, women are at risk if social protection is not raised to meet the increases in the flexibility they are inevitably required to show in their working lives. This is the case in several countries, e.g., the UK, Denmark, and Germany, where income and hours thresholds are used as determinants of eligibility for unemployment support—an arrangement that is particularly problematic for women, especially in the case of discontinuous careers and short-hours part-time work.

Figure 4.4 shows that there is a positive correlation between the percentage of GDP spent on unemployment benefits and the EUGEI; hence relative

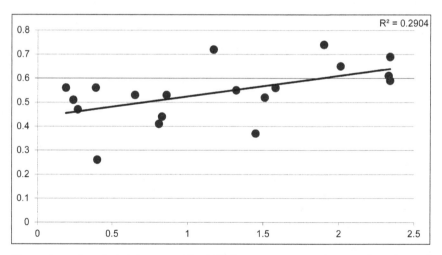

Figure 4.4 Correlation between % of GDP spent on unemployment benefits and EUGEI, 2005.
Source: OECD (2006) and Platenga et al (2009).
Countries: Austria, Belgium, Czech Republic, Denmark, Finland, France, Germany, Greece, Hungary, Ireland, Italy, Luxembourg, Netherlands, Poland, Portugal, Slovak Republic, Spain, Sweden, United Kingdom.

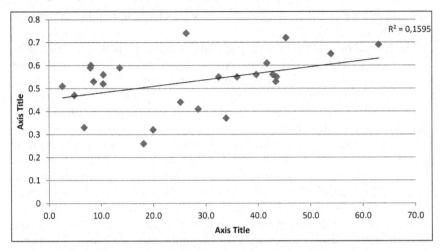

Figure 4.5 Correlation between childcare enrolment for children 3–5 years of age and EUGEI, 2005.
Source: OECD Family Database (2010) and Platenga et al. (2009).
Countries: Austria, Belgium, Cyprus, Czech Republic, Denmark, Estonia, Finland, France, Germany, Greece, Hungary, Ireland, Italy, Latvia, Lithuania, Luxembourg, Malta, Netherlands, Poland, Portugal, Slovak Republic, Slovenia, Spain, Sweden, United Kingdom.

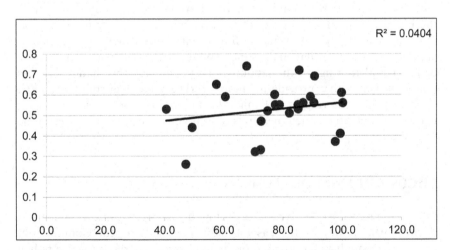

Figure 4.6 Correlation between childcare enrolment for children below 3 years of age and EUGEI, 2005.
Source: OECD Family Database (2010) and Platenga et al. (2009).
Countries: Austria, Belgium, Cyprus, Czech Republic, Denmark, Estonia, Finland, France, Germany, Greece, Hungary, Ireland, Italy, Latvia, Lithuania, Luxembourg, Malta, Netherlands, Poland, Portugal, Slovak Republic, Slovenia, Spain, Sweden, United Kingdom.

higher spending on unemployment benefits goes hand in hand with reduced gender gaps.

The second indicator, the percentage of children enrolled in formal childcare, is presented for two age-groups: children below 3 years and those aged 3–5. Childcare is firmly promoted by the European Commission, as well as by scholars working on gender issues, as being one of the key factors in enabling men and women to combine work and private life. Surprisingly, both Figure 4.5 and Figure 4.6 show rather low correlations with the EUGEI, thus implying that there is little correlation between reduction of gender gaps and provision of formal childcare. It should be noticed that the correlation is strongest for childcare provision for children aged below 3 years of age, which is precisely the group of children for whom the provision of childcare is very low. One way of interpreting this result is that childcare will enable women and men to participate in the labour market and can hence reduce the gender gaps in employment and unemployment. However, to reduce the employment gender gap is far from ensuring gender equality. Much more far-reaching measures are needed to guarantee a situation in which women's entry into employment will lead to a reduction in gender gaps and hence gender equality.

The correlations between six indicators for the flexicurity strategy as promoted by the European Commission and the EUGEI show us that EPL does not correlate with gender equality; that LLL and childcare correlate very little with gender equality; and that spending on ALMP and unemployment benefits are the indicators that have the highest correlation with the EUGEI. A preliminary way of interpreting these results is to say that reducing gender gaps is intimately linked with the existence of an encompassing welfare state that enables men and women to participate on a more or less equal footing on the labour market. On the other hand, whereas policy measures that provide for more market-enhancing solutions, LLL, childcare, or a lowering of ELP might lead to an increase in female labour-market participation, such measures offer no guarantee with respect to the achievement of gender equality.

DISCUSSION AND CONCLUSIONS

In this chapter we set out to explore the link between the four components of the flexicurity policy strategy, as it is defined by the European Commission, and gender equality. We focused on five indicators representing the policy issues that lie at the heart of the strategy: EPL, LLL, ALMP, unemployment benefits, and childcare. Our evidence can be no more than tentative, as our data are cross-sectional and we rely solely on correlations; we cannot, as such, draw conclusions as to causal effects of policy measures. Our data do, nonetheless, suggest that an encompassing welfare state is closely interlinked with gender equality. Measures that enable women to enter and adapt to the labour market cannot, taken alone, ensure that the resulting increase in female employment rates will increase gender equality.

Although our evidence is by no means exhaustive, these findings are supported by research on work–life balance (see Crompton and Lyonette, 2006; Eurostat, 2009). Countries that support mothers' employment in general but do not link this to a gender-equality agenda will not necessarily reduce gender gaps beyond the gender employment gap. By framing security for individuals in terms of decreasing barriers for efficient labour-market participation, one fails to address the root cause of the problem. It is thus that there will be no automatic reduction or disappearance of inequalities in terms of flexibility, income, access to social protection, paid and unpaid work with implementation of the flexicurity agenda. This then questions the concepts of ALMP, LLL, and work–life balance as providing security in themselves as well as guaranteeing employment security, in the sense that employment as a road to adequate security is a reality for rather few women. Interruptions in career paths, on the one hand, and labour-market segregation, on the other, compounded by the unequal distribution of paid and unpaid work, mean that many women are far from achieving financial independence and adequate entitlement to social security provision. What this means is that providing security in terms of the needs of the labour market will not necessarily empower women or help them to become autonomous. Although gender awareness and women's role in the economy as well as society has increased, this has not necessarily translated into policies and institutions that guarantee gender equality by equalising the roles between men and women (Jenson, 2009). It has, rather, rationalised the role of women into one of tension between modern societies' dependence on raising female employment and the fact that women are having fewer children. This state of affairs results in a translation of gender issues into the need to combine family and work without considering who bears the risks associated with childbearing and rearing and how this contributes to promoting, or rather militates against, gender equality (Jenson, 2009).

In view of the above conclusions, it also seems reasonable to question whether inequalities for other vulnerable groups in the labour market are likely to decrease with the flexicurity policy strategy. In short, a conceptualisation of security for workers and families in terms of labour-market needs leaves little scope for reducing inequality and segmentation either within or beyond the labour market. Because it is not through more equal access to employment that inequalities will necessarily be reduced, security needs to be rethought in terms of how it is a means of reducing inequalities in a multitude of different spheres and not only in terms of employment rates.

Vielle (2007) embarks on an analysis of how it would be advisable to reconsider elements that could constitute a new way of reflecting upon and conceiving of security and social protection as a way of responding to collective and individual challenges. She pleads for the inclusion of housing, early education, energy, credit, communication and information media, etc., thereby acknowledging that security should be granted along the multitude of inequality fault lines that are present in modern society. She insists, further, that services of general interest are an important element in constructing such a new model of security and protection.

Turning to the link between gender equality and security, there is a need to include and acknowledge the root causes of forms of inequality such as labour-market discrimination or the unequal distribution of power and unpaid work in order to ensure that women can function as independent individuals in a society. Flexicurity could indeed represent a tool to establish a new gender contract and gender divide, but, for this to be the case, the way in which the concept is currently handled would have to be redefined. The flexicurity approach does not currently deal with the problem of financial independence (lack of adequate wages) associated with working only a few hours a week or a few weeks a year. Nor does it consider the problems arising from atypical employment and their repercussions in the social protection system where benefits are becoming increasingly individualised and based on the contribution record. Nor does it deal with the problem of persistently gender-segregated labour markets that serve to reinforce the current gender pattern. In essence, there is a danger that flexicurity, rather than proposing a new gender contract able to enhance equality between men and women, will have the effect of reinforcing the current gender contract based on unequal participation in paid and unpaid work.

Women and men enter the labour market on unequal terms due to the uneven distribution of the provision of unpaid care and, no matter how secure non-standard working time arrangements may be or may become, this will not change the distribution of unpaid work. In other words, the successful combination of work and family life will continue to be based on the adaptations and adjustments made by women.

By expanding the flexicurity approach to take into account the gender perspective and break the existing gender divide, it might prove possible to establish the conditions for a new work culture that would not only engage women in paid work, but would legitimise and normalise men in unpaid work, at the same time as it would emphasise the need for quality employment for all. However, this approach and discussion is marginalised in the current academic research and policy debate, and this marginalisation makes the flexicurity approach worrying from a gender perspective as it obstructs options for ensuring an evolution in gender role models and their definition. This, in turn, restrains any move towards incorporating a collective social manifestation of these changes.

If gender equality and flexicurity are to go hand in hand, we need a conceptualisation of security that would enable it to be rethought in terms of balancing equality and encompassing issues such as the individualisation of social and tax rights, the redistribution of paid and unpaid work, housing, compensation for excessive flexibility, gender-assessed rights for de-commodification for care and up-skilling (Jepsen, 2005, 2006, 2007). Equally important is the need for a better understanding of the public services required to provide the basis for gender equality and to address workplace practices that hamper gender equality (Lewis and Plomien, 2009).

A flexicurity strategy based on supply-side measures and on the assumption that women and men have equal power in the labour market is bound, by neglecting the issue of inequalities in the policy setup, to exacerbate cases of inequality rather than limit them.

ANNEX 4.1 EUROPEAN UNION GENDER-EQUALITY INDEX

1. Equal sharing of paid work
   Differences in employment rates between women and men in percentage points
   Differences in unemployment rates between women and men in percentage points
2. Equal sharing of money
   Gender pay gap
   Poverty gender gap for single households
3. Equal sharing of decision-making power
   Difference in the share of women and men in Parliament
   Gender gap among legislators, senior officials, and managers
4. Equal sharing of time
   Gender gap in caring time
   Gender gap in leisure

NOTES

1. The European Pact for Gender Equality sets out the European strategy on gender equality.
2. In order not to measure phenomena influenced by purely cyclical developments, we use the latest pre-crisis comparable data, which are from 2005. This is due to lack of timely comparable data for the EUGEI index (Platenga et al., 2009).
3. The result is similar when the correlation is established with the percentage of working age women participating in any form of LLL.

BIBLIOGRAPHY

Bonoli, G. "Varieties of Social Investment in Labour Market Policy." In *What Future for Social Investment?*, edited by Nathalie Morel, Bruno Palier, and Joakim Palme, 55–66. Stockholm: Institute for Future Studies, 2009.

CEC. *Employment in Europe 2006*. Luxembourg: Office for Official Publications of the European Communities, 2006.

CEC. *Communication from the Commission to the Council, the European Parliament, the European Economic and Social Committee and the Committee of the Regions. Towards Common Principles of Flexicurity: More and Better Jobs through Flexibility and Security.* COM (2007) 359 Final, 2007a.

CEC. *Flexicurity Pathways. Turning Hurdles into Stepping Stones.* Report by the European Expert Group on Flexicurity, 2007b.

CEC. *Towards Common Principles of Flexicurity.* 15497/07, SOC 476, ECOFIN 483, 2007c.

CEC. *Gender Mainstreaming of Employment Policies, Social Inclusion and Social Protection Policies.* DG Employment, social affairs and equal opportunities, equality between men/women, 2008.

CEC. *Commission Staff Working Document. 'Open, Dynamic and Inclusive Labour Markets'.* SWD(2012) 97 final, 2012a.

CEC. *Commission Staff Working Document. 'Progress on Equality between Women and Men in 2011'.* SWD(2012) 85 final, 2012b.

CEC. *Communication from the Commission to the European Parliament, the Council, the European Economic and Social Committee and the Committee of the Regions. Towards a Job-Rich Recovery.* COM(2012) 173 final, 2012c.

Council of the European Union. *Brussels European Council 23/24Mmarch 2006. Presidency Conclusions.* 7775/1/06, REV 1, 2006.

Council of the European Union. *Towards Common Principles of Flexicurity—Draft Council Conclusions.* 15497/07SOC 476ECOFIN 483, 2007.

Crompton, Rosemary. *Employment and the Family.* Cambridge: Cambridge University Press, 2006.

Crompton, Rosemary and Clare Lyonette. "Work–Life 'Balance' in Europe." *Acta Sociologica* 49(4) (2006): 379–493.

Dar, Ami, and Zafiris Tzannatos. *Active Labor Market Programs: A Review of the Evidence from Evaluations.* Washington, DC: World Bank, 1999.

EESC. *Opinion of the European Economic and Social Committee on Flexicurity Internal Flexibility Dimension—Collective Bargaining and the Role of Social Dialogue as Instruments for Regulating and Reforming Labour Markets.* SOC/272, 2007.

Eurostat. *Reconciliation between Work, Private and Family Life in the European Union.* Luxembourg: Office for Official Publications of the European Communities, 2009.

Fraser, Nancy. *Justice Interruptus. Critical Reflections on the 'Postsocialist' condition.* New York: Routledge, 1997.

Fredman, Sandra. "Women at Work: The Broken Promise of Flexicurity." *Industrial Law Journal* 33(4) (2004): 299–319.

Hansen, Lise Lotte. "From Flexicurity to FlexicArity." *Journal of Social Sciences* 3(2) (2007): 88–93.

Hemerijck, Anton. "The Political Economy of Social Investment." In *Economy and Society in Europe. A Relationship in Crisis*, edited by Luigi Burroni, Maarten Keune, and Guilliermo Meardi, 40–60. Cheltenham: Edward Elgar, 2012.

Holford, J., S. Riddell, E. Weedan, J. Litjens, and G. Hannan. *Patterns of Lifelong Learning: Policy and Practice in an Expanding Europe.* Berlin: Lit Verlag GMBH, 2009.

IILS. *World of Work Report 2012 'Better Jobs for a Better Economy'.* Geneva: ILO, 2012.

Jenson, Jane. "Lost in Translation: The Social Investment Perspectives and Gender Equality." *Social Politics* 16(4) (2009): 446–483.

Jepsen, Maria. "Towards a Gender Impact Analysis of Flexicurity?" In *Employment Policy from Different Angles*, edited by Thomas Bredgaard and Flemming Larsen, 339–350. Copenhagen: DJØF Publishing, 2005.

Jepsen, Maria. "Work Flexibility and the Reconciliation of Family and Working Life. What Is the Role of Flexicurity?" In *Trends in Social Cohesion no. 16*, edited by Council of Europe, 159–178. Strasbourg: Council of Europe Publishing, 2006.

Jepsen, Maria. "Quand la dimension de genre entrera-t-elle réellement en jeu?" *Travail, Genre et Sociétés* 17 (2008): 15–21.

Jepsen, Maria. "Work–Life Balance, Flexicurity and Gender." Paper presented at the Portuguese presidency conference "Reconciling Professional, Personal and Family Life—New Challenges for the Social Partners and for Public Policy," Lisbon, 12 and 13 July 2007.

Keune, Maarten and Maria Jepsen. "Not Balanced and Hardly New: The European Commission's Quest for Flexicurity." In *Flexicurity and Beyond*, edited by Henning Jørgensen and Per Kongshøj Madsen, 189–211. Copenhagen : DJØF Publishing, 2007.

Knijn, Trudie and Arnoud Smit. "Investing, Facilitating, or Individualizing the Reconciliation of Work and Family Life: Three Paradigms and Ambivalent Policies." *Social Politics* 16(4) (2009): 484–518.

Leschke, Janine. "Are Unemployment Insurance Systems in Europe Adapting to New Risks Arising from Non-Standard Employment?" DULBEA working paper, No. 07–05. Brussels: Université Libre de Bruxelles, 2007.

Leschke, Janine and Maria Jepsen. *The Economic Crisis—Challenge or Opportunity for Gender Equality in Social Policy Outcomes?* WP 2011–04. Brussels: ETUI, 2011.

Lewis, Jane. *Work-Family Balance, Gender and Policy*. Cheltenham: Edward Elgar, 2009.

Lewis, Jane and Ania Plomien. "'Flexicurity' as a Policy Strategy: The Implications for Gender Equality." *Economy and Society* 38(3) (2009): 433–459.

Löfström, Åsa. *Gender Equality, Economic Growth and Employment*. Stockholm: Swedish Ministry of Integration and Gender Equality, 2009.

OECD. "How Good Is Part-time Work?" In *OECD Employment Outlook 2010*, edited by OECD, 211–256. Paris: OECD, 2010.

OECD. "Labour Market Programmes and Activation Strategies: Evaluating the Impacts." In *OECD Employment Outlook 2005*, edited by OECD, 173–208. Paris: OECD, 2005.

OECD. *OECD Employment Outlook 2006*. Paris: OECD, 2006.

OECD Family Database. www.oecd.org/els/social/family/database. 2010.

Platenga, Janneke, Chantal Remery, H. Figueiredo, and Mark Smith. "Towards a European Union Gender Equality Index." *Journal of European Social Policy* 19(1) (2009): 19–33.

Plantenga, Janneke, Chantal Remery, and Jill Rubery. *Gender Mainstreaming of Employment Policies—A Comparative Review of Thirty European Countries. European Commission*. Luxembourg: Office, 2007.

Rubery, Jill, Damien Grimshaw, Mark Smith, and Rory Donnelly. *The National Reform Programmes and the Gender Aspects of the European Employment Strategy*. The Coordinator Synthesis Report Prepared for the Equality Unit. European Commission. University of Manchester, 2006.

Vielle, Pascale. "Flexicurity: Redefining the Security of European Citizens. Observatoire social européen." Policy paper, 1, Brussels, 2007.

5 Beyond Flexibility

Active Securities for Flexible Employment Relationships

Günther Schmid

INTRODUCTION

'Flexicurity', the flagship of the European Employment Strategy, lacks conceptual rigour. It often invites cheap talk, opportunistic use for various political interests, the mistake that flexibility is only in the interest of employers and security only in the interest of employees, or considering 'good practices' as a menu à la carte. Although these weaknesses may be considered a strength (conceptual openness inviting debates and different adaptations), their potential damaging effects pervade. The concept lacks especially a normative background that enables to assess or to properly guide the so-called balance of flexibility and security; a sound empirical background to evaluate the reasons for an alleged increasing demand of flexibility and the related insecurities for people affected by 'flexible' employment relationships; an explicit governance framework that guides the potential win-win game of 'flexicurity'; and, finally, a theory of the interrelationship between various forms of flexibility and security.

The aim of this chapter, therefore, is to contribute to conceptual clarity by using the theory of transitional labour markets (TLMs). In this perspective, active securities—understood as legally guaranteed social rights to participate in decisions over work and employment and to share equally their fruits as well as their risks—are an essential precondition for bringing flexibility and security to a right balance. These securities are 'active' in the sense that they require deliberative interaction (and often negotiation) between individual or collective actors on the labour market.

The chapter starts with the normative basis of TLM grounded on four principles of justice and emphasising a gender-sensible life-course perspective (work-life-balance) as the new orientation for labour market and social policy (1). The empirical basis of TLM is set through a comparison of non-standard employment relationships as the alleged core of flexible employment relationships in Europe at two points of time (1998 and 2008) using the European Labour Force Survey (2). From this normative and empirical backdrop, the role of active social security is derived on the basis of the new behavioural theory of intuitive choices and decisions and from the theory of learning by monitoring (3). The final section exemplifies—especially by good practices from the so-called German job miracle—the potential role of 'active securities' on the basis of two regulatory ideas: rights and obligations to capacity building and coordinated flexibility as functional equivalent to external (numerical) flexibility (4). A summary and outlook conclude with special reference to lessons for the new European Employment Strategy.

NORMATIVE FOUNDATIONS OF TRANSITIONAL LABOUR MARKET THEORY (TLM)

The theory of TLM aims in general at a strategy of ex ante risk sharing through empowerment of both employers and employees understood as enhancing their adjustment capacities to the risks related to product or business cycles, on the one hand, and to life cycles, on the other hand.[1] The first element of such an empowerment is to extend the insurance principle beyond the risk of unemployment and to include volatile income risks connected with critical transitions over the life course, for instance, the transition from school to work, from labour market to unpaid family or civil work (or combining both), from full-time to part-time work, from dependent to own account work (self-employment), from work to retirement. This extension of the risk horizon implies not only 'making work pay' (the transition from unemployment to—implicitly full-time—employment) but also *making transitions pay* (the transition between various employment relationships). A second important element of this empowerment strategy is to enhance the adjustment capacity of both employers and employees not only through investing in human capital, but also through investing in the workplace or work environment. This extension of the risk horizon implies to complement the supply strategy of 'making workers fit for the market' with the demand strategy of *making the market fit for workers.*[2]

As a *normative concept*, TLM theory redefines the social dimension of the labour market by focusing on solidarity through ex ante risk sharing as a way to enhance the transition capacity instead of only compensating ex post the losers of market dynamics through more or less generous transfers. This ex ante solidarity distinguishes the social market economy from a liberal ('capitalist') market economy for which the 'social' consists only in charity. *As an analytical concept*, TLM theory redefines the allocation function or matching dimension of the labour market by focusing on sustainable transitions (work-life careers) over the life course instead of optimising only single job-to-job matches. The right to a career stands for giving individuals a voice in choosing their jobs and work conditions instead of directing them into jobs common in 'socialist' economies and instead of pure workfare common in 'capitalist' economies.

From the *normative perspective*, the core idea of TLM is to empower individuals by enabling them to change from one work situation to another in case of economic and social change or in case of shifting individual preferences. *Work*, in the TLM perspective, includes all activities of an obligatory character, independent of whether they are contractually paid on the market (employment) or socially imposed but not paid. Because participation in deliberations is an essential ingredient of democracy, even taking part in such processes can be considered as 'work' in its widest sense. In fact, historically one of the first measures introducing the work-oriented right of deliberative participation was the granting of time off to employees holding a position of collective responsibility (staff representative) in companies that work with established works councils.

Thus, TLMs also aim at extending options of combining paid and unpaid work (especially care work) according to changing life-course needs and preferences. An important side effect of such empowering would be that people can also take over more risks over the life course, enhancing thereby the dynamics of the whole economy. New active labour-market policy (ALMP) aims not only at *freedom from want*, which means at 'negative freedom' in the sense of being free from fighting for the living necessities of food, water, housing, and health. The policy aim of TLM goes further by including the *freedom to act*, which means 'positive freedom' to determine one's own life through the endowment of capabilities.[3]

The consequence of this perspective is an ontological and ethical emphasis on *individual autonomy embedded in discursive communities*. Applied to the world of work, this means not to emphasise risks we want to avoid but risks we want to take, for instance, when moving from one job to the next, from one employer to the next, from one combination of activities in work, care, and education to the next, and so forth. Here the counterpart of risk is not danger but trust. We do not want only security for external risks, but also security for internal or 'manufactured' risks (Giddens, 1996). In other words, we do not want to insure only for accidents, ill-health, unavoidable old age, or other undesired mishaps; we want to insure for moves we want to make during the life course.

And as we make such moves in the expectation that they conform to the common goal of more flexibility and security in employment, we want to be able to cash in on our insurance when these expectations are disappointed. Thus, the TLM approach aims, finally, at extending unemployment insurance to a system of employment insurance, which means to a system that transforms risks from external attribution (events that we undergo, such as involuntary unemployment) to internal attributions (events we bring about, such as educational or parental leaves). Its basic elements would be ex ante redistribution through establishing collective funds beyond unemployment insurance, embedded in a system of negotiated flexicurity that allows flexible implementation of such funds backed up by the security of fair procedures.

This leads to a further central behavioural assumption: Most people accept changes (including transitions) more easily if risks are shared in a just way. That's why the theory of justice plays an important role in TLM. Four principles of justice underlie this theory.[4] The first principle is *justice as fairness*. Concerning the goals of policy intervention, the concept of TLM is opposed to the utilitarian assumption of maximising happiness for all. TLM theory rather emphasises the difference principle by John Rawls (2001), according to which inequality is only justified if it improves the lot of the least advantaged. This suggests turning around Tolstoy's famous introductory statement in his novel *Anna Karenina*: "Happy families are all alike; every unhappy family is unhappy in its own way" (Tolstoy, 1960: 1). There are many ways to happiness, but the main reasons for unhappiness are few. Maximising happiness is a moving and often futile target as the booming happiness research shows (Layard, 2005; Offer, 2006), but reducing unhappiness, especially caused by long-term unemployment, poverty, and miserable working conditions (low pay, lack of career perspectives) is something that can be achieved.

The second principle is *justice as solidarity*. TLM theory follows Ronald Dworkin (2000), who discovered an important blind spot in John Rawls's theory of justice. The strategy of maximising welfare of the most disadvantaged is ethically insensitive. People are and have to be concerned about the responsibility of their choices. Rights and obligations have to be balanced. Demanding more individual responsibility, however, requires endowing all individuals with equal opportunities. It also requires ex ante solidarity in the sense of periodically redistributing resources over the life course in favour of equal opportunities. The main reason for such redistribution is the fact that market forces regularly distort distributive justice because much depends—in the market game—on sheer luck.

However, Dworkin's concept of periodic redistribution and his hypothetical insurance scheme lack direction in terms of substance, which leads to the third principle of *justice as agency*. Following Amartya Sen (2001) and its adaptations (e.g., Salais and Villeneuve, 2004), TLM theory assumes great differences in the individual ability to convert resources for a fulfilling personal life course. Labour-market policy, therefore, has to concentrate on capabilities, which include not only individualised endowments of resources, but also a supportive economic, social, and political infrastructure. In fact, under the agency perspective, the focus shifts from the means of living to the actual opportunities a person has (Sen, 2009: 253). The civil dialogue in general (free deliberation in media accessible to everybody) and the social dialogue in particular (free deliberation and bargaining/negotiating between social partners/industrial relations) are considered as essential elements of such an infrastructure. Institutional capacity building, therefore, is of utmost importance for sustainable development and prosperity for all.

The fourth principle is *justice as inclusion*. This principle relates, on the one hand, to established social communities. Because labour markets inherently tend to social exclusion of the least competitive members, social integration of all willing to participate is a central element of justice as inclusion. The principle of inclusion, however, also encompasses the relationship between established communities. TLM theory assumes an increasing interdependency of local, regional, and national economies. Globalisation (including Europeanisation) of labour markets in particular requires a spatial expansion of the principle of social inclusion, in other words, an expansion of risk-sharing communities beyond ethnic, regional, and national boundaries (Ferrera, 2005). The reason is that open and opening market economies produce winners and losers in an asymmetrical way.[5]

EMPIRICAL FOUNDATIONS OF
TRANSITIONAL LABOUR MARKETS (TLM)

As an *analytical concept*, TLM theory emphasises the dynamics of labour markets. The analytical focus is on flows between different employment relationships rather than on stocks, and on transitions over the life course rather than on one-way job-to-job changes. Distinction is made between integrative, maintenance, and exclusionary transition sequences or job careers (O'Reilly et al., 2004). This concept of TLM has stimulated a rich set of empirical research on life-course transitions which cannot be presented here.[6]

TLMs, however, emphasise also transitions within employment relationships. The often quoted fact that international research finds no remarkable downward trend in job tenure and no remarkable increase in job-to-job transitions (Auer and Cazes, 2003) is completely in line with the concept of TLM. The reason is that many transitions can be performed within stable employment relationships through internal flexibility as a functional equivalent to external flexibility. Instances are the shift from full-time to part-time work due to parental leave or the combination of part-time work with off-the-job training, or internal job rotation through multiple skills or retraining.

Such flexibility within a continuing employment relationship explains, for instance, the fact that the *nominal employment rate* in Sweden is about 76 per cent, whereas the *effective employment rate*—which means the rate of employed people who actually work in a week—varies between 64 and 68 per cent. The observation of such a (probably increasing) discrepancy between nominal and effective employment rate might even be turned into a normative statement: The more transitions within an employment relationship are allowed or demanded, the higher must be the employment rate to keep the 'machinery' of economic prosperity running. Under this perspective, the Lisbon objective of 70 per cent employment rate in 2010 is too modest in the long run. Some countries, therefore, for instance, the Netherlands and Sweden, have already set the full employment goal at 80 per cent in their national employment programmes, and also the EU-2020 strategy now has reacted to this gap.[7]

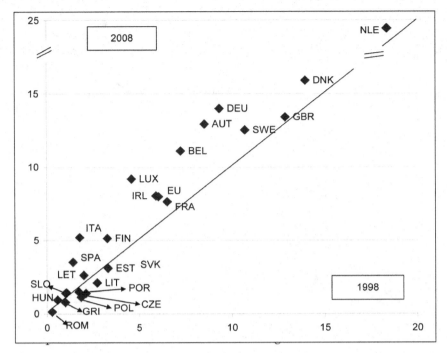

Figure 5.1 Part-time employees (only with open-ended contracts, and without self-employed) as per cent of working age population (age 15–64), 1998 and 2008.

their deviation from the majority of the 'old European member states' is their moderate or low employment protection regulation. The two countries are therefore counterexamples for the otherwise strong positive correlation between employment protection and fixed-term contracts, especially among men. Furthermore, fixed-term contracts, especially in form of temp-agency work, is concentrated among young adults and often combined with low skills and low wages. Many make the transition to open-ended contracts, but also many get stuck and become members of the new precariat. Again: Good and actual comparative data on transition rates are missing.[9]

However, two overall conclusions seem to be uncontested. The higher the share of temporary contracts, the higher the unemployment elasticity (and therefore the unemployment risk) to cyclical variations of demand, a fact well documented by comparing—for instance—the unemployment performance of Spain (drastic increase) and France (moderate increase) during the last crisis (Bentolila et al., 2010).[10] Finally, the increasing concentration of fixed-term contracts on young adults raises serious concerns about how these young people might be able to plan their life (including family formation and long-term careers) in the future.

Third, the number of self-employed—measured here as own account workers without additional employees and working without an employment

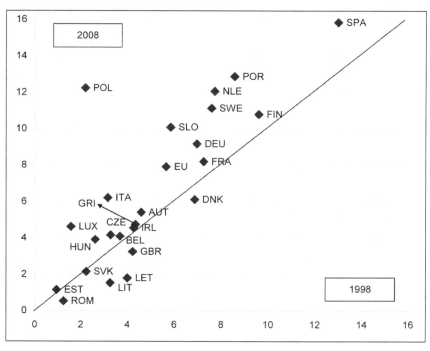

Figure 5.2   Temporary employees (including part-timers) as per cent of working age population (15–64 years), 1998 and 2008.

contract—as per cent of working age population, lies between 2 per cent in Luxemburg and 13 per cent in Greece (Figure 5.3).

There is no clear pattern of the dynamic. In many countries, self-employment is falling mainly due to the decline of traditional small farming; in some countries self-employment is still increasing in the so-called creative sector or because of disguised self-employment and to some extent because of enforced self-employment of unemployed people. Many of these own-account workers face a high risk of volatile income and lack of health or social insurance in old age. We know little about transition rates from self-employment to wage work and vice versa, but some anecdotic evidence, especially from Sweden, tells that this dynamic may be strong. Especially the combination of open-ended part-time employment with self-employment seems to be a promising strategy for enhancing employment and income security beyond the standard employment contract.

If we combine these three forms of non-standard employment and control for overlapping (for instance, some part-timers have fixed-terms contracts; some self-employed are part-timers), we get the aggregate non-standard employment rate. This rate varies between 7 per cent in Estonia and—of course the champion—43 per cent in the Netherlands (Figure 5.4).

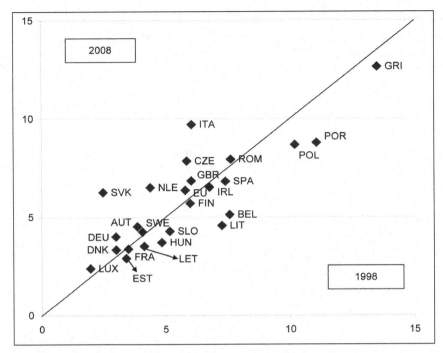

Figure 5.3   Self-employed (full-time or part-time, own-account workers) as per cent of working age population (15–64 years), 1998 and 2008.

A deeper systematic comparison of employment relationships in the EU member states, their dynamics, and their relationship with other performance measures of employment systems over the last decade reveals further insights (Schmid, 2010a, 2010b).

First, through differentiation by gender, the picture becomes more telling. Both the level (EU average of about 15 per cent for men, 21 per cent for women in 2008) as well as the dynamics (EU average of about 2 percentage points change from 1998 to 2008 for men, about 4.5 percentage points change for women) hint to the fact that non-standard employment mainly affects women. It may, thereby, come to a surprise that this combined indicator for 'flexible employment' is highest both in the so-called social democratic systems (Sweden, Denmark, and the champion Netherlands, as a hybrid system, included) and in the 'liberal' systems (UK, Ireland).[11] The family-centred continental 'conservative' systems (e.g., Austria, Belgium, France, and Germany) as well as the Mediterranean systems (e.g., Italy and Spain) are in the middle; all the new member states (e.g., Czech Republic, Hungary, the three little Baltic states)—with the exception of Poland[12]—are at the bottom.

Second, non-standard employment increased in almost all EU member states, especially in the Netherlands, Germany, and Italy. On the other

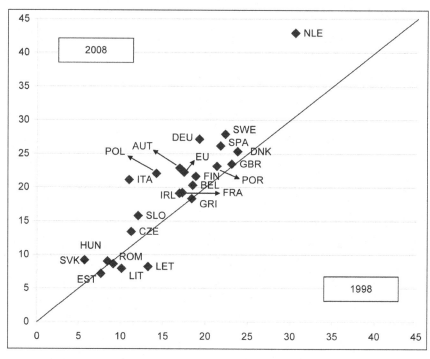

Figure 5.4   Aggregate non-standard employment rates in Europe, 1998 and 2008.

hand, it is remarkable that most of the new EU member states (the 'transition countries') not only cluster together, but that some of these countries, especially Latvia, Lithuania, and Romania, experienced even a decline in the aggregate non-standard employment rate. The most likely explanation for this feature is the fact that work in the informal economy serves as a functional equivalent for formal non-standard employment. In addition, in countries with low economic prosperity, part-time work (the most important component of 'non-standard employment') does not provide enough earning for women engaged in formal labour-market work.

Third, the fact that 'social democratic' as well as 'liberal' systems rank high in terms of non-standard employment can be taken as circumstantial evidence that non-standard jobs are related with very different regulatory frameworks. Whereas the Dutch or Danish non-standard employees seem to be well covered by employment and income security arrangements, this cannot be said, for instance, for their counterparts in Britain, Germany, and Italy.[13]

Furthermore, not all of these jobs are precarious or exclusionary. They can serve as stepping stones or as intermediary jobs within a meaningful work-life career. One can also argue that the concentration of non-standard employment on young adults reflects the renaissance of occupational labour markets (Marsden, 1999), requiring a series of job-to-job transitions in order to gain professional experiences and competitiveness on the labour market. Nevertheless, even in countries with high security standards, non-standard jobs often involve higher risk of exclusion than standard jobs.

Fourth, related to the Lisbon Strategy's goal of social inclusion, the good news is the fact that aggregate non-standard employment correlates both positively with employment and labour force participation as well as with prosperity in terms of gross domestic product per capita. Although correlations cannot be taken as a causal proof, this observation (especially the positive relationship in the dynamic perspective) nevertheless indicates that increased variety of employment relationships supports higher inclusion of people into the labour market as well as a higher level of market transactions. The bad news is that non-standard employment and the related higher risks are heavily concentrated on women, young people, and low-skilled, i.e., on the more vulnerable part of the labour force. In some countries, especially in Germany, the extension of non-standard jobs is closely related with the extension of low-wage jobs.

Fifth, and related to the ambitious Lisbon claim of world-class competitiveness, empirical evidence seems to indicate that rising non-standard employment does not lead to increased productivity. On the contrary, the relationship of employment growth and labour productivity (GDP per employed worker) from 2000 to 2007 is slightly negative. There is no EU member state obtaining simultaneously very high employment and productivity growth (European Commission, 2008: 37–39). As a consequence, the capacity for redistribution (and with it the possibility to compensate the losers in a highly dynamic economy) is weakened instead of strengthened. In other words, trading in higher income security through redistribution (an essential element of the Danish 'flexicurity' model) for taking over higher risks related to flexible jobs (either in form of non-standard employment or in form of high job turnover) becomes a void option if no better balance of flexibility and security can be found.

The proof that it is non-standard employment which retards productivity growth has yet to be brought about. A recent study, however, partly hints in this direction. Zhou, Dekker, and Kleinknecht (2010) report from a sophisticated study for the Netherlands that firms with high shares of workers on fixed-term contracts have significantly higher sales of *imitative new products* but perform significantly worse on sales of *innovative new products* (first on the market). High functional flexibility in insider–outsider labour markets enhances a firm's new product sales, as do training efforts and highly educated personnel. The authors found weak evidence that larger and older firms have higher new product sales than do younger and smaller firms. Their findings, they conclude, should be food for thought to economists making unqualified pleas for the deregulation of labour markets.

To sum up, the increasing contractual variety of employment relationships and the tendency of shifting the related risks to the weakest members of the workforce combined with low productivity gains is the empirical starting point of TLM. Against this backdrop, the aim of TLM-oriented labour-market policy is, metaphorically, to provide 'social bridges' that compensate for the higher risks of increasing contractual variety and ensure that non-standard jobs either are intermediate stages in the work-life or become 'stepping stones' to sustainable job-careers. New ALMP, thereby, has to ensure that these institutional bridges contribute to (or, at least, do not negatively affect) productivity growth. One strategy to realise this objective might be to exploit more systematically the flexibility potential of open-ended contracts (internal numerical as well as functional flexibility, especially in terms of education and training).

TLM theory claims that the implementation of the EU's eight common principles of 'flexicurity'[14] requires following consistent normative and analytical principles as well as taking into account the way people perceive their life-course risks and the way they act in situations of uncertainty. In order to establish such institutional arrangements, the theory of TLM uses the concept of social risk management, elaborated elsewhere (Schmid, 2008: 213–241). The following exemplifies this approach by deliberating on the implications of important restrictions of rational economic behaviour.

ON THE GOVERNANCE OF BALANCING
FLEXIBILITY AND SECURITY

The general question is: How should labour-market policy take account of real behavioural traits—instead of 'ideal' traits assumed by pure theory—such as bounded rationality, asymmetric risk perception, and risk aversion? Two questions are of special importance in the TLM framework: First, how can risk aversion be overcome in order to induce people to take over more risks and the increased responsibility that goes with them? Second, how can the uncertainty entailed in negotiated agreements or contracts be overcome in order to maintain the mutual trust required for continuous cooperation under conflicting interests? Prospect theory, or the theory of intuitive judgements and choices (Kahneman and Tversky, 2000), provides interesting insights to the first question. The theory of learning by monitoring, going back to Albert Hirschman's (1967) development theory and further developed by Charles Sabel (1994), supplies useful hints to the second question.

The way how people perceive risks determines much their real daily choices. Most people tend to myopic risk perceptions. They overestimate small-scale risks in foreseeable future, and they underestimate large-scale risks that seem far ahead in the future. Most people buy, therefore, more easily travel insurance than occupational disability insurance. Most people underestimate also the risk of unemployment or the risk of large income losses over the life course due to the erosion or lack of skills.

Another important psychological insight is that losses loom larger than gains in risk perception. On the one hand, most people prefer small certain gains over large uncertain gains; in other words, they prefer the bird in the hand instead of two birds in the bush. On the other hand, most people are extremely loss averse. They don't like to give things away even if the prospect of gains is bright. Psychologists have found out that the loss to gain ratio is about two to one. It makes thus a difference in perception whether one frames a risk in terms of losses or gains.

From these insights, important conclusions for the policy design of risk sharing can be drawn. Daniel Bernoulli, one of the founders of probability theory and thus of risk management, gives the clue. He made the observation: "A beggar will not give up begging for a workfare job because he would lose his ability to beg. He has to be offered something more" (Bernstein, 1996: 119–20). This "more"—what could that be? TLM theory suggests a specific solution to this psychological problem: the extension of the expectation horizon through a set of opportunity structures available in the most critical events during the life course.

The first pillar of extending the expectation horizon would be the establishment of new social rights that go beyond employment. A solution could be the transformation of the employment contract to a citizen-based 'labour force membership' status (*statut professionnel*) that includes *all* forms of work.[15] The 'statut professionnel', therefore, would also embrace income and employment risks related to transitions between various forms of employment and work. This concept was formulated most forcefully in the Supiot-Report already ten years ago. The authors of this report start with the observation that the terms of the trade-off on which the classical employee status was based—that is, subordination in return for security—are now turned on their heads without any new ones taking their place. This creates the problem of adapting labour force membership to the new employer–employee relationship. Where the Fordist model hinged on the stable organisation of groups of workers, the new model is based on the opposite idea of the coordination of mobile individuals. It has to react to the necessity (and difficulty) of defining a membership of the labour force that integrates individualisation and the mobility of professional careers. To the extent that this individual mobility becomes the dominant characteristic in tomorrow's world, labour law has to ensure employment stability and thereby guarantee workers recognition as labour force members. The paradigm of employment would thus be replaced by a paradigm of labour force membership for individuals, not defined by pursuit of a specific occupation or a specific job, but covering the various forms of work which anyone might perform during his or her life (Supiot, 2001: 25–26, 55).

The new social rights are new in that they cover subjects unfamiliar to industrial wage-earners: rights to education and training, to appropriate working hours, to a family life, to occupational redeployment, retraining or vocational rehabilitation, and to fully participate in the civil and social dialogue. Their scope is also new because they would cover not only 'regular' wage-earners, but also the self-employed, temp-agency, contract, and marginal workers. They are new in nature, because they often take the form of social drawing rights, which allow workers to rely on solidarity, within defined and (possibly) collectively bargained limits in order to exercise the new freedoms.

These new securities can no longer be seen as being given in exchange for subordination (as in the old employment contract), but as the foundations of a new freedom to act. They can be considered as *active social securities*, which go hand in hand with workers' initiatives to shoulder the risks of flexible employment relationships instead of restricting them. Whether the institutional guarantee of security takes the form of open-ended contract with inbuilt flexibilities or fixed-term contracts with fair risk-sharing devices depends on the situational configuration and on institutional path dependency. We will come back to this point in the last section.

The *second pillar* for extending the expectation horizon would be—to put it metaphorically—stepping stones and bridges to overcome critical events during the life course. The tendency of overestimating small-scale risks immediately in sight and underestimating large-scale risks in the long distance leads, for instance, people to perceive the risk of being stuck in the low-wage sector to be greater than the risk of long-term unemployment resulting possibly from being too choosy about the jobs they will accept. ALMPs, therefore, should not be confined solely to offering jobs and placing individuals in work. Follow-up measures are required for *transforming sheer workfare measures into stepping stones* to sustainable job-careers.

The *third pillar* for extending the expectation horizon would be psychological bridges to overcome asymmetric risk perception. Acceptance of risky jobs means often abandoning familiar certainties, even though they may have a lower value than the new employment prospects. These 'familiar certainties' may be of various kinds. The reliability of social assistance benefits possibly supplemented by a small amount of clandestine employment may be one example, the confidence in one's own *productive capacities* another. Taking on a risky new job, however, brings with it the fear of losing these capacities.

To give an example: Risk aversion of people coming from a relatively poor background has a financial as well as a psychological dimension. Paradoxically, the psychological dimension can be even more important than the financial, as Bernoulli's example of the beggar had already signalled. From motivation studies we know that poor people are especially dependent on the sociability of their peer groups. Training and education, however, implies often a change of the peer group, especially when job mobility is required at the end. The consequence of this insight might be to arrange group measures instead of individualised measures in order to stabilise trust within an established social network.

The financial implication is to take care in the programme design that fallback positions remain always in sight. It is therefore important for these target groups to have the opportunity to try out several jobs without benefits withdrawn immediately if one option does not lead to success at once. Trust in such opportunity sets rules out rigid workfare strategies that do not allow trial and error as a productive job search strategy. For the same reason, the implementation of training measures for these target groups should also avoid raising too high expectations, for example, through the requirement of passing formal examinations.

The *fourth pillar* for extending the expectation horizon would be the establishment and reinforcement of *learning communities*. Learning communities are a paradigm of negotiated flexibility and security, but they differ from traditional collective bargaining in at least two ways. First, they include not only trade unions and employers associations, but also other parties that play a key role in the regional economy. Second, learning communities usually involve a representative of public authorities at local, regional, or national levels.

Learning communities are a relatively recent phenomenon and known under different names, for instance, in Germany under 'Alliances for Jobs' (*Bündnisse für Arbeit*), and in the Netherlands as 'covenants'. In a seminal paper, Ton Korver and Peter Oeij (2008) define—and the following relies heavily on their intriguing rhetoric—a covenant as an undersigned written agreement, or a system of agreements, between two or more parties, at least one that is or represents a public authority, meant to effectuate governmental policy. There is not one format of covenants, but they share common features: enough overlapping interests of participants, mechanisms bringing about both definition and the machinery of achievements, the parties cooperate, and formal sanctions are absent, yet parties have the opportunity to go to court in case of another party's default.

Covenants are needed where issues are at stake in which it is not, or not yet, clear what exactly is required of which participants to achieve commonly set and shared values and targets. And because this is unknown, it is quite premature to invoke the regular process of bargaining and thus of deciding on the distribution of the eventual net advantages of the joint effort. In fact, what the net advantages are, how they can be achieved by whom, and how they are then to be distributed, can only be clarified along the way—i.e., through learning by monitoring.

Learning means acquiring the knowledge to make and do things that (labour) markets value (and therewith *un*learning the things not so valued). Monitoring means the assessment of the partner-in-learning in order to determine whether the gains from learning are distributed acceptably. This leads to a dilemma. Learning may undermine stable relationships due to changing identities. The result is conservatism because winners and losers are not known in advance: The advancing knowledge economy, for instance, very likely will increase the inequality of incomes, further strengthening the trend of the past two decades. That may lead to a decision trap: When outcomes are uncertain and where the odds are that some will lose and others will win, with the distribution of odds unknown, conservatism is more likely than innovation. In respect to employment and work, conservatism means that parties revert to their already established identities (*I am a manager, I am a craft worker*, and so on) and to the interests associated with those identities, including social hierarchies and rank and ideas of equity. When monitoring is steered by already established identities and vested interests, learning is sure to be hampered, if not immobilised, for learning entails a redefinition of identity and interest. New partnership arrangements, therefore, are needed to overcome such decision traps.

To summarise and to set these observations into the TLM framework, covenants defined and designed as learning by monitoring are a strategy of policy sequencing. Instead of planning we get exploring (Hirschman, 1967), and risks are transformed from danger to trust. And it is precisely this transformation that needs to be made in order to tackle the opportunities of flexibility, transitions and training, and the problems (bottlenecks, linkages) these give rise to. It is the same transformation that underlies the problem of employability, with its emphasis on personal responsibility, as distinct from the collective or public responsibility derived from the traditional case of involuntary unemployment.

The paradigm of learning communities, however, cannot be applied to all situations of collective choice. We have to come back, therefore, to the original concept of transforming the classical employment contract into a citizen-based labour-market status which broadens the flexibility–security nexus by further elements of 'active securities'. In the following, I will elaborate on two regulatory ideas: first, on rights and obligations to capacity building and, second, on coordinated flexibility as functional equivalents to (numerical) external flexibility.

ACTIVE SECURITIES AS FUNCTIONAL EQUIVALENTS TO (NUMERICAL) FLEXIBILITY

The first example related to 'active securities' can be put under the headline: *Capacity building through ex ante redistribution*. The general strategy would be to remind policymakers of the forgotten part of insurance, which means to stimulate 'innovative hazard' instead of only concentrating on the control of 'moral hazard'. This is what is meant by the slogan 'making transitions pay', in other words, rewarding and ensuring risk taking.

Under the perspective of new social risks related to critical transitions over the life course, it would make sense to extend unemployment insurance to a system of employment insurance. Mobility insurance, either in the form of wage insurance like in Switzerland or in the form of the severance payment scheme (*Abfertigungsrecht*) in Austria (Schmid, 2008: 293) is already good practice to make transitions pay. In Germany, I have proposed to link parts of former UI-contributions to a training fund matched by resources from general taxation for ex ante redistribution in favour for high-risk, low-skill workers. Each worker would be entitled to the same drawing rights from this fund over his or her life course independent of his or her savings capacity (Schmid, 2011). As the reasoning about transforming danger to trust made clear, such virtual capacities and monetary incentives would have to be complemented through public infrastructures ensuring reliable and efficient implementation.

The second example can be put under the headline: *Capacity building through accommodation*. The general strategy would be to extend work opportunities through 'making the market fit for workers' with the aim of greater social inclusion. This would mean to enrich the standard employment contract by imposing duties of reasonable adjustment on employers in favour of workers, especially those with reduced work capacity.[16] In other words—and recently also formulated by Simon Deakin in his recent book with Alain Supiot—rather than requiring the individual to be 'adaptable' to changing market conditions, the employment contract requires that employment practices be adapted to the circumstances of the individual (Deakin and Supiot, 2009: 28).

Simon Deakin interestingly provides illustrations for this principle mainly related to disability policy in Europe, an emphasis correctly reflecting the salience of this problem, noted also by Amartya Sen (2009).[17] A good example in this direction, too, is the recent modification of the German law for severely disabled people, which stipulates the right of disabled against their employer to:

- An employment which enables them to utilise and to develop further their abilities and knowledge
- The right to privileged access to firm-specific training
- The rights to facilitation the participation in external training
- The right to disability-conform work environment
- The right to equipping the work place with required technical facilities[18]

It is evident that these kinds of adjustments duties require support through collective agreements or social pacts between firms and other key actors at the local or regional labour market. The new German law makes provisions for this task through 'integration agreements' to be concluded between employers, works councils, and representatives of severely disabled people[19]; however, representative experiences of this relatively new procedural instrument are not yet available.

The first example for 'coordinated flexibility' can be put under the headline *enhancing internal flexibility through mutual obligations*. The general strategy is to enhance internal adjustment capacities through continuous and—possibly—anticyclical investment. This would mean imposing duties for reasonable adjustment not only on employers, but also on employees, especially in terms of investing continuously into their employability over the life course.

I know this is a sensitive and difficult question. Duties may easily over-burden either side of the employment contract or restrict freedom of choice. However, negative externalities for not investing into the future may be one justification, for instance, the danger of work accidents, health risks, or functional illiteracy through inability to use new technologies. Positive externalities through individual investment, on the other hand, may not be fairly distributed in case of bad luck on the market if no provision is taken for periodic redistribution, for example, through progressive taxation.

The second example for coordinated flexibility can be put under the headline: *Enhancing internal flexibility through risk sharing or pooling of human resources*. The general strategy here is to enhance internal flex-ibility and security through risk sharing within the internal labour market or through extending the internal labour market beyond the firm through resource pooling.

An example for risk sharing within the internal labour market is the German *Kurzarbeit* ('short-time work'). This instrument has a long tra-dition in Germany but can nevertheless still be counted as a 'best prac-tice' case for the concept of employment insurance. Dismissals or layoffs are avoided through sharing the income risk of falling demand between employees, employers, and the state (via the public unemployment insur-ance system). When the worldwide financial crisis started, the number of short-time workers rocketed within a few months to its top of about 1.5 million in May 2009, averaging 1.2 million for the whole year, of which 700,000 were related to the (export-oriented) metal-electric sector. The cri-sis hit especially skilled men in economically strong firms and Germany's hot spot regions (Baden-Wuerttemberg, Bavaria). It is estimated that work-ers, so far, carried about 3 billion euros of the costs,[20] employers about 5 billion,[21] and the federal employment agency about 4.6 billion.[22] The new regulatory idea connected with this instrument is to protect not individual jobs per se but to ensure the preservation of accumulated 'human capital' and to enhance this capital through further employability measures, espe-cially training and education.

Kurzarbeit, so far, has prevented—in combination (!) with other work-sharing measures,[23] plus a demand stimulus for the automobile indus-try[24]—mass unemployment in an astonishing way. Despite at least 5 per cent decline in economic output, unemployment rose only by 150,000 (0.35 percentage points) in 2009, whereas employment remained stable or even slightly increased. This induced the global media industry to celebrate the German job miracle,[25] which certainly is correct compared to the crisis response of many other countries (e.g., Spain or the US) but an exaggeration considered the (potential) side effects. The intended combination with training measures, for instance, was not really successful. In October 2009, the employment agency counted only 113,272 workers combining short-time work and training (cumulated entries). The instrument is also quite dangerous for it may preserve industrial structures which in the long run are not competitive. There is also concern about the fact that, for the first time in German history, productivity fell during a recession due to additional labour hoarding (Herzog-Stein and Seifert, 2010), but possibly also due to the steady decline of private or public investments in Germany during the last decade.[26] In any case, the flip side of this kind of employment security was that the majority of job recovery during the following upswing was related to insecure non-standard forms of employment.[27]

A more innovative example of pooling human resources outside risky temporary or fixed-term employment contracts is the recent collective agreement in NRW's metal and electric industry. This agreement allows firms to lease redundant workers (by keeping the standard employment contract) to firms with labour or skill deficits. The social partners adopted with this agreement a good practice already familiar in the soccer business.[28] The story has yet another interesting side issue. If one agrees that this practice should also be possible between industrial sectors (for instance, between main contractors and subcontractors falling under different collective agreements), the German law on temp-agency work (*Arbeitnehmerüberlassungsgesetz*) would have to be changed because it allows such a personnel change only within the same sector.

A final good practice example for coordinated flexibility (and related to an important challenge all EU member states are facing) is the German collective agreement in the chemical industry in April 2008 setting up so-called demography funds (*Demografiefonds*). This overall framework agreement at the sectoral level of the chemical industry (including mining and energy companies) will be implemented basically through further negotiations at the company level.[29] With the beginning of 2008, all employers in this sector were obligated to yearly contribute €300 for each employee into a fund, which can be utilised after corresponding negotiations and deliberations at the firm level for various aims, among others for early retirement under the condition of building a bridge for young workers entering employment or for buying occupational disability insurance. From now on, building up a corresponding and transparent information system reflecting the age and qualification structure of the companies' workforce is also required for all firms, thereby extending the expectation or planning horizon for employers as well as for employees. The concentration of these funds on early retirement instead on broader issues of 'humanisation of work' (e.g., work–life balance, continuous education and training), however, has to be considered a flaw from the TLM perspective.

SUMMARY AND OUTLOOK

The starting point—to sum up—was that 'flexicurity', the flagship of the European Employment Strategy, lacks conceptual rigour. It often invites, therefore, cheap talk, opportunistic use for various political interests, the mistake that flexibility is only in the interest of employers and security only in the interest of employees, or considering 'good practices' as a menu à la carte. The aim of this chapter was to contribute to conceptual clarity by using the theory of TLMs. In this perspective, active securities— understood as legally guaranteed social rights to participate in decisions over work and employment and to share equally their fruits as well as their risks—are an essential condition for bringing flexibility and security to a right balance. These securities are 'active' in the sense that they require deliberative interaction (and often negotiation) between individual or collective actors on the labour market.

One reason for the ambiguity of the 'flexicurity' concept is its lack of a clear normative orientation. Its usual appeal to a 'win-win game' between employers and employees is naive in the sense that it does not recognise the still existing power gap between the two classes of actors or within these two classes (multinationals versus small enterprises, high-skilled versus low-skilled people). The metaphor of 'balancing' flexibility and security remains void without taking account of such differences. The chapter started, therefore, with the normative basis of TLM, which is grounded on four principles of justice. Considering *justice as fairness*, for instance, requires concentrating policy intervention on the lot of the most disadvantaged in order to guarantee freedom from want for all. *Justice as solidarity* requires endowing all individuals with equal opportunities, especially embedding equality into a gender-sensible life-course perspective (work–life balance). *Justice as agency* hints at the need of building up individual capacities or capabilities in the sense of providing an opportunity set for the freedom to act. An important consequence of this agency perspective is the emphasis on transition securities that encourage workers to make risky transitions through the availability and reliability of proactive labour-market policies and effective public employment services, which are oriented towards sustainable job careers. *Justice as inclusion*, finally, demands the extension of risk-sharing communities beyond conventional social borders (including, for instance, people with restricted work capacities) and—due to globalisation—especially beyond national borders.

The second reason for the conceptual vagueness of 'flexicurity' is its lack of a systematic empirical background able to explain the sources of (new) insecurities and the sources of (new) demands for flexibility on both sides— employers as well as employees. This was the motivation to contribute to this background by systematically comparing the structure and dynamic of non-standard employment relationships as the alleged core of flexible employment relationships in Europe at two points of time (1998 and 2008) using the European Labour Force Survey.

Among the 'non-standard' forms of employment, *part-time work* is the most important driver for the—at least partly successful—inclusion of mature-aged workers and (especially more) women into the labour market. Whereas its flexibility potential is uncontested related to employees, part-time work—especially in its open-ended and substantive form (more than twenty hours)—does not necessarily increase employers' flexibility, partly on the contrary. The most important insecurity aspect related to part-time (especially in its marginal forms) is reduced accumulation of pension entitlement.

Temporary work is basically driven by the wish of employers to manage (new) uncertainties related to volatile demands and—especially—to cut down wage costs by avoiding, for instance, insurance-related wage increases of open-ended contracts (e.g., seniority wages). High dismissal costs through employment protection regulation are important drivers, too, explaining to some extent systematic national differences in utilising temporary work. The most important insecurity aspects related to temporary work is its higher risk of unemployment and low wages, and the danger of getting stuck in a downward spiral of precarious fixed-term contracts.

Self-employment, as the third most important element of 'non-standard' employment, is on the decline related to its traditional components (farming, petty bourgeois business), but thriving—at least in the more prosperous EU member states—in terms of 'modern' forms related especially to the so-called creative sector, and often also in combination (or sequence) with dependent wage work. Whereas the latter form of self-employment opens some interesting opportunities for employers to (cheaply) outsource tasks and services, it seems to be an interesting playing field for young adults to try individual autonomy and agency, or for parents to combine family work with gainful employment. In any case, however, the related risk of social insecurity (low and volatile income and under-insurance in case of illness and old age) is high.

Among many more interesting facets of this exercise, two important conclusions came out: First, there is still a tremendous lack of information on transitions and transition sequences between 'non-standard' and 'standard' forms of employment, especially in terms of life-course careers, which inhibits firm conclusions on the flexibility and security implications of non-standard employment. What is clear, however, is that these implications are quite different related to the various forms of non-standard contract. Second, (still anecdotic) evidence seems to hint at the failure to improve overall productivity and competitiveness based on 'flexible' employment relationships via 'non-standard' forms, especially related to fixed-term contracts.

The third gap in the 'flexicurity' concept is its neglect of behavioural traits in terms of individual perceptions and choices related to (new) employment risks. Any policy, however, intending to support labour-market actors in preventing, mitigating or coping with (new) employment risks must consider these traits in designing the right policies or institutions. Thus, this matter of 'flexicurity-governance' was taken up in the third step by briefly summarising insights of new behavioural economics and the theory of learning by monitoring. As most people are myopic related to high risks with low probability and—depending on the situation and the framing of the problem—either risk averse or unreasonably speculative risk takers, the strategy of extending the expectation (and corresponding planning) horizon seems to be a useful guideline for policy intervention. Four (mutually not exclusive but complementing) possibilities were presented and discussed: First, the establishment of (new) social rights beyond employment; second, stepping stones for navigating through various risks over the life course; third, group instead of individual employability measures; fourth—and especially promising—the establishment of learning communities through social pacts or covenants.

Agreeing covenants (the most interesting element of 'active securities') is rather different than issuing rules and laws. Instead of enforcing institutional forms of 'insurance', in particular through sanctions or penalties, covenants build on trust and social cohesion, thus, on forms of 'ensurance' through fair procedures. They are examples of what is nowadays called 'soft law' or 'soft regulation' and fit in with the larger European trends on coordination. Although it may be too early to advocate covenants for the European level, if only because none of the more essential partners (Council, Commission, European trade unions, and employers) possesses the muscle to bring them about, many EU member states dispose of these conditions, and the new European Employment Strategy might at least play a midwife role in supporting such social pacts, European border regions even might start pilot projects in this direction.

A fourth weakness in the 'flexicurity' concept is its neglect of the interrelationship between flexibility and security. In many cases, security provisions are the precondition for normal 'human animals' taking over risks. However, securities can be of different kind and may have different incentives. As theory tells us, any (social) insurance contract leads people to think of their contributions as kinds of investment that must have some pecuniary return (even in case they are lucky by not being affected by the risk, e.g., unemployment, over their life course). It is, however, wrong to consider only the negative incentives related to (in fact any kind of) insurance and to concentrate all policies to get this 'moral hazard' under control. Much neglected are the positive incentives, which we may call the 'innovative hazard' of insurance and which encourages people to take over risks (with positive externalities for the society) they otherwise would not take. Such innovative hazard requires a corresponding safety net either in terms of monetary benefits or in terms of social infrastructures on which workers can rely with trust if they are caught by the negative side of the risks they have taken over.

The real art of *balancing flexibility and security*, therefore, is to balance 'moral hazard' as well as 'innovative hazards' in such a way that society indeed reaches a higher level ('equilibrium') of flexibility and security. As the empirical part of this chapter has shown, the concentration of flexibility measures on external flexibility such as fixed-term contracts and out-contracting (among others to own account workers) has shifted risks to individuals or small enterprises without, yet, persuasive compensations of security and without producing persuasive evidence of increased sustainable productivity and competitiveness. This gave reason to look to alternatives for which I presented two regulatory ideas on the basis of 'active securities', which means institutional support enhancing the 'innovative hazard' instead of controlling 'moral hazard' related to securities: rights and obligations to capacity building and coordinated flexibility as functional equivalents to (numerical) external flexibility. The final section exemplified the potential role of such 'active securities' with special emphasis on good practices from the recent 'German job miracle', which, however, had to be partly qualified considering their real or potential dangerous side effects.

A final caveat, therefore, seems to be in order: As successful countries demonstrate, balancing flexibility and security has to be embedded in sound macro-economic and macro-social policy. Without sustainable job creation dynamics, all employability and stepping stone strategies are in danger of ending up in a cul-de-sac or of displacing other categories of workers. Without new active securities, envisaged and represented perhaps in a 'social progression clause' of a revised Lisbon Treaty, all 'flexicurity' strategies might end up in new forms of labour-market segmentation.

The current rescue efforts to solve the economic and fiscal crisis demonstrate in a dramatic way that the process of Europeanisation, in particular through the Eurozone, increases interdependencies, urgently requiring coordinated efforts to stimulate sustainable economic growth, especially through investments in a better European economic and social infrastructure. Related to our emphasis on 'active securities' (and in a bit of speculative mood), the extension of the European Social Fund to a European Employment Insurance Fund, or at least a complementation of the European Social Fund through a focused European Knowledge Lift Fund,[30] would not only make the European Social Model more visible and tangible, but might also develop into a new level playing field for balancing flexibility and security through an enhanced civil and social dialogue.

NOTES

1. By using the term 'theory', I am well aware that TLM has not yet reached the status of a unified theory. However, as the following might demonstrate, theoretical elements of various strands are existent and invite the reader to develop further.

2. These slogans have been coined by Gazier (2007). In this vein, see also the recent literature on capacity building, e.g., Deakin and Supiot (2009).
3. The distinction of 'negative' and 'positive' freedom goes back to the social philosopher Berlin (2002).
4. For an explication at proper length, see Schmid (2006) and Schmid (2008: 224–231).
5. To give just one telling example: Thanks to mass production in hog farming (killing the small hog farming), pork prices dropped by about one-fifth in the US between 1970 and 2004, providing annual savings of about $29 per US consumer. With the opening of borders, the US giant Smithfield storms into Eastern Europe with the same intent and comparable effects on a global scale. In Romania, the number of hog farmers has declined by 90 per cent—to 52,100 in 2007 from 477,030 in 2003. In their place, the company employs or contracts with about 900 people and buys grain from about 100 farmers (*International Herald Tribune*, 6 May 2009: 1).
6. See, among others, Schmid and Gazier (2002), Schmid (2006, 2008), and various contributions in six recently published rich volumes on 'flexicurity' and TLMs by Anxo, Erhel, and Schippers (2007), Jørgensen and Madsen (2007), Koning (2007), Lassnigg et al. (2007), Muffels (2008), and Rogowski (2008). For complementarities and differences between the TLM approach and the capability approach, see Rogowski, Salais, and Whiteside (2012); related to labour-market issues, the main difference is TLM's greater emphasis on transition capacities, whereas the capability approach puts greater emphasis on labour-market conventions, in particular on the company responsibility for workers' professional development.
7. The EU-2020 strategy set the target at 75 per cent, however, by correcting the denominator ('working age population') to the age of 20–64, European Commission (2010).
8. For more figures and data, see Schmid and Protsch (2009); Schmid (2010a, 2010b).
9. Some figures based on the European Community Household Panel (ECHP) for the period 1994–2001 can be found in Klammer, Muffels, and Wilthagen (2008); Leschke (2008) provided an excellent four-country study on non-standard employment (Denmark, Germany, UK, and Spain) based on the same data source. Statistical monitoring of transitions is still a desideratum, both at national and international levels.
10. The authors argue that labour-market institutions in the two economies are rather similar, except for the larger gap between dismissal costs of workers with permanent and temporary contracts in Spain, which led to huge flows of temporary workers out of and into unemployment. The authors estimate in a counterfactual scenario that more than one half of the increase in the unemployment rate (about 6 percentage points!) would have been avoided had Spain adopted French employment protection institutions before the recession started. The case of the German 'unemployment miracle'—to which we come later—is different. Here it was less employment protection than the availability of 'active securities' which prevented a drastic increase in unemployment.
11. Non-standard employment is not necessarily flexible in all respects: Part-timers, for example, are less flexible than full-timers in terms of numerical working time (overtime, short-time); fixed-term workers are often less flexible than open-ended full-timers in terms of multiple tasks.
12. Although Poland's employment rate is low like in most of the transition countries, its share of temporary work is very high. Fixed-term employment rocketed from 514,000 (1998) to 3,207,000 (2008), whereas total employment

stagnated. The reason probably is the lax regulation of temporary work which allowed fixed-term chain contracts without any limit until 2003. Only in 2004, Poland introduced stricter regulation, except in the seasonal and temp-agency sector. In fact, the height of fixed-term contracts was in 2007, and the number of temporary workers declined slightly in 2008.

13. See Schulze Buschoff and Protsch (2008) on comparative security arrangements for non-standard forms of employment.
14. The eight common principles decided—after a Green Paper induced consultation of member states—by the European Council in December 2007 are: (1) good work through new forms of flexibility and security; (2) a deliberate combination of the four 'flexicurity' components: flexible and reliable contractual arrangements, comprehensive lifelong learning (LLL) strategies, effective ALMPs, and sustainable social protection systems; (3) a tailored approach according to the member states' specific circumstances; (4) overcoming segmentation through stepping stones and through managing transitions both in work and between jobs; (5) internal as well as external 'flexicurity'; (6) gender equality in the broader sense of reconciling work, family, and private life; (7) the crucial importance of the social dialogue in implementing 'flexicurity', which means—in TLM terms—negotiated flexibility and security; and, finally, (8) fair distribution of costs and benefits (European Commission, 2007).
15. This official English translation is not satisfactory; the original French term 'statut professionnel' would be translated in German as *Arbeitsmarktbürger*.
16. Such duties can be derived (in contrast to all utility related approaches of justice) from the principle of *justice as agency*, called "responsibility of effective power" (Sen, 2009: 270), or from the concept of "individual solidarity" in my own terminology (Schmid, 2008: 226).
17. Sen (2009: 258–260) draws attention to the fact that for people with disabilities, the *impairment of income-earning ability* is often severely aggravated by a *conversion handicap*. He cites a study for the UK showing that poverty drastically jumps by 20 percentage points for families with a disabled member if taking account of conversion handicaps, whereby a quarter can be attributed to income handicap and three quarters to conversion handicap (the central issue that distinguishes the capability perspective from the perspective of incomes and resources).
18. SGB (*Sozialgesetzbuch*) IX, § 81 (4).
19. SGB (*Sozialgesetzbuch*) IX, § 83 (1).
20. The replacement rate of earnings for the reduced working time corresponds to the unemployment benefit scheme: 60 per cent (without children), 67 per cent (with children) related to the 'normal' net earnings.
21. For the employer, *Kurzarbeit* does not reduce labour costs proportionally with working hours. Some of the fixed costs of labour remain, estimated between 24 per cent and 46 per cent per reduced working hour, depending on the size of state subsidies. These remaining costs, practically, increase through many collective agreements topping up short-time allowance as an additional kind of wage insurance through negotiated flexibility (Bach and Spitznagel, 2009).
22. Financed by unemployment insurance contributions and partly through tax financed subsidies by the federal government, the latter targeted mainly social security contributions (employers, otherwise, would have to pay) and training costs as far as they occurred.
23. Melting down accumulated time accounts (saving the equivalent of 244,000 jobs), overtime work (285,000 jobs equivalent), and other forms of working time reductions (equivalent of about 500,000 jobs) through flexible working

time corridors allowed by collective agreements; Herzog-Stein and Seifert (2010), Möller (2010).

24. A wreck-bonus (*Abwrackprämie*) of 2,500 euros for buying a new car (supposed to be less polluting) in exchange for a car at least nine years old. The German government spent altogether about €5 billion; however, the bonus also benefitted imported non-German cars.

25. For instance, the magazine *Economist* devoting a special issue (13 March 2010) to the German job miracle, as well as Nobel Prize winner Paul Krugman in his columns in the *New York Times* and *International Herald Tribune*.

26. This alarming trend reflects the probably too heavy reliance of the German employment system on the export industry.

27. Seventy-five per cent of the increase in jobs from 2009 to 2010 were 'nonstandard', especially temp-agency work.

28. Pundits of German *Fußball* were curiously following up a prominent example: *FC Bayern München* lent *Toni Kroos* to *Bayer Leverkusen*. This example is especially telling because it hints to a sensitive issue and to potential limits of this model. *Bayern München* and *Bayer Leverkusen* are both at the top of the German league (*Bundesliga*). The decisive game between these two clubs took place on 10 April 2010; *Toni Kroos* turned out to be decisive in preparing the one goal for Leverkusen to reach a draw, which means that he helped to score against his employer to whom he later on returned.

29. Information can be uploaded in the website of IGBCE trade union under *Demografiefonds*.

30. According to the Swedish example (see Albrecht, van den Bert, and Vroman, 2005).

BIBLIOGRAPHY

Albrecht, James, Gerard J. van den Berg, and Susanne Vroman. *The Knowledge Lift: The Swedish Adult Education Program That Aimed to Eliminate Low Worker Skill Levels.* Bonn: IZA Discussion Paper No. 1503, 2005.

Anxo, Dominique, Christine Erhel, and Joop Schippers, eds. *Labour Market Transitions and Time Adjustment over the Life Course.* Amsterdam: Dutch University Press, 2007.

Auer, Peter. "In Search of Optimal Labour Market Institutions." In *Flexicurity and Beyond—Finding a New Agenda for the European Social Model*, edited by Henning Jørgensen and Per Kongshoj Madsen, 67–98. Copenhagen: DJØF Publishing, 2007.

Auer, Peter and Sandrine Cazes, eds. *Employment Stability in an Age of Flexibility.* Geneva: ILO, 2003.

Bach, Hans-Uwe and Eugen Spitznagel. *Betriebe zahlen mit—und haben was davon.* Nuremberg: IAB-Kurzbericht No. 17, 2009.

Bentolila, Samuel, Pierre Cahuc, Juan José Dolado, and Thomas Le Barbanchon. *Two-Tier Labor Markets in the Great Recession: France vs. Spain.* Bonn: IZA-Discussion Paper No. 5340, 2010.

Berlin, Isaiah. *Liberty.* Edited by Henry Hardy. Oxford: Oxford University Press, 2002.

Bernstein, Peter L. *Against the Gods. The Remarkable Story of Risk.* New York: John Wiley and Sons, 1996.

Deakin, Simon and Alain Supiot, eds. *Capacitas—Contract Law and the Institutional Preconditions of a Market Economy.* Oxford: University of Oregon Press, 2009.

Dworkin, Ronald. *Sovereign Virtue—The Theory and Practice of Equality*. Cambridge, MA: Harvard University Press, 2000.

European Commission. *An Agenda for New Skills and Jobs: A European Contribution towards Full Employment*. Communication from the Commission, COM(2010) 682 final, Strasbourg, 23.11.2010, 2010.

European Commission. *Council Conclusions towards Common Principles of Flexicurity*. Brussels: COM(2007) 359 final, 2007.

European Commission. *Employment in Europe 2006—Recent Trends and Prospects*. Luxembourg: Office for Official Publications of the European Communities, 2006.

European Commission. *Employment in Europe 2008*. Luxembourg: Office for Official Publications of the European Communities, 2008.

Fehr, Ernst and Armin Falk. "Reciprocal Fairness, Cooperation and Limits to Competition." In *Intersubjectivity in Economics*, edited by Edward Fullbrook, 28–42. London: Routledge, 2002.

Ferrera, Mauricio, ed. *The Boundaries of Welfare—European Integration and the New Spatial Politics of Solidarity*. Oxford: Oxford University Press, 2005.

Gazier, Bernard. "'Making Transitions Pay': The 'Transitional Labour Markets' Approach to 'Flexicurity.'" In *Flexicurity and Beyond—Finding a New Agenda for the European Social Model*, edited by Henning Jørgensen and Per Kongshoj Madsen, 99–130. Copenhagen: DJØF Publishing, 2007.

Giddens, Anthony. *Beyond Left and Right—The Future of Radical Politics*. Cambridge: Polity Press, 1996.

Herzog-Stein, Alexander and Hartmut Seifert. *Deutsches "Beschäftigungswunder" und flexible Arbeitszeiten*. Düsseldorf: Hans-Böckler-Stiftung, WSI-Diskussionspapiere Nr. 169, 2010.

Hirschman, Albert O. *Development Projects Observed*. Washington, DC: Brookings Institutions,1967.

Jørgensen, Henning and Per Kongshoj Madsen, eds. *Flexicurity and Beyond—Finding a New Agenda for the European Social Model*. Copenhagen: DJØF Publishing, 2007.

Kahneman, Daniel and Amos Tversky, eds. *Choices, Values and Frames*. Cambridge: Cambridge University Press, 2000.

Klammer, Ute, Ruud Muffels, and Ton Wilthagen. *Flexibility and Security over the Life Course: Key Findings and Policy Messages*. Dublin: European Foundation for the Improvement of Living and Working Conditions, 2008.

Kok, Wim, Carlo Dell'Aringa, Federico Duran Lopez, Anna Ekström, Maria João Rodrigues, Christopher Pissarides, Annette Roux, and Günther Schmid. *Jobs, Jobs, Jobs—Creating More Employment in Europe. Report of the Employment Task Force Chaired by Wim Kok*. Luxembourg: Office for Official Publications of the European Communities, 2004.

Koning, Jaap de, ed. *Evaluating Active Labour Market Policy—Measures, Public Private Partnerships and Benchmarking*. Cheltenham: Edward Elgar, 2007.

Korver, Ton and Peter R.A. Oeij. "Employability through Covenants: Taking External Effects Seriously." In *The European Social Model and Transitional Labour Markets—Law and Policy*, edited by Ralf Rogowski, 143–169. Cheltenham: Edward Elgar, 2008.

Lassnigg, Lorenz, Helen Burzlaff, Maria A.D. Rodriguez, and Morton Lassen, eds. *Lifelong Learning—Building Bridges through Transitional Labour Markets*. Apeldoorn Antwerpen: Het Spinhuis, 2007.

Layard, Richard. *The New Happiness*. London: Penguin Press, 2005.

Leschke, Janine. *Unemployment Insurance and Non-Standard Employment—Four European Countries in Comparison*. Wiesbaden: VS Verlag für Sozialwissenschaften, 2008.

Madsen, Per Kongshoj. "How Can It Possibly Fly? The Paradox of a Dynamic Labour Market." In *National Identity and the Varieties of Capitalism—The Danish Experience*, edited by John L. Campbell, John A. Hall, and Ove K. Pedersen, 321–355. Montreal: McGill-Queen's University Press, 2006.

Marsden, David. *A Theory of Employment Systems: Micro-Foundations of Societal Diversity*. Oxford: Oxford University Press, 1999.

Möller, Joachim. "The German Labor Market Response in the World Recession—De-Mystifying a Miracle." *ZAF (Zeitschrift für Arbeitsmarktforschung)* 42 (2010): 325–336.

Muffels, Ruud J.A., ed. *Flexibility and Employment Security in Europe—Labour Markets in Transition*. Cheltenham: Edward Elgar, 2008.

Offer, Avner. *The Challenge of Affluence: Self-Control and Well-Being in the United States and Britain since 1950*. Oxford: Oxford University Press, 2006.

O'Reilly, Jacqueline, Immaculada Cebrián, and Michel Lallement, eds. *Working-Time Changes—Social Integration through Transitional Labour Markets*. Cheltenham: Edward Elgar, 2000.

Rawls, John. *Justice as Fairness—A Restatement*. Edited by Edward Kelly. Cambridge, MA: Belknap Press of Harvard University Press, 2001.

Rogowski, Ralf, ed. *The European Social Model and Transitional Labour Markets—Law and Policy*. Farnham: Ashgate, 2008.

Rogowski, Ralf, Robert Salais, and Noel Whiteside, eds. *Transforming European Employment Policy—Labour Market Transitions and the Promotion of Capabilities*. Cheltenham: Edward Elgar, 2012.

Sabel, Charles F. "Learning by Monitoring: The Institutions of Economic Development." In *Rethinking the Development Experience: Essays Provoked by the Work of Albert O. Hirschman*, edited by Lloyd Rodwin and Donald A. Schön, 231–274. Washington, DC: Brookings Institutions and the Lincoln Institute of Land Reform, 1994.

Salais, Robert and Robert Villeneuve, eds. *Europe and the Politics of Capabilities*. Cambridge: Cambridge University Press, 2004.

Schmid, Günther. *Full Employment in Europe—Managing Labour Market Transitions and Risks*. Cheltenham: Edward Elgar, 2008.

Schmid, Günther. "Non-Standard Employment and Labour Force Participation: A Comparative View of the Recent Development in Europe." In *Bridging the Gap—International Database on Employment and Adaptable Labour*, edited by Ernest Berkhout and Emina van den Berg, 123–162. Amsterdam: Randstad & SEO Economic Onderzoek, 2010a.

Schmid, Günther. "Non-Standard Employment in Europe: Its Development and Consequences for the European Employment Strategy." *German Policy Studies* 7 (2010b): 171–210. http://spaef.com/file.php?id=1273 (accessed 28 April 2012).

Schmid, Günther. "Social Risk Management through Transitional Labour Markets." *Socio-Economic Review* 4 (2006): 1–37.

Schmid, Günther. *Übergänge am Arbeitsmarkt—Arbeit, nicht nur Arbeitslosigkeit versichern*. Berlin: edition sigma, 2011.

Schmid, Günther and Bernard Gazier, eds. *The Dynamics of Full Employment—Social Integration through Transitional Labour Markets*. Cheltenham: Edward Elgar, 2002.

Schmid, Günther and Paula Protsch. *Wandel der Erwerbsformen in Deutschland und Europa*. Wissenschaftszentrum Berlin für Sozialforschung: Discussion Paper SP I 2009–505, 2009. http://bibliothek.wzb.eu/pdf/2009/i09–505.pdf (accessed 28 April 2012).

Schulze Buschoff, Karin and Paula Protsch. "(A-) Typical and (In-) Secure? Social Protection and 'Non-Standard' Forms of Employment in Europe." *International Social Security Review* 61 (2008): 51–73.

Sen, Amartya. *Development as Freedom.* New York: Alfred A. Knopf, 2001.
Sen, Amartya. *The Idea of Justice.* London: Allan Lane and Penguin Books, 2009.
Supiot, Alain. *Beyond Employment—Changes in Work and the Future of Labour Law in Europe.* Oxford: Oxford University Press, 2001.
Tolstoy, Leo. *Anna Karenina.* New York: Bantam Classic, 1960 (first published 1877).
Wilthagen, Ton and Frank Tros. "The Concept of 'Flexicurity': A New Approach to Regulating Employment and Labour Markets." *Transfer* 10 (2004): 166–186.
Zhou, Haibo, Ronald Dekker, and Alfred Kleinknecht. *Flexible Labor and Innovation Performance: Evidence from Longitudinal Firm-Level Data.* Rotterdam: Research Paper 2010–01–21 of the Erasmus Research Institute of Management (ERIM), 2010.

6 Labour, Capabilities, and Situated Democracy[1]

Robert Salais

INTRODUCTION

The global crisis at work originates in the 1980s, following the disqualification of the Keynesian model of full employment and, more generally, of socialism and planning. These theories have been replaced by a generalised belief in market efficiency as a general system of governance for all human activities. This has raised a dilemma. On the one hand, the current crisis is the outcome of such beliefs in market efficiency. On the other hand, times have changed, and it is impossible to return to the Keynesian model of full employment as it was. What should be done? Should we undertake nothing beyond rhetoric, thus allowing market apologists to continue their race towards the abyss, or should we search for a new political path that would be capable of overcoming this dilemma? The issue involves more than merely finding an alternative to flexicurity. More fundamentally, it involves discovering the foundations for a new economic and social model. In this chapter, we trace several elements of such a model by reviewing the potentialities of the capability approach. We begin by presenting several general guidelines. We then specify the most prominent characteristics of work policies based on capabilities, and we draw conclusions regarding desirable reforms to democratic practices with regard to the transformation of work.

TOWARDS NEW TYPES OF WORK POLICIES BASED ON FULL EMPLOYMENT?

Since the Second World War, the search for full employment has traditionally been considered a task for Keynesian monetary, fiscal, and budget policies. In contrast, the proposal developed here centres on the implementation of work policies for this purpose. Such policies could systematically reallocate public resources that were previously dedicated to Keynesian employment policies towards the lifelong development of individual capabilities, whether within or outside the context of work.[2] To be socially just and economically efficient, such policies should be defined and implemented through a profound process involving the democratisation of economic, political, and social life.[3] This would allow collective decisions to be taken closer to situations of life and work.

It is important to note that, until 1980, the category of 'unemployment' was at the core of social policies seeking to provide citizens with a minimum floor of security in life and work. The 'Keynesian policies' (which, in practice, greatly simplified the theoretical ideas of John Maynard Keynes) were largely 'passive'. They were aimed at compensating for the ex post social consequences of economic recessions; they were not intended to develop ex ante actions to prevent economic and social hazards. From the 1980s to the 1990s, the European institutions progressively shifted from unemployment as the key concept and objective towards the maximising of the rate of employment, individual employability and the monitoring of public policies through quantitative performance indicators. Such orientations are part of the broader European policy shift towards neoliberalism and deregulation that has accompanied the convergence towards the single currency, the euro. Far from disappearing, mass unemployment has been taking other forms (e.g., precariousness and exclusion). Such changes in employment policies have come to resemble a sort of conservative 'revolution'—a return to a past in which individuals bore sole responsibility for their own fate. In contrast, it is necessary to develop really new policies with new goals and new instruments. Maintaining a path toward social progress and employment requires new collective instruments that go beyond social compensation and that are more ambitious: work policies based on the development of capabilities throughout life.

How could this work? The operational character of such policies is obvious: six guidelines should be followed. Each of these guidelines is described in detail in the course of the chapter. The section below provides a brief overview of their most important features.

Guidelines for Thinking and Acting

1. The new type of full-employment policy should have a universalistic character, neither organised along the lines of old corporatist social groups nor subdividing social recipients into the deserving or undeserving poor.

2. The individuality and accomplishments of human beings cannot be neglected, as had been the case with the standard macro-economic views. It is becoming less and less acceptable to split the individual into many parts, each targeted by specific policies and institutions developed independently of others. For individuals, families, local communities, and companies, life and work are becoming increasingly intertwined. Reuniting the separate parts of individuals and restoring continuity throughout their lives in a logic of development

should be at the heart of any new economic and social model (see also Méda and Zimmermann, this volume). In economic terms, this would make work fairer and more efficient, thereby making it easier to meet the increasing demands of companies with regard to flexibility and autonomy of action.

3. Allocation of public resources for the development of capabilities should not be undertaken purely as a means of providing security. In essence, the objective should be to equip all individuals—here and now—with true freedoms with which to achieve the lives that they value and the work that they would like to do. Such a constraint is demanding. Although work should be a valuable activity for personal fulfilment, it can no longer be considered as the only valuable activity. Work is not a commodity sold in a market, nor is it the sole purpose of life. Individuals should have the opportunity to reconcile their work in a positive manner with other activities that are of value to them.

4. Such an institutional framework implies that, in their work, workers should no longer be seen as machines or purely as factors in the process of production. They must become citizens who have a say (both individually and collectively) about the organisation, remuneration, and aims of their work, particularly with regard to the values, common goods, and basic goals of the broader society in which they live. Backed with individual and collective rights and duties, their capabilities for voice should be recognised and their voices heard in all collective decisions. Workplaces must thus be open to the world around them.

5. As stated above, the implementation of such policies and social practices requires in-depth democratisation. The voice of those concerned must be heard and taken into account during deliberative procedures. Such procedures should include appropriate and sufficient resources and rights, with the underlying goal of establishing a 'situated' democracy. In other words, democratic practices should combine representative democracy (particularly at the national level) with forms of participatory democracy that rely upon the mobilisation of various 'publics' through collective deliberative enquiries.

6. Finally, the guidelines stated above do not imply that economic and market activities should be impeded. However, the ways in which firms and markets are organised will require extensive changes in order to fulfil the purpose of capability development. The necessary changes must be driven by a combination of revised and new regulations at the national and European levels. It will be necessary for labour markets to become less dominant, such that they no longer determine the future of individuals in any circumstances of social and economic life. Firms, public agencies, and collective bargaining should receive additional responsibilities with regard to capability development. Regulations should help firms and markets to include

capability development in their operations as a standard for evaluating their strategies and organisation. Concerns about capability should not be limited to people at work, however, but should extend as well to all people.

Transcending the Instrumental Conception of Work

According to the instrumental conception of work, capitalism alone is assumed capable of transforming labour into a process of emancipation by developing productive forces, by imposing the learning of discipline and productivity at work and by centralising workers into organised masses within large firms (Honneth, 1980). In this view, the role of the labour movement is essentially to follow (and be led by) the movement of capital, as well as to struggle with it while pursuing the conquest of the state and political power. The instrumental conception of work includes beliefs about technical progress and its political neutrality (i.e., 'the productive forces'), and the virtues of central planning are considered the only 'provisions' to be adopted by social movements in their quest for labour emancipation. Despite several important exceptions, the instrumental view of work is dominated by two broad versions of the same argument: the reformist version (which calls for a peaceful, gradual transition) and the revolutionary version (which calls for the conquest of political power by any means possible). Both of these versions are based on the same preconceived notion that freedoms are of no value to labour, and they both claim that any actual development of such freedoms would serve the interests of capital alone, and not those of labour. Both the reformist and the revolutionary versions have ultimately failed. We know the disastrous consequences of such conceptions in the formerly socialist countries. In capitalist systems, new forms of management have subjugated aspirations for freedom and accomplishment at work to the service of refined labour exploitation.

Although resistance to the domination of capital and its consequences has played an essential role in the labour movement (especially in the interests of the movement's own development), it ultimately appears to have been insufficient. It has failed to achieve the emancipation of labour (let alone of humanity as a whole). In retrospect, the struggles led by labour, social, or political organisations appear to have been valuable only for particular economic systems (roughly those of large rationalised capitalist industries).[4] Such struggles have proven to have little or no value for the other systems (e.g., territorially anchored SME production systems or high-tech industries or services). The labour movement has thus remained largely powerless to cope with the transformations of economic systems led by *fin de siècle* capitalism and its globalisation at the dawn of the twenty-first century. Large mass industries based on integrated firms have declined. Instead, the global division of labour has expanded, setting individuals, firms, national systems, and peoples in competition against each other. Market mechanisms have been introduced at the core of production and work, thereby thwarting and invalidating the predictions of Marx.

The resulting developments are contradictory. The literature highlights a long list of disadvantageous consequences (e.g., unemployment, job insecurity, downward pressure on wages, time pressure, feelings of being overburdened, individualisation, rising demands from managers with regard to work intensity, and submission to ever higher standards of corporate profitability and to capital markets). Work pathologies have developed, characterised by such terms as 'suffering at work' and 'moral harassment'. The weakening of social and legal protections for labour is now supported by European monetary, economic, and employment policies. In contrast to the Lisbon strategy's call for 'more and better jobs', we are now observing the proliferation of bad jobs that are poorly paid and that offer no future to those who perform them.

A series of factors nevertheless underscores the possibility of an alternative future for work, in which aspirations for personal accomplishment and human development are rising, despite the contradictions generated by capitalism and its crisis. The demand for individual capability development has emerged from this alternative future, which is accompanied by increasing aspirations for less constrained work that could allow professional development and, ultimately, equality and effective freedoms in life and work. In the interest of efficiency, an increase has been observed in the number of jobs involving autonomy, initiative, and responsibility, all of which contribute to individual and collective freedoms. In fact, capitalist strategies have been revised (at least in developed countries) through the introduction of management methods based on the concept of individual competence. For capitalism, this has taken place out of necessity, as well as in order to serve various interests. The necessity involves the need to master complex environments of production and markets, which demands space for autonomy at work. The interests served by these developments are based on the assumption that such management methods are needed in order to be successful in the pursuit of profitability. Unfortunately for workers, however, these developments are generating work processes that generate extreme stress, and precariousness, poor working conditions, and low wages are becoming the rule.

THE PRIMARY CHARACTERISTICS OF WORK
POLICIES BASED ON CAPABILITIES

In retrospect, therefore, history has shown that the issue is not (nor has it ever been) a matter of finding a third way between capitalism and socialism; it is simply a matter of finding the way. More and more voices and collectives (both within and beyond labour movement organisations) are now becoming aware of this situation. This raises the question of which mode of development should be sought. The capability approach is one of several serious candidates.[5] The value of this approach is that it embeds the emancipation of labour within a wider and possibly more tractable process: the implementation of a capability-based mode of development.

Reinventing Labour[6]

After 1945, labour was allowed to enjoy and to participate in at least some freedoms, largely in the social domain. The freedoms at stake were negative freedoms (labelled as 'freedom from want' by Beveridge in the UK and Roosevelt in the US): protection against the hazards of life and work, job security (at least to some extent), and social security, in addition to protective labour and social legislation. Despite conflicting ideologies, the same overall programme was operating in both capitalist and socialist countries, largely as an outgrowth of their competition. Despite perceptible differences (notably the status of freedoms), both systems used these programmes to pursue the same political goals: general adherence to the system and social peace. At its roots, however, the participation of labour in freedoms was a response to Nazi barbarity. Extending well beyond social freedoms, fundamental human rights were recognised, extending to the guarantee of economic, political, and civil freedoms through a series of charters and international organisations (especially the UN and the ILO) (Supiot, 2011). To date, these charters have remained a medium for a politics of freedoms, along with its universalistic legitimacy.

Social protection, which was largely brushed aside in formerly socialist countries several years after the fall of the Berlin Wall, is now under attack in Western Europe as well, under the impetus of European authorities and governments, austerity policies, and reduced public spending. These attacks reveal the weaknesses of the post-war implementation of social liberties. First, their initial formulation in terms of negative freedoms was insufficient for coping with the transformations of labour. For example, the rise of social precariousness and poverty in work undermines the tenure of stable jobs, which is often a prerequisite for benefitting from normal social protection. Fewer and fewer people are fulfilling the necessary conditions (e.g., contributions, entitlement to benefits, number of years worked over a lifetime). Negative freedoms should be transformed into positive freedoms, with the goal of preventing social hazards and providing people with the capability of controlling their lives. Second, and more importantly, the social liberties conceived or claimed during the post-war period were not intended as part of a more ambitious move to achieve the coherent expansion of all freedoms. Such an avenue was nevertheless potentially opened when charters of fundamental rights were established and signed at the end of the Second World War.[7]

The challenge today is to provide labour with renewed social freedoms, along with economic, political, and civic freedoms both within and outside of work activity. Labour must be reinvented through a politics of effective freedoms and the development of capabilities.

The best way to grasp the issue is to start from the current valuation of individuals in capitalist regimes. Briefly stated, the public value accorded to individuals is now a direct function of the quantity of work they deliver to the economy. Such a measure of value is essentially utilitarian. Individuals are useful when they are or can be employed; the concept of employment thus refers to the possibility of using the individual as a tool for producing wealth. Employment is essentially a utilitarian concept. If people are not employable, they are of no value. The structural reforms of labour markets and social protections pushed by the OECD and the European authorities are centred on this mode of valuation. In a capability approach, the value of the individual is different and richer. This approach represents an attempt to respect the variety of goals that people may have in their lives. It recognises the worth of these goals and their achievements. Work can no longer be considered the sole criterion for valuing people. Although this value obviously varies according to individuals and the societies in which they live, work cannot be considered the only goal. People have many other activities, the accomplishment of which has value for them. Examples include having and raising children, participating in various aspects of community life, remaining in good health, engaging in creative activities, and acquiring knowledge (and thus developing their effective freedom of choice). Any fair valuation should consider all of these activities, and not only (or even primarily) employment. The ultimate goal of any work policy should be to provide people with opportunities and resources with which to increase their value, as understood in this way. Amartya Sen and the capability approach have developed a formal structure and methodology for this type of value measurement. It is important to note that this methodology, formal structure, and implementation are closely related to the human rights movement that developed during the post-war period. The capability approach preserves this aspect of reform and helps to make it operational.

Work cannot be isolated from life; it is an integral part of life. In order to develop their capabilities for work, as well as for their other activities, individuals must be able to find the necessary resources, time, and freedom within their living and working situations in order to choose and achieve the goals and activities that they value. They should have the freedom to combine raising children with holding a job, to combine training and work, to have time for participating in the public debate and local community life, to have time within the context of work to discuss the situation within the firm with their colleagues and to make their voices heard on these topics. The challenge is to ensure that all individuals, here and now, are capable of living the lives that they value. This implies that the entire society should be organised such that all individuals are able to benefit from some freedom to choose within their own living and working situations. At the micro level (e.g., within the firm), this would require designing jobs that make it possible for people to learn, to enhance their capabilities, and to voice their opinions. Such a design assumes that basing labour on the requirements for justice and providing it with effective freedoms and autonomous spaces available for discussion and action would create a positive dynamic between responsibility and autonomy. This would enhance the efficiency of labour in terms of content, outcomes, and execution, in contrast to participative management in which labour is subjugated to quantitative performance indicators.

Labour, Citizenship and a New Model of Development

The model of development resulting from a politics of effective freedoms no longer centres on economic growth relying upon accelerating the accumulation of capital, mobilising labour power, and increasing the hourly rate of labour productivity. Such a model of growth no longer exists (and is unlikely to return) in developed countries, and the situation is likely to be similar everywhere else in the foreseeable future (presumably after many tensions and conflicts).

Investments should be based on non-market criteria other and broader than the rate of return on capital. Their design, content, procedures, and efficiency measures should incorporate the gains and costs that they will generate from the perspective of developmental objectives (human capabilities and the development of nature). Work must be considered as one of many valuable activities. Such a shift would require the discovery of compromises and combinations (both individual and collective) between work and other valuable activities. It would be necessary to overcome many constraints (particularly with regard to available resources, preferences and commitments, optimal location, and distribution). It would open a wide field for democratic deliberation at different levels and on various issues (see below). The outcomes of such compromises and combinations would determine the array and scope of valuable lives that would be open to people. Such outcomes are of crucial importance for people. It is important to remember that, in a capability approach, valuable lives are those during which individuals can expect to achieve a sense of personal accomplishment. People equate living such a life with making the right choices at the right time and place; they associate it with changing direction from one activity to another and varying combinations of activities throughout their lives. The relevant political benchmarks in such an approach are not predefined, quantitative macro-indicators. Instead, they consist of the judgements that individuals make, relative to their degree of life accomplishment. These are the tests of any politics of freedoms, and they condition the political and social sustainability of any capability-based model of development.

The concept of citizenship also requires extensive revision. According to the standard formulation by T.H. Marshall, citizenship (and consequently the citizen) is divided into different parts—political, civil, and social—each having no organic relationship to the others. In contrast, capable citizens become both holders and actors of a set of freedoms in concomitant and mutual development. Unlike Marshall's citizen, the capable citizen cannot be fragmented, and such a citizen would refuse such a divided life. The capable citizen cannot be a worker at one moment, a consumer at another, an owner or tenant at a third moment, or a voter from time to time. In the quest for unity in their lives, capable citizens intend to use both synergies and tensions to link the contributions that they can and would like to make towards the realisation of the societal and developmental objectives in which they are stakeholders. Through such engagements, citizens acquire knowledge, gain convictions, and form expectations, all of which are valuable in terms of the quality and intensity of democratic deliberation.

According to the capability approach, individuals who work are considered as citizens with opinions to be stated and heard (and to be recognised as such by virtue of explicit rights) on matters relating to their work: organisation, remuneration, and societal objectives. In these matters, working individuals have the capability, both individually and collectively (through their representatives), to voice their views, not only in relation to issues within their own firms, but also with regard to the societal objectives to which their firms have the means to contribute. One of the democratic outcomes of a politics of freedoms is that capable citizens become not only the voices of their own claims (or those of their local labour communities); more broadly, they become the voices of the actual process of development. In the political debate, they are its interpreters. They have the capability to formulate the objectives that development must achieve at their own level and within their own spheres of activity. Because they possess part of the necessary knowledge (i.e., the practical part), the participation of citizens in collective choices is required, in the usual political sense and, more generally, for the sake of the actual process of development.

Representing Labour and Its Voice

If making voices heard and mobilising practical knowledge as a resource in life and work situations are to become crucial to the process of development, it will be necessary to address at least one basic issue: the representation of labour wherever collective issues are debated and resolved. Such issues are linked to democratic practices and to the state, as discussed below. The simplest way in which individuals can represent themselves is through the latitude offered by direct expression in public forums and assemblies. Whereas citizen assemblies need to be carefully prepared in order to be productive and avoid being manipulated, direct expression is arguably preferable wherever possible (e.g., in workshops, establishments, districts, or any collective based on proximity). In our large and complex societies, however, the mediation of representation is usually necessary. Representatives, whether individuals or organisations (e.g., parties, trade unions, interest groups, or associations), are supposed to speak for us and to express a voice that, in a perfect world, would be our voice as well. How can we ensure that their voice will be ours?

There are urgent needs in this regard. In the current crisis, we have reached the limits of generalised financial evaluation—the most abstract, dehumanised principle ever imagined for representing and evaluating human activities. The criterion of financial return has invaded every activity, including work, through quantitative performance indicators. Even Europe has been infected. The European 2020 Agenda claims to evaluate the future of European economy correctly according to five macroeconomic global indicators. This is nonsense. Such a claim is far removed from the realities that are lived and perceived by Europeans. In contrast, a capability-based democracy would assign priority in evaluative practices to the human and concrete dimensions of labour, providing people with capabilities and a voice in collective choices. Such a democracy aims to reinstate diversity and specificity, in contrast to financial evaluation, which considers only standardisation and abstraction.

The representation of labour should thus be understood in its full scope and scale. The standard view focuses on ensuring the social and political representation of labour at all levels of decision making, from firms and territories to the national, European, and international levels. Specialised organisations (i.e., unions and parties) exist for this purpose. These organisations have their own agendas and formulate mottos and demands for their members, to be adapted on the ground. In case of unions, this standard view neglects three difficult issues. First, as noted above, the traditional foundations of membership have been profoundly undermined and eroded by the decline of large, integrated industries, as well as the rise of small firms with no unions and precarious jobs. Second, the capability approach is aimed specifically at recreating the unity of individuals in their lives and work. To become capable, people at work should not be divided into parts, with each part represented by a special, vertical organisation. Instead, they require 'horizontal' representation, which allows them to link their claims as workers, consumers, users of public services, voters, and other entities, in addition to identifying synergies between them at a 'situated' level. In this regard, unions are challenged either to cooperate with civil society associations or (as some organisations already do) to include wider claims within their scope. Third, governance based on the tools of New Public Management (e.g., performance indicators, benchmarking, reporting) proceeds from an informational foundation, which is associated with serious biases when representing labour. In most cases, labour is treated as a quantity and a cost,[8] and it is therefore not adequately represented with regard to its transformations, needs, and capabilities.

All three of these issues underline the cognitive dimension of representation and the urgent need for unions and associations to re-create dense links between building relevant knowledge about work and formulating claims. To represent is to re-present. For unions and associations, this means building up their own knowledge about work and life (and the intersection between them), as well as considering this knowledge wherever decisions are made with regard to work and its future. It is important to recall that a claim essentially aggregates the diversity of individual situations into general proposals. Such aggregation should be relevant to the action that is to be undertaken upon returning to workplaces or firms. In a capability approach, claims have normative, cognitive, and pragmatic moments and dimensions. With regard to labour transformations and the challenge they are currently posing to collective action, the cognitive moment appears increasingly central. These issues involve both representation and representativeness.

DELIBERATIVE DEMOCRACY AS A TOOL FOR SOCIAL JUSTICE AND ECONOMIC EFFICIENCY[9]

The capability approach thus places democracy and its full exercise at the core of collective decision making in every field, in the cognitive and social mechanisms of representation, and in the production of public knowledge. Moreover, the search for efficient solutions from the perspective of development and its needs must rely on deliberative democratic procedures. This is obviously not the common view. Today, the true centres of decision making are becoming increasingly remote from workshops, plants, or territories. It is striking to note the extent to which multinational companies, international organisations (e.g., OECD, IMF, World Bank, EU authorities) and national administrations are now using essentially the same tools and methodologies to address problems that have nothing in common in terms of specificity, content, quality, scope, scale, location, or the population concerned. All of these organisations use standardised tools that are based on abstract, quantitative, and financial criteria, benchmarking, and low-cost competition. Such a dogmatic (i.e., unquestioned), 'universal' approach to collective problems is inevitably inefficient, especially for development. Even worse, it generates widespread waste of resources, human suffering, job destruction, and lasting social and economic stagnation. The more decisions are made in close consultation with the people involved and their practical knowledge about the situation, the better they will be in terms of development. This requires deliberative procedures in which a relevant plurality of voices can be heard around the table and in which a debate on criteria is possible. In any case, such a debate on criteria would help to keep financial criteria in check and to identify compromises that would be more favourable to human and sustainable development. As a precondition, methods and criteria that are favourable to such development must be represented by voices around the table. It is also important to note that the table in question should be positioned in the right place, at the right level (depending upon the issue at stake), and with the right question. The search for the right place and question is at the core of what we call a 'situated' approach.

This opens a series of possible traps. In such deliberations, it would be unproductive to ask participants about their opinions or wishes. To be truly justified and understandable, each statement should be backed by information and data, clarifying how the proposed criteria would work. Individuals should have a voice, as should objects (at least those whose characteristics are relevant to the problem), and they should therefore be represented by accredited spokespersons (usually associations or the state). This is particularly true for nature, the environmental and developmental interests of which should be heard (see also Méda, this volume). The same holds for other contexts as well, including heritage objects (e.g., historical buildings). Actors around the table have unequal resources and unequal capabilities to express their voices correctly and to be truly heard. Procedures should be designed in order to ensure understanding between people who consider each other as equals. The state and its institutions could avoid most of these traps through the application of procedural rules and the distribution of rights to deliberate on which access to resources will be given to whom. As long as effective solutions are expected instead of pure discussion or consultation, the deliberative rule should start by assuming the autonomy of the participants, and the resources allocated should be determined through deliberation. The entire process calls for a situated state, the only one capable of and interested in implementing such procedures.[10]

How decisions are to be made at the end of the deliberative process is not hard to determine in technical terms. It depends upon the rules selected: unanimity or majority rule, the assignment of equal or differential weights to the various voices, or the legal accreditation of one particular actor or person to decide. Regular procedures can also be organised for revising decisions based on the evaluation of outcomes at a later point. In our view, the most neglected issues in the literature concern the formulation of the question to be addressed and the informational basis upon which to rely in examining the question, debating solutions, and evaluating outcomes (e.g., Which data are appropriate? Where can they be obtained?). The key issue for the development model advocated by Sen involves the democratisation of the processes leading to formulating the question and building the relevant knowledge to address it. It involves the objectivity of data and information. Once the question and its informational basis have been determined, they outline the corridor in which the solutions are to be discovered.

Unlike the hard sciences, socioeconomic matters cannot guarantee objectivity solely through the application of scientific rules of observation and deduction.[11] In particular, statistical data on these issues can never be considered objective in this sense. Such information is socially constructed from start to finish, from the questionnaire (it is well known that answers are influenced by the way in which questions are formulated) to the categories, the choice of tables, the selection of key figures (e.g., in case of indicators), and their interpretation. A plurality of modes of constructing questions, categories, and data is the rule, not the exception; the same holds for the hierarchy or relative weight assigned to empirical statements. Since their inception, scholars in the area of social enquiry and statistics have developed methodologies for coping with such subtleties (e.g., the representativeness of random samples, the neutralisation of biases emerging from the situation of interviews, the detection of imprecision and ambiguity in the wording of questions or the definition of categories). Nevertheless, norms and value judgements are inevitably embedded in *a priori* technical choices (ultimately due to their social nature). Amartya Sen underscores this point by emphasising that "description is choice" (1982) and by noting that individuals, communities, even nations differ with regard to the relative weights they attribute to objects that are generally considered of value in society (1993).

In a universe containing a plurality of voices, the solution we offer with regard to discovering the relevant question and its informational basis revolves around the concept of deliberative enquiry.[12] The worst thing would be to rely upon recourse to experts (as is currently quite common). Experts are useful only for the first approach to problems, as they deliver information according to a supposed scientific truth, which neglects the plurality of possible objectivities and leaves knowledge out of any debate. What is needed is neither expertise nor the addition of subjective opinions, but true knowledge that everyone could share. For this purpose, deliberative enquiry should combine two distinct fields: enquiry and deliberation. Enquiry is necessary, as we must follow the methodology and deontology of the social sciences. Deliberation is necessary as well, given that both the questioning and its implication in terms of politics should be publicly debated in a democratic arena. Moreover, the combination of enquiry and deliberation adds a third dimension: a collective process by which the people involved build up a cause on their own, along with the question to be resolved and the required knowledge concerning what matters. In this process, the cause, question, and knowledge become their own, providing structure to their state of belonging within the same community, as well as their awareness of this belonging, which ultimately channels action and coordination in the future. In other words, deliberative enquiry seeks to create a public in the sense described by Dewey—a public that is capable of taking part in public deliberation through its representatives. With an informational basis thus constructed, the public could achieve a knowledge-based compromise, with leeway for assigning different weights according to the facts. A public with its own legitimate and collectively agreed knowledge can back its voice with facts, as well as with claims founded on empirical evidence (and not on ideology). Deliberative enquiry thus appears capable of avoiding the traps associated with direct expression without falling into the biases of institutionalised or inadequate cognitive representation. Many deliberative enquiries should be at work, depending upon the number of common goods and the degree to which their implementation is situated. By requiring deliberative enquiries, unions and associations could improve or update the formulation of claims, back them with facts, and, presumably, increase both their audience and membership.

The Situated State

At the outset, it is important to note that, as used here, the term 'state' does not refer to a bureaucracy that is external to the people, but to the materialised and publicly institutionalised expression of some 'convention of the state', which is shared by the people. Briefly stated, such a convention defines what citizens expect their state to do with regard to defining and realising common goods, as well as what they are expected to (and should) do themselves with regard to such tasks. As with other systems of conventions, there are many possible ways of dividing and coordinating labour between the state and the citizenship.

Michael Storper and I define a 'situated' state as one that distances itself from both an interventionist state (characterised by socialism and a planned economy) and an absent state (characterised by self-regulation and a market-based economy). Its defining characteristic is that its policies are based on the premise that people are autonomous and capable of acting in favour of the common good (Salais and Storper, 1993: part IV.2; Storper and Salais, 1997). In such a state, freedoms are not opposed to the achievement of the common good. The situated state relies upon (and reciprocally encourages) the conceptions of citizenship and voice that we have attempted to define above. In essence, it wagers that the effective development of capabilities requires engaging in a process of 'capacitation', which can lead to collective learning. Such processes allow people to demonstrate their confidence in their own capability to themselves and to others. Several conditions relative to the state's action are required for the proper functioning of this process:

- Formulating objectives at the central level with regard to common goods, as expressed in qualitative terms only, and not predetermined in terms of performance indicators
- Allowing autonomy for the concretisation of these goods through deliberative procedures between people at appropriate levels
- Engaging substantial and procedural resources (deliberative rights) at the relevant levels (depending upon the nature of the common good involved) at which such concretisation is pursued through the mobilisation of the citizenry
- Intervening only as a last resort and in a non-predictable way for cases involving the proven failure of the collective in charge of concretising the common good

European social philosophy (largely from continental Europe) contains a variety of approaches to such situated states, depending upon the foundations that are favoured for the capability to act towards the common good (e.g., proximity, dignity, awareness of the potentialities of the situation, or human development). Each of these types of states has its own way of implementing the pragmatic assumption that each person is potentially capable of acting towards the common good. Such states attempt to create institutional frameworks that foster the emergence of such capability (e.g., by developing devices based on mutual expectations and reflexive learning). Instead of deciding everything in advance or instrumentalising freedom towards the achievement of predefined goals (as in governance schemes), such states seek to develop free collective spaces of reflection, initiative, deliberation, coordination, and achievement. Such spaces are expected (and deliberately designed) to generate an apprenticeship of democracy, innovation, capability, responsibility, and, ultimately, individual and collective control of development.

CONCLUSION: TOWARDS SITUATED DEMOCRACY IN EUROPE?

European democracies have already incorporated some elements of the capability-based approach to development, notably with regard to voice and deliberative democracy, whether in critical movements or in institutions. This raises the question of how far Europe still has to go in order to have any true possibility of implementing something like a situated state. In this regard, it would be quite interesting to determine the distance between existing states and democracies in Europe from such a situated state and the democracy that it would entail.

The situated state relies on deliberative democracy at all levels as an efficient means of public action and as an efficient mediation between ends and means. For this purpose, it focuses on the development of capabilities. The distance between this type of state and the existing ones could be roughly evaluated according to two measures: the degree of 'horizontal' representation and the role of participatory versus representative democracy. The true picture is obviously much more complicated and detailed than is the sketch provided below.

With regard to the new and enriched citizenship required by a capability-based form of development, the autonomous spaces of deliberation and achievement that it demands cannot be the same as those already instituted by existing organisations. The existing institutions are based predominantly on the principle of vertical representation by sector or field. In most cases, unions represent labour primarily as the most relevant human activity, regardless of all others, according to a definition that excludes an increasing proportion of workers. Other human activities (e.g., housing, urbanism, family, childhood, transport, environment) or social problems (e.g., poverty, illness, social exclusion) are largely represented by associations belonging to civil society. Municipalities, towns, and other local constituencies try to coordinate all of these separately represented activities. Such tasks are impossible to undertake in as fair manner, especially when the state (and Europe) is exerting control from above. Capable citizens cannot be adequately represented by such verticality. They require more horizontality, with organisational efforts to re-create and represent the unity of individuals and their voices. This could be achieved through various reforms. Examples include enlarging competencies (e.g., with unions developing their own associations), redefining categories of thought and action, and improving coordination at situated levels (or a combination of these reforms). This constitutes the first measure with which to evaluate distance from the situated state.

The second measure involves the distinction between 'participatory' and representative democracy, as well as their connection within European countries. In this context, we are defending a specific conception of participatory democracy (the one explained above), which focuses on the emergence and mobilisation of publics through deliberative enquiry. It is not something marginal and manipulated from above; it is a political tool for expressing the voice of citizens (including those who work) and considering them publically whenever collective decisions are to be taken. The type of voice favoured by such participatory democracy is backed by relevant knowledge and claims, both constructed autonomously as outcomes of deliberative enquiries of the sort we describe. Although this could enhance direct democracy in firms and territories to a significant extent, it would necessarily be limited. People who are external to such publics (for good reasons) cannot exercise their voices or have them heard. The choices made by existing publics could have negative consequences (spillover effects) for the lives and choice space of these people, who would thus have grounds for protest. Although representative democracy at higher, more general levels would have the capacity to address such problems, it also has disadvantages, including excessive abstraction (leading to poor construction of the problems to be addressed), increasing difficulty achieving 'enlightened' votes (that reflect true knowledge of the issue and respect the general interest), and biased cognitive representation.

Further questions concern the extent to which and the forms in which situated democracy (which seems to the most appropriate political regime for capability-based development) could be successful in implementing the representative and participatory democracy (as defined here). For example, representative democracy at the central level could be used to determine the basic objectives of the community, its resources (or at least the central part of them), and their breakdown at lower levels. Participatory democracy (in our understanding) could be applied in order to concretise the common goods, using central resources, possibly supplemented by individual resources according to the conditions discussed above (mobilisation of publics through deliberative enquiry). Representative democracy would continue to belong to the standard, yet revised political order, complete with its electoral systems. Participatory democracy would be used to stage and implement the convergence between the economic, the social, and the financial 'on the ground', along with their common focus on the development of capabilities. Through the application of 'horizontal' deliberative procedures aimed at involving all relevant actors, participatory democracy could use specific systems for choosing representatives and establishing voting procedures, while retaining the flexibility inherent in processes of mobilisation.

Finally, it is important to emphasise that European institutions, law, and policies in their current state simply do not help. Although this issue falls beyond the scope of this chapter,[13] it is important to mention it briefly. Instead of regulating markets and addressing concerns about new modes of development (except in environmental directives, to some extent), the European authorities are playing the opposite role during the current crisis (and were presumably doing so long before it began). Their preference for deregulation has weakened both states and democratic practices throughout Europe. Without a political and social impulse, this state of affairs will continue indefinitely, and the opportunities and resources needed in order to find new paths of development for Europe will be sterilised and perhaps lost. Nothing is more urgent and necessary than is the task of finding such paths. At least in my view, the future of Europe will depend upon the capability for voice amongst European citizens and their representatives (e.g., governments, parliaments, parties, social organisations, associations, local constituencies) in various domains and at different levels. Urgent questions to be addressed concern the political and institutional conditions that are needed in order to develop the capability for voice, how this capability would intimately link individual and collective freedoms, and how we should construct new understandings and liberate the space necessary for the emergence of new modes of development.

NOTES

1. The redaction of this chapter was enhanced by a presentation in the colloquium *L'approche par les "capabilités", une réponse concrète aux inégalités?*, organised by the MOC-ACW (Mouvement Ouvrier Chrétien–Koepel van Christelijke Werknemersorganisaties [Association of Christian Employees' Associations]) held in Brussels in January 2012 (with support from the European Commission). A different version of this chapter has been published in De Leonardis, Negrelli, and Salais (2012).
2. Human development should also be symbiotically connected to the development of nature. Only then can we speak of development and not of growth.
3. Such questions formed an underlying theme for the presentations and debates held at the final Conference of the CAPRIGHT European Research Programme, which took place in Nantes on 2–3 December 2010 (see Bourgouin and Salais, 2011, notably the roundtable session and the conclusion).

4. This statement should obviously be considered in relation to the historical specificities of particular countries (e.g., the role of political freedoms or the types of collective organisation); see Trentin (1997, 2012).
5. The concept of capability is presented in a number of works. For example, see Sen (1993) and, more recently, De Munck (2008). The extent to which the capability approach could be interpreted as a politics of freedoms is the object of Jean-Michel Bonvin and Nicolas Farvaque (2008).
6. Title borrowed from the publication of the final Conference of the European Research Program CAPRIGHT (Bourgouin and Salais, 2012).
7. Amartya Sen (2004) has conducted extensive work on human rights theory.
8. For example, compare the sets of indicators promoted by the European Central Bank or the European Employment Strategy.
9. Deliberative democracy has already generated a long chronicle of publications (for a survey—rich in references, but somewhat oriented, see Mansbridge, 2010). I am grateful to Michele Lamont for this reference. To my knowledge, the literature has not yet addressed the economic efficiency of deliberative democratic procedures.
10. See the section below entitled "The Situated State."
11. This statement could even be disputed for hard sciences as well.
12. More in Salais (2009). Links between democracy and enquiry are also developed in Bohman (1999). Many experiments have been conducted with deliberative, participative, or experimental democracy, and their results should be read in light of the concept of deliberative enquiry. This largely remains to be done.
13. See Salais (2012).

BIBLIOGRAPHY

Bohman, James. "Democracy as Inquiry, Inquiry as Democratic: Pragmatism, Social Science, and the Cognitive Division of Labour." *American Journal of Political Science* 43 (1999): 590–607.

Bonvin, Jean-Michel, and Nicolas Farvaque. *Amartya Sen, une politique de la liberté*. Paris: Michalon, 2008.

Bourgouin, Agnes and Robert Salais, eds. *Le travail réinventé. Un défi pour l'Europe*. Nantes: CAPRIGHT Edition, 2011.

De Leonardis, Ota, Serafino Negrelli, and Robert Salais, eds. *Democracy and Capabilities for Voice*. Brussels: PIE Peter Lang, 2012.

De Munck, Jean. "Qu'est-ce qu'une capacité ?" In *La liberté au prisme des capacités. Amartya Sen au-delà du libéralisme*, edited by Jean De Munck and Benedicte Zimmermann, 21–50. Paris: Editions de l'Ecole des Hautes Etudes en Sciences Sociales, 2008.

Honneth, Axel. "Travail et agir instrumental. A propos des problèmes catégoriels d'une théorie critique de la société." In *Arbeit, Handlung, Normativität, Theorien des Historischen Materialismus*, edited by Axel Honneth and Urs Jaeggi, 285–333. Frankfurt: Suhrkamp, 1980.

Mansbridge, Jane. "The Place of Self-Interest and the Role of Power in Deliberative Democracy." *Journal of Political Philosophy* 18(1) (2010): 64–100.

Salais, Robert. "Deliberative Democracy and Its Informational Basis: What Lessons from the Capability Approach." Paper presented at the SASE Conference, Paris, July 2009. http://halshs.archives-ouvertes.fr/halshs-00429574 (last accessed on 30–09–2013).

Salais, Robert. "Employment and the Social Dimension of Europe: What Constitutive Conventions of the Market?" In *Transforming European Employment*

Policy: Labour Market Transitions and the Promotion of Capability, edited by Ralf Rogowski, Robert Salais, and Noel Whiteside, 255–282. Aldershot: Edward Elgar, 2012.

Salais, Robert and Michael Storper. *Les mondes de production. Enquête sur l'identité économique de la France*. Paris: Editions de l'Ecole des Hautes Etudes en Sciences Sociales, 1993.

Sen, Amartya. "Capability and Well-Being," In *The Quality of Life*, edited by Martha Nussbaum and Amartya Sen, 30–66. Oxford: Clarendon Press, 1993.

Sen, Amartya. "Description as Choice." In *Choice, Welfare and Measurement*, edited by Amartya Sen, 443–449. Cambridge, MA: Harvard University Press, 1982.

Sen, Amartya. "Elements of a Human Rights Theory." *Philosophy and Public Affairs* 32(4) (2004): 315–356.

Storper, Michael and Robert Salais. *Worlds of Production. The Action Frameworks of the Economy*. Cambridge, MA: Harvard University Press, 1997.

Supiot, Alain. *L'esprit de Philadelphie. La justice sociale face au marché total*. Paris: Seuil, 2011.

Trentin, Bruno. *La cita del lavoro. Sinistra e crisi del fordismo*. Milan: Feltrinelli, 1997.

Trentin, Bruno. *La cité du travail*. Paris: Fayard, 2012.

7 From Flexicurity to Capabilities
In Search of Professional Development

Bénédicte Zimmermann

INTRODUCTION

Although there is a broad consensus today regarding the need to reconcile flexibility and security, there is profound disagreement with respect
to the means to be used in achieving it. One widely held idea is to situate
flexibility internally within the enterprise, in the economic sphere, and to
situate security externally within the social sphere. Security thus functions
as an external shock absorber of the social consequences of an enterprise's
flexibility. Whatever might be their particular nuances, the discourses on
'flexicurity' adopt this logic of externalisation. But there is an alternative
conception that refuses to limit the question of security to employment,
extending it to work and the internal workings of an enterprise.

In this chapter I will take up this second approach. In the first section, I
will discuss the limits of the concept of flexicurity and underline the importance of including a company perspective. Then, in the second section I
will show the contribution of the capability approach to a reappraisal of
the equation between economic efficiency and social justice (see also Salais,
this volume). The very point of the capability approach is to introduce,
alongside flexibility and security, a third element into the debate, namely,
freedom. I will show how capabilities and freedom bring a shift of focus
to the debate, taking the case of professional development as a concrete
example. Capability-based professional development offers another way
of articulating flexibility and security. Among the capabilities involved in
professional development, that of expressing one's views and making them
heard ranks first. From such a perspective, the conditions of work and
workers' participation at the workplace constitute a component of security.
that is as decisive as the very conditions of employment.

Thus, reassessing the flexibility–security debate in terms of workers'
capabilities means to go beyond the institutional level and focus on companies' internal flexibility as well as reconsidering the role of the company in
any modus vivendi between flexibility and security; it amounts to placing
the company and the worker at the heart of the analysis, as core actors in
the flexibility–security nexus.

WHAT IS WRONG WITH THE CONCEPT OF FLEXICURITY?

In 2007 the European Commission identified the principles of a common EU flexicurity policy, defined as "an integrated strategy to enhance, at the same time, flexibility and security in the labor market." The aim was to combine economic flexibility with "successful moves [i.e., transitions] during one's life course: from school to work, from one job to another, between unemployment or inactivity and work, and from work to retirement. . . . It is about progress of workers into better jobs, 'upward mobility' and optimal development of talent" (European Commission, 2007: 5).

According to this declaration, flexicurity is not intended merely to combine flexibility and security but also to transform flexibility itself, turning it into a two-way process that will be equally beneficial to employers and employees and in which not only free enterprise, but also freedom to work and develop at work become fundamental values and goals. It was to this end that the European Commission identified four components as essential to any EU flexicurity policy:

1. "Flexible and reliable contractual arrangements . . . through modern labor laws, collective agreements and work organization"
2. "Comprehensive lifelong learning strategies to ensure the continual adaptability and employability of workers"
3. "Effective active labor market policies that help people cope with rapid change"
4. "Modern social security systems that provide adequate income support, encourage employment and facilitate labor market mobility" (2007: 6)

Centred on employment and labour-market policy, i.e., on the legal and institutional dimensions, these components would however seem to rule out the very activity of work as a locus for reconciling flexibility and security.

Employability as a New Paradigm of the European Welfare State

A closer look at the policy of modernisation of the welfare states as initiated by the European Commission makes this absence even more striking, because this policy makes out of employability the cornerstone of national social-protection reforms and a pillar of flexicurity (European Commission, 2000). Employability is called upon to establish a preventive logic—designed to be an "active" one—and to replace the inherited collective logic of social insurance, which is denounced as being merely a 'passive' logic. One goes from a model based on job security to a model based on security through employability; that is to say, on a model that is no longer linked with a position on the labour market but to a process that permanently demands its maintenance and consolidation by the workers themselves.

The guiding concepts of this new social model based on employability are activation, adaptability, competence, development, and individual responsibility. These concepts profoundly redefine the relationship between work and social issues as well as the place of work in constituting the links between individual and collective in at least two respects that prove highly ambivalent.

On the one hand, the activation policies impute to a worker the responsibility of finding and retaining a job in his role as entrepreneur of his own career, thus setting the new normative framework for the politics of the labour market (Bröckling, 2007). As a result, the absence of professional development and long-term unemployment are no longer ascribed to structural causes or to a social risk enlisting collective responsibility but rather to the worker himself. Thus, the notion of responsibility is never far from that of culpability; it infers a moralisation of social problems and places a moral burden on the shoulders of those who—for a variety of reasons—are unable to develop their employability.

On the other hand—this is the second way in which social issues are redefined—the figure of the employee entrepreneur of his own career carries the promise of the valorisation of each individual person. This goes hand in hand with a process of subjectivation of work which creates hope and expectation of recognition—and this in line with the idealised vision of a world in which each is able to achieve solely by virtue of their desire to do so.

Because the activating social state makes individual responsibility the condition for both self-realisation and securement of the individual's future, crucial questions arise regarding the conditions pertaining to the exercising of that responsibility. To what degree can employees effectively access the means to exercise such responsibility, to be actors of their own future? These questions reflect the ambivalence of a model of justice that privileges individual distinction over collective solidarity—thus making the exercise of responsibility a central object of the investigation.

But how to conduct an enquiry into responsibility? Notably John Dewey (1991) and Amartya Sen (1993) have shown us that the exercise of responsibility is not solely an affair of individual will but in the first instance requires freedom—the freedom to choose among different options but also the freedom to convert these options into valuable achievements, which in turn require the power to take effective action. But nothing is more problematic for an employee than the freedom to choose and the ability to take effective action—even in those matters that concern him as directly as his professional development.

Is there not then a contradiction in enjoining employees to be free and responsible entrepreneurs of their own career even if they remain employees in a subordinate relationship to their employer—that is to say, in a situation in which they abdicate a certain portion of their freedom?

Institutions, Individuals, and the Company's Responsibility

I contend that a flexicurity policy which makes no mention of the company's role, specifically in connection with fostering employees' professional development, is condemned to asymmetry from the start, and its promise of achieving two-way flexibility and security can be no more than a pious hope. Employee security does not lie exclusively in establishing ways of making transitions on the labour market.[1] It is also forged through work itself and the possibilities for professional development that this work then offers. This puts the question of company responsibility for employees' professional development—a question that is generally neglected—at the heart of the flexicurity debate. An unemployed person's employability largely depends on the employability of the employee he or she used to be. Both employability and skills are developed first and foremost in the course of work and occupational experience.[2] Most companies prefer not to take this fact into account, remitting to the labour market all would-be employees whom they deem unemployable and without necessarily affording them a chance to develop occupationally, or, in some cases, actually aggravating their 'unemployability' by confining them to non-quality work. The fact is that insecure employment is related not only to the job and its legal form (i.e., the type of contract), but also to real working conditions, which can be a source of professional development or, obversely, vulnerability. Far from being a matter of the worker's personal qualities alone, development and vulnerability are highly dependent on the opportunities and means for professional development that the company makes available to its employees.

Because companies are the main actors in matters of flexibility, one can with good reason consider them as playing a decisive role in calibrating flexibility and security—but most of them refuse to assume a role that requires a professional-development policy for their employees. Statistical sources show that whereas the proportion of trained employees in France has skyrocketed since 1977, the amount of training time provided by French companies has dwindled drastically and certification practices have collapsed (Bérêt, 2009: 72). Between 2005 and 2009, together with Delphine Corteel and Dilip Subramanian, I conducted qualitative studies of employees' professional development in thirteen French companies.[3] In companies where employees are provided opportunities and means to develop occupationally, it emerged that this works in favour of both their security and flexibility, in internal and external labour markets alike. These studies furthermore showed that when companies do commit to their employees' professional development, they in turn benefit from it—and regardless of the sector.

Employability: The Logic of Short-Term Skills Development

The development of skills and competence is one of the main ways of preserving and improving employability. In theory, skills development "is about equipping people with the skills that will enable them to progress in their working lives and help them find new employment" (European Commission, 2007: 6). However, our enquiries into the practices of French companies firstly show that companies make their employees responsible for updating and developing their skills without necessarily offering the conditions required for the exercise of such a responsibility (Zimmermann, 2004; Corteel and Zimmermann, 2007). Secondly, they show that the point of reasoning in terms of skills and competencies is above all to satisfy a company's short-term needs with regard to workers' adaptability and with no consideration given as to their employability.

The logic of skills and competence places a person in the service of economic efficacy and performance. It aims to increase the output of 'human capital' in the enterprise by only retaining so much of the human as can directly serve this object—versatility, adaptability, individual initiative, and responsibility. To be competent means knowing how to react in the appropriate manner, to be capable of confronting a new or unaccustomed situation.

Company skill-development policies are therefore first and foremost a response to the economic imperative of reactivity and just-in-time adjustment, whereas in most cases remaining disconnected from individuals' choices and projects—that is, from the temporal and social dynamic of individual pathways. In the company, one's superior decides who will be trained to do what and how. The individual's entitlement to training (*Droit Individuel à la Formation* or DIF), instituted in France in 2004, has not changed this situation.

PROFESSIONAL DEVELOPMENT AND CAPABILITIES

To approach employability via the notion of capability rather than competence allows us to escape that facile reduction of the individual to a resource designed to yield a profit along the lines of market regulation. Capability invites us to take into account every aspect of the individual worker—his performance and skills but also his own need for recognition, fairness, respect, and security. It opens the way for conceiving enterprises' economic development in relation to development of their employees. It takes into account not only what a person is capable of doing—their skills—but the actual possibilities for developing and implementing these skills—that is to say, the opportunities and the means of action accessible to employees in a given organisation. If being competent denotes the exercise of responsibility in a work situation, capability denotes withal the means of exercising this responsibility.

In *Development as Freedom* (1999), Sen reminds us that the purpose of economic activity is not simply to produce goods and services but to contribute to the welfare of persons and also that freedom is not simply a means toward development but its very purpose. In opposition to the reduction of development to a factor of economic growth, he puts forward a more demanding definition that makes of development "a process of expanding the real freedoms that people enjoy." Over and above mere economic output measurable in terms of utility and monetary value, Sen argues the need for taking into account the social opportunities created as well as the individual well-being that is generated. By defending the integration of economic and social development in this way, the capability approach calls for a reconsideration of human beings in the workplace—to view them as the final goal of economic activity. Seen from this perspective, the possibilities and conditions of professional development in the workplace constitute a crucial issue.

But what is to be understood by professional development? From the capability standpoint, professional development cannot be reduced to occupational or vocational development; it cannot be limited to an increase in skills, for it entails an extension of employees' freedom to work by broadening the range of roles, positions, and careers open to them. Nor can it be restricted to the notion of career development but includes considerations of personal development. Accordingly, professional development will be defined here—from the standpoint of both personal and career development—as the outcome of the combined exercise of different capabilities: the capability for performing a job and work that one has reason to value, the capability for training and learning, the capability for participating (in the sense of having a 'voice', i.e., expressing oneself and being heard) and finally the capability for combining private and working life (Zimmermann, 2011: 178ff.).

From a capability perspective there is neither an *a priori* meaning of development nor is it unidirectional, linear, or cyclical; rather, it implies trials, ordeals, and revolutions. These defining features lead to two fundamental conclusions—by including contingency, they break with simplistic functionalist or evolutionist models; by emphasising relations between the person and his or her environment, they introduce the idea that development is socially constructed. Understood in this way, individual development is simultaneously a singular transformation and a relational process that takes place through contact with others and more generally the environment. In the broadest sense, the environment refers here to material, human, organisational, institutional, political, and policy realities (apprehended at the level of company, territorial area, or sector) as well as familial ones. It is this meaning of development—as an interactive, eminently social practice, a process co-produced by the person and his or her environment—that underlies and informs the following analysis.

I am basing this analysis on the case of Bigtrucks, which in our sample was the best enterprise at fostering its employees' capabilities.[4] Bigtrucks is an assembler of trucks with more than four hundred employees. The assembly line is organised along Taylorian lines but monitored by a system of participatory management. The vast majority of employees work on a non-automatised assembly line. The extremely dense pyramid of functions offers few opportunities for a worker to vacate his operator status via the internal market, but being employed at Bigtrucks gives him a good chance of mobility on the external market because of the enterprise's reputation for professional development of its employees. Even if professional development does not necessarily translate into career advancement, it is achieved by means of participatory management and a training policy that imbues employees with a reputation for 'quality' on the external market.[5] The example of Bigtrucks shows how the securement of individual pathways through employability can be all the more effective by being associated with the exercise of real freedom when it comes to professional mobility. Training is an important factor, but it is not a sufficient one; it still needs to contribute to the employee's effective professional development. Training that contributes both to the security and professional freedom of employees earns the label 'capability enhancing' in that it is a source of development and power to act.

Using Sen's (1999) conceptualisation, I will define capabilities with respect to three main dimensions: freedom of choice, empowerment, and collective responsibility.[6] It is within these dimensions that capabilities conjointly reframe the question of professional development in terms of choice, the power to achieve, and developmental potential. In so doing, they broach a crucial question, namely, the degree to which an understanding of persons as ends in themselves is reconcilable with a conception of the individual as a means, consubstantial with capitalist economic activity.

Possibility of Choosing

The capability for choice approaches professional development from the standpoint of freedom of choice; it raises the question of the extent of possibilities and their accessibility. Even in matters where labour law accords a formal liberty to the employee, in practice such liberty often remains inaccessible to him. For example, this difficulty is encountered in France with respect to personal leave for training (CIF), which permits "every worker, and for the duration of his professional life, to pursue training initiatives independent of the enterprise's training plan." In principle, this law can be considered as capability enhancing, for it aims to give access—at instigation of the employee—to a higher level of qualification, to a change in activity or profession that is independent of the enterprise's policy. But recent surveys show a great disparity in the various regional implementations of the law. They also reveal a clear tendency on the part of enterprises to hijack the law by placing it in service of their own needs and to formulate training plans to the detriment of individual professional-development projects (Podevin et al., 2008). Bigtrucks distinguishes itself in this regard by encouraging individual training projects leading to a qualification and in offering its employees the real possibility of enlisting in these projects, even if their aim is an occupational reconversion that will eventually see the employee leaving the enterprise. The enterprise rarely finances degree courses of long duration, but its human resources office lends its support to the formulation of personal development or retraining projects funded externally, such as personal leave for training (CIF). Thus, three of the thirty workers that we met up with were engaged, at the time of the interviews, in the preparation of a personal-leave-for-training dossier. They underscored the complexity of the task and the importance of the support provided by the company's human resources office in an area where other enterprises let their employees turn to staff representatives or simply manage things themselves. This support helps make up for individual inequalities in accessing both information and those necessary skills for building one's résumé; it additionally increases the chances of successfully fulfilling demands. Without this support, certain operators would not have been in a position to obtain training leave that was formally open to them. This example illustrates the importance of collective support for creating possibilities and extending the latitude of individual choice, in particular for those persons least equipped with qualifications and social resources.

Power to Achieve

The power to achieve thematises professional development from the standpoint of accomplishments. It is related to the means of action—both individual and collective—and to the conditions of the implementation in a given situation. Freedom as the power of being and doing implies that a person be enabled to convert the opportunities and available resources into valuable achievements—for instance, the conversion of a personal training project into skills training—and presupposes that the various elements, both personal and environmental, which shape one's capability to act, are adequately combined. What Sen calls the conversion factors contribute to producing this appropriateness, and individual occupational pathways evince their variety. A sole factor rarely suffices in establishing the capability of a person, which tends to be the result of the interaction of various factors.

Let us take the case of Olivier. Thirty years of age and holder of an intermediate qualification as a lathe operator, Olivier came to Bigtrucks ten years ago as a warehouseman. Subsequently he became a forklift truck operator and rose through the ranks of the skilled workers. At the top of his grade he "dreamt of going further, not staying at the same level." His "ideal" was to become a foreman, but his determination, investment in work, and the recognised skills that he exhibits are not enough in this regard. In an enterprise where the coveted foreman posts are limited, one's qualifications act as a filter, with a high school diploma or its equivalent as the minimum requirement for transcending one's 'worker' status. Encouraged by his superior to take up his studies again, Olivier left the factory for eight months to pursue training as a stocking technician and to pass the equivalent of a high school diploma within the framework of a personal leave for training. The project was made possible by the confluence of various conversion factors—those of institutional type (the existence of personal leave for training, which permits access to skills training while still drawing one's salary), those of personal and familial type (one's determination, skills, and the support of one's companion), those of interpersonal nature (the support of one's superior, who offers counsel and operates as an intermediary between Olivier and the human resources office of the enterprise), and finally those along organisational lines (human resources office, which is there to answer Olivier's questions, to assist in building his résumé, and to support his project). Olivier's example clearly shows that legal and institutional entitlements are insufficient in sustaining one's capability for training if they are not combined with other factors that create the power to achieve within an enterprise.[7]

Developmental Potential

The potential for development seizes upon work and training via the values that underlie them and the objectives people associate with them. In the case of Olivier, this potential is gauged in terms of the impact of work and training on his professional development and career. When we interviewed him, Olivier summed up very clearly the goal of his training: "I'm not undergoing the training for another post awaiting me at the end. It is rather so as to have the skills to apply for other posts." Training does not automatically mean promotion; it is an asset in the competition for a possibly better position on the internal market or in searching for another one on the external market. Such is the capability-enhancing dimension of training in the case of Olivier—a dimension that is not easily compatible with a conception of training solely designed for the short-term adaptation of an employee to the needs of the enterprise.

Olivier's pathway is representative of the factory's most successful cases of professional development—that of young people recruited for their first job, who have adhered to the 'Bigtrucks spirit' instilled by the participatory management and know how to take advantage of it. From this point of view, Bigtrucks empirically refutes the conventional discourse on the impossibility of employing young people—their lack of seriousness and perseverance—which we often heard from the side of other enterprises in the course of our enquiry. The motivation and capability for work are not attributable solely to the person of the worker; these are forged in the relationship to others and the organisation of work. Respect and trust, the opening of future prospects, notably through training, as limited as they may be—these are decisive elements.

NO SECURITY WITHOUT FREEDOM

Professional development can be considered both an objective and a result of capabilities in the enterprise. Contributing to employability, it is a source of security and entails the expansion of the real freedom a person enjoys; capabilities are both a means and an end. Professional development does not therefore necessarily signify the making of a career or increasing responsibilities; neither is it reducible to the development of knowledge and know-how. It also integrates considerations of personal development and the balance between professional and private life (see also Salais and Méda, this volume). It calls for the possibility of the employee expressing a choice, of constructing a professional project that is not solely in accord with the needs of the organisation but with the goals that he himself brings to his work. This presupposes the existence of spaces for discussion that permit the expression and defence of these choices as well as the existence of opportunities and means (notably for training) allowing one to realise a chosen option. If the enterprise does not offer these basic conditions, the employee alone cannot create them; that is why professional development is a co-production of both the employee and the enterprise. In order that it not be the sole prerogative of the most resourceful individuals or those most advantageously placed in the organisation, collective support at both the institutional and organisational levels is required so as to sustain an equal freedom to develop professionally. And yet collective agreements and an enterprise's human resources policies are insufficient—these latter have only a small impact if they are not furthered by a management and a work organisation that is favourably disposed toward the four capabilities that we have identified as basic capabilities for professional development: the capability for quality work, the capability for finding a balance between professional and private life, the capability for training, and the capability for airing one's views and being heard (Zimmermann, 2011).

A quality job is defined by means of recruitment modalities, type of contract, working hours, salary, and access to training. As decisive as these characteristics of the wage relation may be, they do not suffice in assuring professional development. The quality of work, understood as how (concrete conditions) a particular job activity is carried out, is just as important. The quality of work is not owing solely to the worker's performance but is also dependent on the environment and the conditions pertaining to the realisation of that work. It is encompassing possibilities for learning by doing and impacts well-being at work. So far, quality work can be seen as a shared good jointly produced by the enterprise and its employees—a collective good in which the interests of different parties converge. As a source of economic development for the enterprise, the quality of work contributes to the securement of individual pathways in the same way as job quality.

The capability for balancing professional and private life concerns the potential for reconciling work with choices in one's extra-professional life. It includes the freedom of choosing *not* to advance a career if one thinks this will mean increased responsibility, greater stress, and more time spent at work and consequently less time available for family life or extra-professional activities. Perceived in terms of capabilities, professional development thus integrates the respect of arbitration and hierarchies that persons are bound to establish amongst work and their various other commitments and that do not necessarily place the career at the centre of their lives. I will now dwell a bit longer on the capability of undergoing training and that of being able to voice one's opinions and be heard—whereas the first is often wrongly considered a self-sufficient condition of professional development, the second is generally ignored—even if it constitutes an inescapable condition.

Training as a Good in Itself and a Means of Opening Up Possibilities

Continuing vocational training, often highlighted as a privileged means of professional development, is only a single element among others. Whatever its focus and quality, training is not automatically a factor in development. It is still necessary that from the very beginning employees have the means to direct their training—that is to say, the capability of expressing their preferences as well as making them count. It is still necessary that, once achieved, this training leads to a quality job and that this work proves itself compatible with that balance between the personal and professional life to which one might aspire.

Training can be conceived of in two ways—as "a good in itself" in the sense of a goal deemed worthy of pursuing as such (Dodier, 2003: 19) and as a means of opening up possibilities and creating developmental potential. Training as a good in itself is measured in terms of distribution, quantity, and quality, and professional development is what it makes possible in the way of later achievement. Rooted in the present as a good in itself, training is also attuned to the future through the possibilities it creates. Workers' capability for training, developing, and renewing their skills is an important component of what I call Bigtrucks's employee-quality. Whereas company training policies are usually evaluated exclusively in terms of training-as-a-good-in-itself, equally important in terms of employee quality is the degree to which training creates new employment prospects for the employees; it shifts attention from training to the professional development that is likely to be generated by that training.

Bigtrucks contributes to professional development by offering access to various combinations of types of knowledge and know-how—that which is specific to the company, that which is specific to the automobile sector, and more general knowledge. The specificity of general knowledge is that it is readily transferable outside the company and even outside the sector. How this knowledge is acquired proves just as decisive as the knowledge itself. General knowledge is not only produced at Bigtrucks through individual formal training—e.g., instruction in the English language—but also through a variety of participatory arrangements that foster on-the-job learning, initiative taking, and responsibility. These arrangements range from the system of delegations and continuous improvement to problem-solving groups. Clusters are organised in such a way that each member—or at least each member who wishes—can leave the assembly line for at least a few hours a month to take on other tasks. This is what is meant by 'delegations'. The amount of time involved varies. Some tasks demand one to two hours a month, others as much as three-quarters of an hour each day. It is a year-long, voluntary system in which the employees rotate. The tasks range from keeping the cluster supplied with tools or dealing with anomalies to acting as an 'auditor' or a guide for visitors to the factory.[8]

The problem-solving groups—made up of workers from different positions in the hierarchy, from operator to head of production—meet on an *ad hoc* basis to tackle problems of different sorts, for example, security or productivity on a particular segment of the production line, adapting working methods and organisation to a new model or even to personal relations within a cluster. When working alongside other colleagues—operators, technicians, and managers—on the best solution to a problem, an operator may be away from the line for days or even weeks at a time. Laurent, for example, working in the engines cluster, was part of a group that paved the way for the introduction of a new model in 2003–2004. He spent two weeks at the Swedish site of the company, which had already introduced the new model, and on his return he took on the task of training his colleagues.

The decisive characteristic of these participatory arrangements with regard to professional development is that they integrate collective forms of producing knowledge and thereby promote an active attitude and relation to knowledge and learning. Just as important as formal training in establishing the reputation for quality of the Bigtrucks employee is the ongoing informal learning process at the company as organised by the methods of participatory management.

Participation, Capability for Expressing Oneself, and Professional Freedom

The capability of airing one's views and being heard—the capability of having a voice (Bohman, 1996; Bonvin, 2008)—is a decisive element of professional freedom. Beyond access to information and participation, it presupposes that each employee, in his specific situation, knows what is of value for himself in matters of the job, of training, and of the balance between professional and personal life. Capability for voice thus involves a process of valuation in the sense of ascribing value, of determining what is of value, and of prioritising the various options according to these values (Dewey, 1991). Because the capability for voice furthermore implies the capability for making oneself heard, it structures all the other capabilities in a transverse manner.

Training contributes all the more to securising individual pathways if it offers employees the possibility of influencing their future. And that possibility is all the greater if the person is able to clearly assert his preferences. This is a dimension of development and professional freedom too often neglected in the debates on flexicurity and individual securisation through employability. To the contrary, flexicurity discourses tend to promote the idea that a 'bad job' is always better than no job at all and that any training is better than none at all—even if it means imposing these things on people against their will.

Extending the scope of choices for workers, of their capability for aspiring and voicing what they value, raises the central political question as to the governance of the enterprise and the forms that the employee's participation should take. Being an active agent in your own development presupposes being able to participate in decisions that influence your existence—that is, having a degree not only of technical, but also political and moral control over one's environment. In the course of the twentieth century, trade unions offered such a possibility in establishing a type of mediation between employees and their employers based on participation by means of delegation and elected representatives. Peculiar to this mediation was its promotion of a collective approach toward individual destinies within broad socio-professional categories such as the classification of posts or functions by professional branch. Participation under managerial control opposes to this representative strategy the logic of individualised control of the future as based on direct participation and the one-on-one relationship between workers and their superior—practices that are susceptible to opening the way for the worst abuses of power if they are not supplemented by a policy of individual capability collectively guaranteed, as it is partly the case at Bigtrucks.

In creating a space, even if of a limited nature, for deliberation on work, direct participation, in the case of Bigtrucks, is of service to the enterprise by tapping into people's critical capability and their general capacity to express themselves. Conversely, the workers see in direct participation an opportunity to make a contribution to defining just how they wish to work—even if with strict respect to those matters offered for deliberation by the management. In spite of severe limits—strategic decisions do not form part of deliberation, only their implementation—such participation produces amongst workers a feeling of having a say in matters of their own work activity and their professional development alike. By doing so, it produces a general feeling of greater well-being in their work as opposed to other professional experiences that they might have had. Even at Bigtrucks, participatory management is an instrument of the normalisation of behaviours by means of the moral aspect it ascribes to work when participation is presented as a must be, imbuing a sense of belonging to the enterprise. But the manner in which it is implemented also contributes to the professional development and reputation of quality of its employees.

Employee Quality—Another Way of Articulating Flexibility and Security

The case of Bigtrucks is indicative of what training pointed toward professional development can produce. It does not necessarily produce a career but rather employee quality—a quality locally recognised and sought after. Employee quality proceeds not only from the assigning of capabilities that are not restricted to a professional activity or given skills; it also relates to a potential capacity to learn and adapt to changing situations. The capability for training, developing, and renewing one's skills is an important component of it. But more broadly it is professional development—the capability for training, the capability for having and doing a work of quality, for expressing oneself and participating, for balancing professional and private life—which forges the quality of the Bigtrucks employee.

Our survey has permitted us to establish that the Bigtrucks employee enjoys a reputation that is solidly established vis-à-vis other employers and employees in the labour pool. When he seeks a job on the local labour market, the Bigtrucks employee benefits from a positive reputation vis-à-vis those responsible for recruitment at other enterprises. Shared by all the members of the enterprise, Bigtrucks' reputation for the quality of its employees highlights the collective dimension of capabilities. It shows that before being individual attributes, such capabilities are collectively structured and are in turn dependent on conditions and possibilities offered by the enterprise. It is because employee quality is associated with the enterprise's capability-enhancing character that all its employees are given bonus points from the outset—and independent of their function, qualification, or classification. Sought by other enterprises and their employees, the Bigtrucks label opens to its possessors a potential space of mobility that boosts their confidence in the future. The difference between skills for which the individual is the sole guarantor and capabilities for which a collective is answerable—in this case a work collective—would appear to be decisive in the matter of securing individual pathways of employability. This does not mean that capabilities are any substitute for individual competence and skills; they are situated on another level and offer the means that permit, among other things, the expression and development of these latter.

To open the discussion, I should like to give some insights into what distinguishes employee quality understood in terms of the capability for work, capability for learning and training, capability for work–life balance, and capability for having a voice, from the standpoint of job or work quality as discussed within the European Parliament or the International Labour Office. Several recent studies propose a synthetic overview of different sets of indicators that are in competition, showing the different meanings of work quality that each of them fosters with respect to the specific dimension of work or employment or social policies that they are focusing on (Anker et al., 2003; Green, 2006; European Parliament, 2009; Van der Maesen and Walker, 2012). However, my aim here is not to discuss these different sets of indicators and their internal rationale but rather to show what is lacking in the picture of quality work that one gets when putting them all together—and in comparison with the requirements of capability-based employee quality. Two crucial dimensions of the latter are systematically missing in even the most synthetic and complete set of work-quality indicators, namely, individual participation and individual power of valuation, two constitutive conditions of any capabilities. When participation is taken into account by work-quality indicators, it is exclusively under the heading of information or collective participation via social dialogue. Although collective participation is a condition for capabilities to flourish, it is not enough. A capability policy in the workplace cannot be satisfied solely with representative collectives as its fulcrum—it also requires participatory collectives able to create a forum for exchange and to constitute a common pool of knowledge concerning work. The challenge is then to combine the representative logic embodied by trade unions with more direct forms of work participation that are not necessary to be placed under management control. In order to make freedom and professional development into sources for securing individual career paths, the capability approach and the value it attaches to the singular individual call for a renewal of the forms of collective action (Supiot, 2012: 139) in order to enable individual voice and valuation to take their place alongside collective voice.

CONCLUSION

Capability delineates a way of articulating security and flexibility that makes a normative ideal of professional freedom accessible to all. Training is an important element of it, but it attains its full meaning only from the standpoint of the professional development that it authorises and beyond the formal rights that institute it. The capability of acting, of valuating, and of expressing one's views and making them heard within the enterprise are essential components. From such a perspective, aiming to combine flexibility and security thus presupposes that we readdress the question as to both the individual and collective purpose of work in capitalist society as well as the question of the governance of the firm and the participation of employees in that governance.

NOTES

1. "Arranging for pathways" linking one temporary work position or activity to the next is a primary dimension of the transitional markets idea: "Transitions include all possible differences from that of the reference situation of permanent full-time employment" (Gazier, 2003: 131).
2. The present analysis does not include youth unemployment, which raises its own problems precisely because young people are by definition not in a position to have developed employability through work experience.
3. I conducted the 2005 studies with Delphine Corteel as part of the European Union research project "Eurocap: Dialogue Social, Emploi et Territoire: Pour une politique européenne des capacités" (Eurocap, contract HPSE-CT-2002–00132) and the 2009 studies with Dilip Subramanian as part of

the EU research project "Capright: Resources, Rights and Capabilities: In Search of Social Foundations for Europe" (Capright, contract CIT4-CT 2006–028549).
4. The methodology employed in our enquiry was based on observation, the study of documents, and semi-structured interviews with employees at all levels of the hierarchy as well as union representatives. See Corteel and Zimmermann (2007).
5. For a detailed study of the Bigtrucks case, see Zimmermann (2011).
6. For a discussion of the capability approach with regard to work-related issues, see De Munck and Zimmermann (2008).
7. For a non-exhaustive list of conversion factors, see Zimmermann (2011: 195–196).
8. The auditor inspects vehicles chosen at random as they come off the assembly line.

BIBLIOGRAPHY

Anker, Richard, Igor Chernyshev, Philippe Egger, Farhad Mehran, and Joseph A. Ritter. "Measuring Decent Work with Statistical Indicators." *International Labour Review* 142(2) (2003): 147–177.
Bérêt, Pierre. "Formation continue, salaires et transformation des marchés internes." *Travail et emploi* 117 (2009): 67–80.
Bohman, James. *Public Deliberation, Pluralism, Complexity and Democracy.* Boston: MIT Press.
Bonvin, Jean Michel. "Capacités et démocratie." In *La liberté au prisme des capacités*, edited by Jean De Munck and Bénédicte Zimmermann, 237–261. Paris: Editions de l'EHESS, 2008.
Bröckling, Ulrich. *Das unternehmerische Selbst. Soziologie einer Subjektivierungsform.* Frankfurt: Campus, 2007.
Corteel, Delphine and Bénédicte Zimmermann. "Capacités et développement professionnel." *Formation Emploi* 98 (2007): 25–39.
De Munck, Jean and Bénédicte Zimmermann, eds. *La liberté au prisme des capacités. Amartya Sen au-delà du libéralisme.* Paris: Editions de l'EHESS, 2008.
Dewey, John. "Theory of Valuation." In *The Later Works of John Dewey. 1925–1953. Edited by Jo Ann Boydston*, Volume 13: 1938–1913, 189–251 . Carbondale: Southern Illinois University Press, 1991.
Dodier, Nicolas. *Leçons politiques de l'épidémie du sida.* Paris: Editions de l'EHESS, 2003.
European Commission. *Labor Directives 2001.* Brussels: COM 548 final, 2000.
European Commission. *Towards Common Principles of Flexicurity: More and Better Jobs through Flexibility and Security.* Brussels: Com 359 final, 2007.
European Parliament. *Indicators of Job Quality in the European Union.* Directorate General for Internal Policies, Policy Department A: Economic and Scientific Policy, PE. 429.972, 2009.
Gazier, Bernard. *Tous "sublimes." Vers un nouveau plein emploi.* Paris: Flammarion, 2003.
Green, Francis. *Demanding Work. The Paradox of Job Quality in Affluent Society.* Princeton, NJ: Princeton University Press, 2006.
Podevin, Gérard, Sarah Ghaffari, Pascal Caillaud, and Claude Dubard, eds. *Le congé individuel de formation: un droit national, des réalités territoriales.* Rennes: PU Rennes, 2008.

Sen, Amartya K. "Capability and Well-Being." In *The Quality of Life*, edited by Martha Nussbaum and Amartya K. Sen, 30–53. Oxford: Oxford University Press, 1993.

Sen, Amartya K. *Development as Freedom*. Oxford: Oxford University Press, 1999.

Supiot, Alain. *The Spirit of Philadelphia. Social Justice against the Total Market*. London: Verso, 2012.

Van der Maesen, Laurent and Alan Walker. *Social Quality. From Theory to Indicators*. London: Palgrave Macmillan, 2012.

Zimmermann, Bénédicte. *Ce que travailler veut dire. Une sociologie des capacités et des parcours professionnels*. Paris: Economica, 2011.

Zimmermann, Bénédicte. "Competences-Oriented Logics and the Politics of Employability." In *Europe and the Politics of Capabilities*, edited by Robert Salais and Robert Villeneuve, 38–53. Cambridge: Cambridge University Press, 2004.

8 Life-First Welfare and the Scope for a "Eudemonic Ethic" of Social Security

Hartley Dean

INTRODUCTION: NEW CAPITALISM AND THE EROSION OF SOCIAL CITIZENSHIP

Debates in the post-industrial or 'new capitalist' world about flexicurity,[1] labour-market activation (LMA), workfare, and 'welfare-to-work' have been fuelled by a variety of factors. Effects associated with economic globalisation have diminished the security of livelihoods founded on wage labour. And the effect of the 'crisis' of the capitalist welfare state has been to diminish the security once guaranteed through rights of social citizenship.

However, the security afforded to wage labourers by industrial capitalism was always tenuous. The security afforded during the 'golden age' of the welfare state was never unconditional. Nevertheless we are led to believe that in today's labour market there is no such thing as a job for life,[2] that universal social protection may no longer be sustainable.[3] The coming of the 'risk society' has entailed a loss of commitment to the institutions of the welfare state.[4]

When Claus Offe claimed 'we no longer live in a class society, but a risk society',[5] he was challenging the essential optimism of T.H. Marshall's celebrated account of the development of social citizenship.[6] Marshall's contention had been that the advent in the twentieth century of the welfare state concluded the evolution of 'modern' citizenship. Industrial capitalist societies had by stages developed first civil rights and the rule of law, followed by political rights and the reign of democracy. But, finally, the emergence of social rights and the welfare state made it possible to achieve a degree of substantive equality "not so much between classes as between individuals within a population which is now treated for this purpose as though it were one class."[7] However, social divisions and inequalities did not then melt away. And Offe—drawing on Polanyi[8]—considers that Marshall was mistaken. He suggests that "the owner of labour power first becomes a wage labourer as a citizen of a state."[9] The welfare state had been the precondition for, not a civilising embellishment of, liberal-democratic capitalism. For without the welfare state, it would not have been possible to utilise labour power as if it were a commodity. The social citizenship of which Marshall wrote did not eradicate capitalist exploitation so much as reconstitute the individual as an independent subject. The subject becomes a citizen rather than a member of a class. The risk society of which Offe speaks, therefore, is one in which the bonds of class have indeed been weakened, yet the prospectus offered by social citizenship is now exposed to have been a sham. It has become apparent that the welfare state does not, and supposedly ought not, completely or unconditionally protect the citizen against the risks she faces: If the citizen is truly constituted as an ethical individual subject, she must, in part at least, accept responsibility for her own fate.[10] Taylor-Gooby argues that the policy model that is emerging 'damages social citizenship'.[11]

The conventional explanation for the origins of social citizenship suggests that to varying degrees capitalist welfare states elected partially to 'decommodify' the worker.[12] That is to say, by providing for the basic needs of workers, the state not only ensured the efficient reproduction of labour power; it also enabled workers to live independently of the labour market, albeit only up to a point: the point at which s/he would be optimally productive. Following the global crisis of the welfare state, there has been a trend to 'recommodification'.[13] The point at which workers could live independently has been shifting.

At the level of labour-market policy there was a trend away from demand-side policy informed by Keynesian economics to supply-side policy informed by monetarist economics and endogenous growth theory[14]: Put simply, the developed economies sought to compete by maximising domestic labour-market participation and the productivity and flexibility of labour. It has been argued that the resulting economic precariousness and insecurity of labour were never an inevitable consequence of global change, but stemmed directly from neoliberal influences on economic and social policy; influences that exposed the world as a whole to greater risk from market forces.[15] The certainties of policymakers may have been shaken by the scale of the global financial crisis of 2008–2009, but the foundations of economic liberalism's hegemonic discourse appear to have survived.[16]

At the heart of that discourse is the mantra "work is the best form of welfare."[17] The assumption is that state welfare provided as a social right is a suboptimal means of meeting human need, whereas the responsible means of provision is that to be obtained through paid employment. In what follows, this chapter will begin by questioning that assumption; it will then critically examine the meaning that may be attached to the idea of a right to work as a right of social citizenship; and finally it will discuss ethical and practical alternatives to current labour-market policies.

WORK AND WELFARE

Any understanding of the relationship between work and welfare depends—self-evidently—on how each is defined. *Work* as a term can apply not only to paid employment, but also to vital caring and domestic activities and to a variety of educational, creative, and voluntary pursuits that are unpaid. Welfare, if it is taken to refer to human need in its widest sense, depends on states of health, physical security, personal identities, and social relationships that go beyond mere material livelihood. If by work, however, we mean no more than paid labour, work can be bad for human welfare: if it does not pay enough to secure a worker's livelihood and/or that of her family; if it is exploitative, hazardous, or demeaning.

Perhaps the most critical account of the relationship between work and welfare is that originally offered by Karl Marx.[18] In his early writings Marx claimed that capitalism, athough it has advanced the human condition, is inherently alienating and inimical to social humanity. In his later writings, he sought to expose the immanent logic of the commodity form and the wage relation under capitalism and demonstrated how this distorts our understanding of human need. It is supposed by some that there is an element of discontinuity between Marx's earlier and later writings,[19] but others disagree. It is argued by Heller that Marx had assembled a holistic and dynamic account of 'truly' human needs.[20] Geras argues that Marx consistently espoused a permanent or 'trans-historical' normative standard of human need.[21]

The foundation of Marx's argument rests, in the first instance, upon a degree of scepticism towards the Cartesian dualism on which classic liberal thinking is premised. He argued, "Thought and being are indeed distinct, but they also form a unity."[22] It is the dynamic relationship between thinking and being that characterises human action and therefore human history. Following from this, the argument rests on a rejection of utilitarian and psychological accounts of human welfare and an insistence upon what it is that is distinctive about humanity and human industry. By 'industry' Marx was referring not merely to the burgeoning manufacturing technologies of his own time, but to what might be called the human project; to scientific understanding and the self-conscious harnessing of 'Nature' for the benefit of 'Man' (i.e., humanity in general). Marx acknowledged that capitalist industry exploits both Man and Nature, but this represents a particular moment or phase in human history.

> If industry is conceived as an exoteric form of the realisation of the essential human faculties, one is able to grasp also the human essence of Nature or the natural essence of Man. . . . Nature as it develops in human history, in the genesis of human society, is the real nature of Man; thus Nature, as it develops through industry, though in an alienated form, is truly anthropological Nature.[23]

Marx's theory of human need amounts, therefore, to a theory of the essential characteristics of the human species and of its species-being.[24] The account may be summarised in terms of four constitutive features of our species-character and mode of existence: work, consciousness, sociality, and historical development. Most particularly, for the purposes of this chapter, 'work' may be understood in terms of human beings' purposive interaction with the world around them, of their metabolism with Nature. Through work we may satisfy our instrumental needs, but also develop the creative skills and the critical knowledge that defines our humanity. Wage labour, however, as the dominant form of work under capitalist relations of production is, according to Marx, inherently exploitative and a cruel distortion of what work should be.

In Marx's later work, a further strand of his critique of capitalism emerges in which he is not concerned with constitutive needs of individuals as human beings but with the way that social needs are ideologically constituted or by which 'welfare' is socially defined.[25] Through his analysis of the way in which value attaches to commodities under capitalism, he provided the basis on which to claim that capitalism generates false needs and a distorted understanding of welfare. Certain needs, although they are demonstrably and consciously experienced, are illusory rather than real.[26] The exchange value of commodities—including labour— conceals their 'true' value or *usefulness* for human welfare. This theme has been developed, for example, in Illich's account of the way in which advanced industrial societies—both capitalist and communist—either manufactured or imputed the needs of their citizens.[27] Illich speaks out against the tyranny of imputed needs and useless jobs, and in favour of 'useful unemployment' and human fulfilment.

Yet more recently, Richard Sennett has suggested that the new managerial orthodoxies of the flexible, incentivising, reinvented corporation of post-industrial capitalism is more likely to lead to indifference than 'alienation' in the sense that Marx had foreseen in his earlier writings.[28] The recent erosion of craft skills and class consciousness Sennett associates with the 'corrosion of character'. What has been characterised as the 'McDonaldization' of many forms of paid employment strips such work of meaning.[29] Yet, at the same time, the evolution of welfare state capitalism had been associated with a cultural shift that—paradoxically perhaps— was conducive to more individualistic preoccupations and a less solidaristic interpretation of welfare.[30]

One of the important criticisms of T.H. Marshall's social citizenship thesis has been advanced by Tom Bottomore,[31] who emphasised, on the one hand, the historical significance of class struggle and the labour movement to the achievement of social rights and who, *pace* Marshall, attached importance to the maintenance of class struggle—alongside the struggles of other emergent social movements—in order to retain and develop such rights. On the other hand, like Sennett, Bottomore was mindful of capitalism's changing nature and, in particular, the 'new folklore of capitalism' that had then and has since been implicated in the marketisation and managerialisation of welfare provision.[32]

WORK AND SOCIAL CITIZENSHIP

As the new capitalism reconstitutes the relationship between work and welfare is there scope, as Bottomore has urged us, to reimagine a role for social citizenship or for remobilising a discourse of social rights?

A right to work may or may not be expressly recognised as an economic or social right of citizenship within constitutional instruments or by specific legislative provision within any individual nation-state. However, several key international instruments include specific provision in relation to 'work', albeit that in every instance the term appears by implication to refer to self-remunerative work. The Universal Declaration of Human Rights (UDHR) of 1948 declares, "Everyone has the right to work, to free choice of employment, to just and favourable conditions of work and to protection against unemployment" (Article 23[1]). The International Covenant on Economic, Social and Cultural Rights (ICESCR) of 1966 'acknowledges' the right of everyone to the opportunity to gain her living by work which she freely chooses or accepts (Article 6[1]). At the European level, the Council of Europe's selectively ratified Social Charter of 1961 (revised 1996) provides for a right to earn one's living in an occupation freely entered upon and to an economic and social policy designed to ensure full employment. The European Union's Charter of Fundamental Rights of 2007 (now incorporated into the 2009 Lisbon Treaty, albeit with an opt out by the UK and Poland) provides more cautiously for "the right to engage in work and to pursue a freely chosen or accepted occupation" and "the freedom to seek employment [and] to work": By implication, there is no obligation on member states to provide a citizen with a job. Whereas the right to work is established as a human right, its availability as a social citizenship right may not necessarily or unequivocally be guaranteed. It may be noted that the UDHR additionally provides for a right of protection against unemployment and a right to social security (under Articles 22 and 25). In practice, some welfare states have always been more willing than others to protect citizens from the adverse consequences of wage labour through, for example, intervention to regulate wages and the terms and conditions of employment.

Were we to accept that work is part of a person's species-being, the right to work—in whatever form it exists—might be inferred to reflect the sense in which every citizen *needs* to work. However this is not the case: first, because the *right* to work is increasingly conflated with a *responsibility* to work; second, because work is narrowly construed—whether as wage labour or individual enterprise—as legitimately paid work.

The Responsibility to Work

The welfare state has rowed back from the idea that a partial decommodification of labour power provides the worker, as a social citizen, with a degree of independence and the right freely to work under conditions that are 'just and favourable'. Under the 'workfare' state,[33] decommodification has been reconstituted as welfare dependency; the citizen's right work has been reconstituted as a responsibility; and dependency and responsibility have been construed as inherently inimical. I have suggested elsewhere that this shift may take different forms[34]:

- In its crudest authoritarian form, responsibility equates with conditional obedience and the new role for the state is the governance of irresponsibility. This is reflected in sanctioned, 'work-first' types of active labour market policies (ALMP).
- In its republican form, responsibility equates with moral obligation and the role of the state is to prioritise the normative and practical integrity of the social order. This may be reflected in a strong rhetorical commitment to a right, or a freedom, to work, but reluctance to disrupt existing labour relations.
- In its liberal form, responsibility equates with civic duties owed by self-sufficient subjects and the role of the state is to promote equality of opportunity. This may be reflected in types of ALMP that focus on human capital development.
- In its social-democratic form, responsibility equates with shared social responsibility and the role of the state is to ensure that every citizen can participate in and benefit from the labour process. In the past, this has been associated with job-creation policies, but current trends are more focused on supply-side flexibility.

Such a taxonomy can, of course, be no more than a heuristic device. Actual flexicurity, LMA, or welfare-to-work policies are inevitably hybrid in nature and are likely to incorporate elements of more than one approach. Wherever the emphasis may lie, however, the common policy denominator is a shift away from social security towards the imposition of at least some element of individual responsibility. Supply-side flexibility requires that the worker, as a citizen, becomes less independent and more dependent on the vicissitudes of market forces. Although perversely, the process may be promoted or defended as a way of making the worker, as an economic actor, more independent and less dependent on the state. Either way, a person's *need* to work becomes quite secondary.

The Subordination of Unpaid or Informal Work

The other way in which the need to work is marginalised is that formal paid employment becomes not only the dominant form of work, but it is prioritised over other kinds of useful, or indeed essential, work. The following kinds of work—or of 'industry'—may, in different ways, be rendered increasingly subordinate:

- *Care work must be reconciled to the demands of a flexible labour market.* One of the most vital forms of work performed by human beings is the care they provide for other members of the species: the care provided in raising children or looking after disabled or frail elderly relatives. Precisely because it most usually is a labour of love,[35] it is work that is every bit as definitive of our humanity as any other. Human beings can only exist through and with others within networks of care.[36] Care work has been and still is carried on for the most part by women and within families. But it has been suggested that one of the most important issues for post-industrial capitalism is that of how social welfare provision will adapt to the changing dynamics of care within the household economy, as family life adapts to the imperatives of changing labour markets.[37] On the one hand, therefore, we have policies to promote 'work–family reconciliation' or 'work–life balance'[38]; on the other, LMA policies have been increasingly focused on maximising labour-market participation by all those of 'working age', irrespective of caring responsibilities. A case in point is the recent debate in the UK as to the age the youngest child of a lone parent should reach before the parent is required to seek work as a condition of receiving social assistance.[39]

- *Informal work is suppressed to ensure it does not subvert the formal labour market.* The 'great transformation' that characterised the advent of modern capitalism entailed the formalisation of labour markets.[40] The survival of informal work in developed economies is regarded by policy makers as a significant threat to economic competitiveness.[41] Work may be regarded as informal if it is not performed in accordance with a legally regulated contract and/or it is not declared for social security or taxation purposes. It may be paid, but it is not necessarily legal. In practice a great deal of the everyday services that are exchanged between people is informal. In the European Union, it has been estimated, almost a quarter of the population is involved to some degree in 'undeclared work',[42] and of course in many developing countries the great majority of work may be defined as informal. Work does not cease to be work if it is not legally regulated or declared, but as labour markets become increasingly polarised, with ever-greater flexibility at the periphery, the extent to which people resort to informal work may increase.[43] Although policymakers attempt to regularise unregulated work where feasible, the favoured strategy is to clamp down particularly, for example, on informal work carried out by recipients of unemployment benefits, a strategy that tends to impact most on the most marginalised workers.

- *Voluntary work is increasingly harnessed from above.* A considerable amount of valuable work, particularly in social service provision, has long been undertaken in the sphere of 'civil society' on a voluntary and unpaid basis. This may entail a range of activities from providing high-powered professional advice to campaign groups to doing the shopping for an elderly neighbour. Civil society is inhabited by a wide variety of movements and organisations and is a contestable space.[44] It is a space in which, historically, radical social movements have been able to mobilise against the state, but which more recently has been colonised by neoliberals and 'new' communitarians as an alternative to the state. Under the banner of 'active citizenship' essentially conservative principles of *noblesse oblige* may be revived. The solution to structural deficits may be to reduce both taxes and public spending by devolving social provision to the voluntary or 'not-for-profit' sector, where successful citizens can pay something back in kind through unpaid work for their less fortunate fellow citizens. The idea that we might promote a 'Big Society' alongside a smaller state was particularly in evidence in the run up to the recent General Election in the UK,[45] and elements of that approach already feature in the programme of the Conservative/Liberal Democrat Coalition Government.[46]

- *Recreational work goes unrecognised.* Another important form of work that is not necessarily paid relates to creative or cultural endeavour; for example, artistic and musical expression.[47] Amateur and unsponsored forms of such endeavour may be dismissed as mere hobbies, but as a self-conscious form of metabolism with Nature they most certainly meet Marx's definition of work. What is more *recreation*, in its literal sense, has long been recognised as essential to human well-being and can, in a medicalised sense, be recognised as having therapeutic applications.[48] However, the significance of recreational work has to some extent been trivialised through the general 'Disneyfication' of cultural life.[49] And more fundamentally the spectre of, for example, the dole-claiming, free-riding surfer[50]—however artistic she may be—is one that perennially silences arguments that favour unconditional support for unemployed people, particularly those who are young and healthy.

Insofar as these other forms of work are equally constitutive of our species being should they not be valued as rights of social citizenship?

RECONSTRUCTING SOCIAL POLICY

For Marx the achievement of welfare—the realisation and satisfaction of 'radical needs'—must mean that need rather than value should become the measure of things.[51] This would require the revolutionary overthrow of capitalism, which is not going to happen anytime soon! Nevertheless, how might it be possible to challenge the hegemonic creep of neoliberal orthodoxy that puts work before welfare? This chapter suggests two possibilities: an attempt to capture the idea of a eudaimonic welfare ethic and to build this into 'life-first' work-to-welfare practices.

Towards a Eudaimonic Ethic?

The prevailing ethic in social policy—and especially in relation to ALMPs—is essentially 'hedonic'. It assumes the human individual is motivated by the personal desire to maximise pleasure and minimise pain and that people can be governed in this light. In classical Greek philosophy, however, the counterpart to a hedonic ethic was a 'eudaimonic' ethic, which is concerned not with material utility, but spiritual well-being. The ancient Socratic tradition recognised both, but the traditions have diverged. The Epicureans supposed that a good life entailed the pursuit of pleasure (mental as well as physical) and the avoidance of pain or discomfort. The Aristotelian tradition—as expounded in the *Nicomachean Ethics* and the *Eudemian Ethics*[52]—contended that leading a good life means more than pleasure seeking; it entails virtue. Self-realisation comes through the nature of our social relationships, civic duties, and creative activities. I have attempted elsewhere to argue that the hedonic-eudaimonic distinction is reflected in the different ways in which post-Enlightenment concepts of citizenship and associated approaches in social policy have been constructed.[53]

The hedonic tradition found expression in nineteenth-century utilitarianism; in the creation of, for example, the Victorian workhouse and the principle of 'lesser eligibility'; and in the founding elements of a 'welfarist' approach that continues to inform social policy.[54] Welfarism here is taken to refer to a particular kind of thinking that assumes that social policy intervention should be judged by its aggregate effects, rather than the well-being of any particular individual. Policy may be used to induce or to reinforce the behaviour most likely to generate beneficial overall outcomes. It is in one sense an illiberal approach, yet its origins lie perversely in liberal Enlightenment thinking about the nature of the human individual.[55] The starkest of liberal conceptions of the social order regards the human condition as a competition of all against all.[56] Citizenship, therefore, entails a contract: a trade-off between the unrestrained pleasures of individual sovereignty in return for protection against the pain that might be inflicted by the actions of others. Such an interpretation continues to justify a neoliberal 'work-first' approach to LMA.

The eudaimonic approach has been inflected in different directions. One element of it was translated during the eighteenth century onwards into Kantian 'deontological ethics'; that is to say, into notions of universal moral duty and the contention that not only does everybody have a right to well-being, but nobody should be treated as a means of achieving happiness for another. Such thinking opened the door to the social liberal thinking that informed the creation of modern welfare states, to liberal concepts of social justice, such as that espoused by Rawls,[57] for example, and to Sen's capability approach.[58] However, the eudaimonic tradition had also informed the post-Enlightenment republicanism of Rousseau and Montesquieu and, evolving from this, the thinking of contemporary 'radical-democrats' (sometimes referred to as 'left-communitarians'), such as Macintyre, Walzer, and Sandel, who have questioned the abstract nature of the individual 'self' that is posed in liberal deontology and would presume that the mutual obligations human beings owe to each other are grounded in the realities of their social belonging.[59] Underpinning republican traditions lies an assumption that human relations amount to a collaboration between vulnerable but cooperative beings. Citizenship entails solidarity: a pooling of individual sovereignty and the promotion of social order, existential security, and collective well-being.

Social liberalism and European republicanism each therefore embody elements of a eudaimonic tradition: The former is premised more on abstract philosophical doctrine; the latter more on a concern for the inherent integrity of the social order. The former as it evolved became allied to an extent with the politics of social democracy, with an emphasis on promoting social justice. The latter as it evolved became allied to an extent with social conservatism, with an emphasis on preserving the traditional social order. But both, arguably, have succumbed to the hegemonic influence of a hedonic, neoliberal orthodoxy. Social liberalism is retreating from its alliance with social democracy and is preoccupied, for example, with human capital development. European republicanism has sustained its alliance with social conservatism that tends in turn to ally itself not with left-communitarianism, but a more authoritarian communitarianism, which resonates, perhaps, with Etzioni's and Putnam's preoccupations with social capital development.[60]

Nevertheless, the eudaimonic tradition still has roots in contemporary thinking and in those elements of social security provision based on solidaristic principles of risk sharing and social insurance. It is possible to reimagine approaches to flexicurity and/or welfare-to-work from an alternative ethical perspective.

A Life-First Approach?

A few years ago, following an empirical investigation in the UK into the labour-market experiences of people with multiple problems and needs, I suggested that—at a time when policymakers were discussing 'work-first' activation measures, on the one hand, and 'work–life balance' policies, on the other—we ought to consider a 'life-first' approach to welfare-to-work.[61] My concern then and now was that policymakers—certainly in the UK-needed to rethink what is meant by 'work-readiness'. The interviewees in my study, while often harbouring wholly unrealistic expectations, were by and large manifestly unready for employment. Most had had chaotic and disrupted lives and could not be employed. They needed time, space, and extended support. With colleagues I later argued, "The life-first approach requires both a politics of need interpretation, focused on the redefinition of rights, and a politics of capabilities, focused on the re-definition of human autonomy."[62] It is time, perhaps, with the benefit of hindsight, to firm up this concept of a life-first approach.

I should begin by saying that I am now less convinced by the idea of a politics of capabilities. My preference is for a politics of needs interpretation that could remobilise claims to rights-based social citizenship.[63] The capabilities approach associated with Amartya Sen is less amenable to an acceptance of human interdependence; less adept at framing demands for parity of participation in decision making; and less critically resistant to the exploitative potential of wage labour under capitalism.[64]

The capabilities approach, although an advance on the abstract Rawlsian conception of social justice, remains essentially liberal-individualist. Its focus is on the individual's freedom to do and to be that which she would choose and value. The individual subject is conceived as an independent entity existing in the space of her own capabilities. In reality, I would argue, the human subject is defined through her interdependencies with other human subjects; through what Marx refers to as her 'sociality'. Our sociality is constitutive of our individual identities and of the frameworks of intersubjective meaning through which we value the things we can do and be.[65] Our development and our capacity for critical autonomy as individuals is dependent in the first instance on the social or 'interpsychological' processes embodied in human relationships within families, communities and the gamut of formal and informal social institutions that shape our lives and—among other things—the moral value and meaning of work.[66]

Sen does acknowledge that there is a role for 'public reasoning' in the definition of capabilities but does not address the shortcomings of the liberal democratic process when it comes to including voiceless and oppressed social groups in the processes through which our understanding of human needs are negotiated.[67] As Nancy Fraser further contends, it is not merely that some people's voices go unrecognised, but the issues of social justice that affect them are 'misframed'.[68] She argues that frame-setting in the new capitalist order would be best governed according to the principle that "all those affected by a given social structure or institution have moral standing as subjects of justice in relation to it."[69] Those worst affected by the flexibilisation of labour markets are largely excluded from public reasoning as to the kind of work they should do or on what terms and conditions. And here the capability approach is silent as to the implications of the real or potential exploitation entailed by the system of wage labour under capitalism; exploitation made more real as labour markets become more precarious. One interpretation of the consequences is that offered by Guy Standing, who has identified a new class-in-the-making, the 'precariat'.[70] As the traditional working class or proletariat shrinks, an ever-expanding precariat emerges: a diverse socioeconomic group of flexible workers with undervalued skills and little work-based identity. The concept may not be sociologically rigorous, but it captures something essential about the workers whose lives are most likely to be affected by policymakers' concepts of flexicurity.

Lacking a critique of the capitalist labour-market process, the capability approach cannot quite capture the implications of a life-first approach to work and welfare. All work, even wage labour, must have moral value.[71] Not all forms of paid employment can be in every respect congenial or satisfying, but the moral value that attaches to work, regardless of material remuneration, reflects the recognition accorded to the human subject who performs that work. The life-first approach should be about work-to-welfare, not welfare-to-work. It eschews a utilitarian conception of the work ethic, which assumes that 'work' (i.e., paid employment) is the means and 'welfare' (i.e., hedonic well-being) the goal in favour of a work ethic that regards work as constitutive of our social well-being. Restoring a work ethic does not mean compelling people to labour but promoting the self-hood and social identity—or what Sennett refers to as 'character'[72]—that work imparts. The life-first approach gives precedence to human welfare or well-being in the sense that that is the goal. Because well-being depends on work and the recognition of its worth, the need to work must be addressed in order to achieve the goal of welfare. Work is the means; welfare the end. But as we have seen, we must rethink the meaning of both. This would redefine the responsibilities of both employers and the state.

Employers and the State

Though the issue of corporate social responsibility and its relevance for social policy are hardly new,[73] it is a concept ripe for strategic elaboration. If one considers, for example, the International Labour Organisation's 'Decent Work' agenda,[74] here is a global campaign specifically dedicated to promoting just and favourable conditions of work and that directly engages employer organisations. The agenda is underpinned by four 'strategic objectives': employment creation, rights at work, social protection and social dialogue (see www.ilo.org/global/about-the-ilo/decent-work-agenda/lang—en/index.htm.

Of the United Nations agencies, the ILO is the one least in thrall to neo-liberal tendencies, but it has little direct influence. Although there had been recent debate in Europe relating to the related issue of 'job quality',[75] it is striking that the EU's *Europe 2020* strategy document would seem to have dropped all reference to this.[76]

Nevertheless, the campaign for decent work provides a significant platform and lends credibility to a discourse that may be strategically called upon to assert that the provision of decent work is a corporate social responsibility. ILO conventions in relation to the prohibition of all forms of forced labour, the protection of health and safety at work, freedom of association, protection from discrimination, fair and humane disciplinary practices, reasonable working hours, and remuneration are integral to the SA 8000 standard promoted by Social Accountability International.[77] This is an audit standard applied to company practices mainly in relation to their operations in developing countries, but to a limited extent within clothing industries in Europe. It is a discourse which, it seems, is seldom brought into play in the context of debates about flexicurity and LMA. And yet it can be argued that employers ought to be subject to a corporate social responsibility to counter instability in the labour market, to provide more for their workers than is minimally required and to accommodate more vulnerable workers.

Take, for example, the idea that employers might accept a corporate social responsibility for the employment of disabled workers. In the UK, in response to legislation specifically to advance the rights of disabled workers, a standing Employers Forum for Disability was created (see www.efd.org.uk) to advise and support employers and which accepted that there was a business case for unlocking the skills and the potential of disabled people. Similarly, there has been an Employers for Work–Life Balance Forum (www.theworkfoundation.com/difference/e4wlb.aspx). In neither instance, however, was there a clear sense that the responsibilities which employers were accepting were embraced as social responsibilities.

The issue of work–life balance has been presented from the employers' perspective as a contest between the 'win-win' theory espoused explicitly by the UK government and the case supposedly attributable to the European Social Model (Bloom, Krestchmer, and Van Reenen, 2006): The former argues the business case for work–life balance, holding that it can increase productivity in a global free market; the latter argues that measures to promote work–life balance, even if they reduce productivity, represent a cost that ought to be borne to ameliorate the consequences of rampant economic competition. The 'win-win' or business case theory holds that flexible managers who accommodate workers' needs will get better results. Bloom, Krestchmer, and Van Reenen's analysis, based on quantitative data, suggests that good management does indeed lead to better work–life balance outcomes and, subject to good management, work–life balance does not necessarily harm productivity. But the evidence showed that work–life balance does not of itself enhance productivity. From this we might infer that work–life balance ought really to be promoted on the basis of the social, not the business, case.

The same conclusion may be drawn from qualitative research in the UK.[78] Under the UK's prevailing policy regime a satisfactory work–life balance is achievable only for some. In particular, the benefits of the family-friendly working practices operated by employers and the accessibility of employment rights and childcare facilities tend to accrue to more highly skilled and higher-paid workers than to lower-skilled and low-paid workers. Flexible working arrangements require trade-offs between employers and employees, but the indications from a small-scale qualitative study of the experiences of working parents in a low-income neighbourhood in London was that such trade-offs encroach by and large not so much on the work the parents are required to put in, as on the quality of their family life. The reality is that the thoroughgoing changes in the culture and dynamics of the workplace that might be entailed to ensure a satisfactory work–life balance for lower-paid and lower-skilled workers clearly would not bring short-term economic benefits for employers, but the case for doing so could be presented as an issue of corporate social responsibility. By extension it can be argued more generally that employers should be encouraged, enabled, or compelled to accept some responsibility for the needs of a range of workers who cannot become immediately productive. Clearly, the mechanisms for making such demands of employers are better established in European welfare regimes with strongly developed social partnership arrangements. They are demands that are best founded and promoted on the basis of class-based solidarity and progress is likely at best to be incremental, not least because the interests of the precariat are not necessarily best represented by established trades unions.[79]

It is clear that corporate interests can in some circumstances be persuaded to bow to popular demands. The modest successes of the global Fair Trade movement (e.g., www.wfto.org; www.eftafairtrade.org; www.fairtrade.org.uk) in using the power of consumer preferences to change corporate behaviour in relation to environmental protection and child labour practices is an example. Although it is perhaps difficult to envisage a similar form of consumer mobilisation by or on behalf of the so-called precariat, the extent of popular anger across Europe about austerity measures following the global financial crisis suggests that awareness of encroaching risks may provide an inflection point in public opinion. The corporate sector is itself hugely dependent on state support and governments do therefore have points of leverage.[80] A case can be made for seeking to reframe both popular and political discourse in a way that confronts the ethics of employment practices and the role of nation-states in sustaining such practices through labour-market and social security policies. The terrain of the debate could shift towards demands for greater stability and fairness in the labour market, rather than ameliorative flexicurity.

Turning, therefore, from the responsibilities of employers to the responsibilities of the state, the issue here can be portrayed not as corporate responsibility, but collective responsibility for meeting people's need to work. The case for job creation through public infrastructure investment has been accepted by President Obama in the US, but it could be that some limited return to Keynesian ideals is on the cards. Even if this is not to be the case, a shift that embraces a eudaimonic ethic of social security might permit a greater sense of mutual engagement with, and shared concern for, those who are excluded from, unready for, or simply ill-suited to the formal labour market.

At one level, this might simply require a willingness to support people through the benefits system during protracted periods of time while their multiple problems are effectively addressed. At another it would entail a greater acceptance of the value of forms of work other than paid employment. Benefits and social insurance credits to cover periods of time in which people have caring responsibilities could be retained or extended, rather than curtailed, particularly when people consider their care work to be more important than paid employment. The approach to informal work could be made more open. Rather than deter informal work, initiatives that try and regularise some kinds of informal work could be extended. Just as importantly, greater attention could be paid to the sufficiency of out-of-work benefits and this, together with increased accessibility of 'decent work' in the formal sector, should lessen the incentive for people to engage in informal work. Ultimately, however, it must be acknowledged perhaps that a certain amount of informal work is a necessary component of a functioning community. Finally, the general quality of social life—particularly at a local community level—could be enhanced through the promotion and facilitation of recreational work. A case can be made not for marketising amateur creative endeavour, but for acknowledging its life-enhancing and therapeutic possibilities, particularly for those who are not 'work-ready' in the conventional sense.

CONCLUSION

What I have just advocated comes close to a case for some form of Basic Income, or at least a Participation Income,[81] but this is not my principal focus. My concern is whether and how we might reconstruct popular and political understandings of work and welfare. My ostensibly reformist argument concerning the corporate social responsibilities of capitalist employers is similarly an exercise in strategic reframing. At its heart, the life-first approach is about changing the terms and the climate of debate.

Insofar as these are 'times of change'—not just within Europe but globally—it has been suggested that capitalism's most recent crisis of accumulation may, as we embark on an era of austerity and increased exploitation of labour, portend a revitalisation *either* of economic-liberal orthodoxies *or* of some kind of neo-Keynesianism.[82] It is a moment at which a hegemonic 'war of position' might draw for legitimacy upon a variety of strategies.[83] Whether it is founded on a Marxist notion of what constitutes humanity's species being, or an Aristotelian notion of eudaimonic well-being, the central contention of the chapter has been that people need to work. If people need to work, it may be claimed that we share a collective responsibility to *let* them work, whether or not their work takes the form of paid employment. This amounts to an inversion of the prevailing neoliberal assumption that work is an individual responsibility and that people must be *made* to work. Insofar as enforcement is an issue, an individual's need to work translates into an economic or social right. As a human being, this is a human right and all states parties to the UDHR and ICESCR are sworn to strive to respect, promote, and fulfil that right.[84] As a citizen of a welfare state, this is a citizenship right that in *some* circumstances should be demanded of, and enforced against, employers in the context of a shift to new forms of demand-side employment policy. In *other* circumstances it is a right whose substance must be rearticulated with a deeper and more ethical understanding of human welfare or well-being.

NOTES

1. It should be noted that 'flexicurity' as a term is seldom encountered in the UK or other Anglophone countries, although it is widely promoted across continental Europe. The term refers to a combination of active labour-market policy (ALMP) with more or less generous social protection and aspirations to promote lifelong learning (LLL) and work–family reconciliation measures. The interpretation and implementation of the concept varies widely, but the best-known (albeit differing) exemplars of flexicurity are to be found in Denmark and the Netherlands. In its purest form the concept might be regarded as quintessentially 'Third Way'—see Giddens (1998)—but the fact that the term was never adopted, for example, in the UK reflects, perhaps, the extent to which neoliberal influences tended to predominate over New Labour's erstwhile support for a 'Third Way'. In practice, flexicurity may be understood as a version of, if not a synonym for, what throughout much of the world is called 'welfare-to-work' policy.
2. See Doogan (2009) and Sennett (1998).
3. Pierson (1996).
4. Beck (1992).
5. Offe (1996: 33).
6. Marshall (1992).
7. Marshall (1992: 33).
8. Polanyi (1944).
9. Offe (1984: 99).
10. See Bauman (1993) and/or Rose (1999).
11. Taylor-Gooby (2009).
12. Esping-Andersen (1990).
13. Offe (1996: 123–125).
14. Dolowitz (2004: 213–230).
15. Doogan (2009).
16. Jordan (2010).
17. Jones and Novak (1999: 196).
18. Dean (2010: 20–22).
19. For example, Althusser (1994).
20. Heller (1974).
21. Geras (1983).
22. Marx (1975: 351).
23. Marx (1975: 355).
24. Markus (1978: 37–41).
25. Heller (1974) and see Soper (1981).
26. Marx (1970: passim).
27. Illich (1977).
28. Sennett (1998).
29. Ritzer (2004).
30. See Beck and Beck-Gernsheim (2001) and/or Inglehart (1990).

31. Bottomore (1992).
32. Bottomore (1992: 88).
33. Jessop (2002); Lødemel and Trickey (2000); Peck (2001).
34. Dean (2007: 573–589).
35. Finch and Groves (1983).
36. Sevenhuijsen (1998); Tronto (1994).
37. Dean (2008a); Esping-Andersen (1999).
38. Lewis (2006: 420–437).
39. Gregg (2008); Department for Work and Pensions (2010).
40. Polanyi (1944).
41. Mateman and Renooy (2001); Williams and Windebank (1998).
42. Eurobarometer (2007).
43. Dean (2000).
44. Powell (2007).
45. Social Justice Policy Group (2008).
46. H.M. Government (2010).
47. For example, Fischer (1963).
48. Seebohm Rowntree and Russell Lavers (1951).
49. Fevre (2000).
50. Fitzpatrick (1999: 58–66).
51. See Heller (1974).
52. Fitzpatrick (2008: chap. 4); Macintyre (2007).
53. Dean (2003a, 2008b).
54. Jordan (2008).
55. King (1999).
56. Hobbes (1996).
57. Rawls (1972).
58. Sen (1985).
59. Macintyre (2007); Walzer (1983); Sandel (2009).
60. Etzioni (1995); Putnam (2000).
61. Dean (2003b: 441–459).
62. Dean et al. (2005: 3–26).
63. Fraser (1989).
64. Dean (2009: 261–273).
65. See also Deneulin and Stewart (2000).
66. Vygotsky (1978).
67. Sen (2005: 151–166).
68. Fraser (2010: 19).
69. Fraser (2010: 24).
70. Standing (2011).
71. Hegel (1983).
72. Sennett (1998).
73. Brejning (2012); Farnsworth and Holden (2006: 473–494).
74. Standing (2002: 263–265).
75. Leschke, Watt, and Finn (2008).
76. Pochet (2010).
77. Social Accountability International (2004); see www.sa-intl.org.
78. Dean (2002: 3–10; 2008a).
79. Standing (2011).
80. Farnsworth (2012).
81. Atkinson (1996: 67–70).
82. Callinicos (2010).
83. Gramsci (1971).
84. For example, Shue (1980).

BIBLIOGRAPHY

Althusser, Louis. *Althusser: A Critical Reader.* Edited by Gregory Elliott. Oxford: Blackwell, 1994.

Atkinson, Anthony B. "The Case for a Participation Income." *Political Quarterly* 67 (1996): 67–70.

Bauman, Zygmunt. *Postmodern Ethics.* Oxford: Blackwell, 1993.

Beck, Ulrich. *Risk Society: Towards a New Modernity.* London: Sage, 1992.

Beck, Ulrich and Elisabeth Beck-Gernsheim. *Individualization.* London: Sage, 2001.

Bloom, Nick, Tobias Krestchmer, and John Van Reenen. *Work–Life Balance, Management Practices and Productivity.* London: Centre for Economic Performance, London School of Economics, 2006.

Bottomore, Tom. "Citizenship and Social Class, Forty Years On." In *Citizenship and Social Class,* edited by Tom Bottomore, 55–93. London: Pluto, 1992.

Brejning, Jeanette. *Corporate Social Responsibility and the Welfare State.* Aldershot: Ashgate, 2012.

Callinicos, Alex. *Bonfire of Illusions: The Twin Crises of the Liberal World.* Cambridge: Polity, 2010.

Dean, Hartley. "Business versus Families: Whose Side Is New Labour On?" *Social Policy and Society* 1 (2002): 3–10.

Dean, Hartley. "Critiquing Capabilities: The Distractions of a Beguiling Concept." *Critical Social Policy* 29 (2009): 261–273.

Dean, Hartley. "Defrauding the Community? The 'Abuse' of Welfare." In *Social Problems and Social Policy,* edited by Margaret May, Edward Brunsdon, and Robert Page, 248–262. Oxford: Blackwell, 2000.

Dean, Hartley. "Discursive Repertoires and the Negotiation of Wellbeing: Reflections on the WeD Frameworks." WeD working paper 04. Bath: Wellbeing in Developing Countries ESRC Research Group, 2003a.

Dean, Hartley. "The Ethics of Welfare-to-Work." *Policy and Politics* 35 (2007): 573–589.

Dean, Hartley. "Flexibility or Flexploitation? Problems with Work–Life Balance in a Low-Income Neighbourhood." In *Social Policy Review 20,* edited by Tim Maltby, Patricia Kennett, and Kirstein Rummery, 113–132. Bristol: Policy Press/Social Policy Association, 2008a.

Dean, Hartley. "Reconceptualising Welfare-to-Work for People with Multiple Problems and Needs." *Journal of Social Policy* 32 (2003b): 441–459.

Dean, Hartley. "Towards a Eudaimonic Ethic of Social Security." In *Social Security, Happiness and Wellbeing,* edited by Jonathan Bradshaw, 57–76. Antwerp: FISS/Intersentia, 2008b.

Dean, Hartley. *Understanding Human Need.* Bristol: Policy Press, 2010.

Dean, Hartley, Jean-Michel Bonvin, Pascale Vielle, and Nicolas Farvaque. "Developing Capabilities and Rights in Welfare-to-Work Policies." *European Societies* 7 (2005): 3–26.

Deneulin, Séverine and Frances Stewart. "A Capability Approach for People Living Together." Paper presented at the VHI conference "Justice and Poverty: Examining Sen's Capability Approach," Saint Edmunds College, Cambridge, 2000.

Department for Work and Pensions. *Universal Credit, Welfare That Works, Cm 7957.* London: Stationery Office, 2010.

Dolowitz, David, P. "Prosperity and Fairness? Can New Labour Bring Fairness to the 21st Century by Following the Dictates of Endogenous Growth?" *British Journal of Politics and International Relations* 6 (2004): 213–230.

Doogan, Kevin. *New Capitalism? The Transformation of Work.* Cambridge: Polity: 2009.

Esping-Andersen, Gøsta. *The Social Foundations of Post-Industrial Economies.* Oxford: Oxford University Press, 1999.

Esping-Andersen, Gøsta. *The Three Worlds of Welfare Capitalism.* Cambridge: Polity, 1990.

Etzioni, Amitai. *The Spirit of Community.* London: Fontana, 1995.

Eurobarometer. *Undeclared Work in the European Union.* Brussels: European Commission, 2007.

Farnsworth, Kevin. *Social versus Corporate Welfare: Competing Needs and Interests in the Welfare State.* Basingstoke: Palgrave Macmillan, 2012.

Farnsworth, Kevin and Chris Holden. "The Business–Social Policy Nexus: Corporate Power and Corporate Inputs into Social Policy." *Journal of Social Policy* 35 (2006): 473–494.

Fevre, Ralph. *The Demoralization of Western Culture: Social Theory and the Dilemmas of Modern Living.* New York: Continuum, 2000.

Finch, Janet and Dulcie Groves. *A Labour of Love: Women, Work and Caring.* London: Routledge and Kegan Paul, 1983.

Fischer, Ernst. *The Necessity of Art: A Marxist Perspective.* Harmondsworth: Penguin, 1963.

Fitzpatrick, Tony. *Freedom and Security: An Introduction to the Basic Income Debate.* Basingstoke: Macmillan, 1999.

Fitzpatrick, Tony. *Applied Ethics and Social Problems.* Bristol: Policy Press, 2008.

Fraser, Nancy. *Scales of Justice: Reimagining Political Space in a Globalizing World.* New York: Columbia University Press, 2010.

Fraser, Nancy. *Unruly Practices: Power, Discourse and Gender in Contemporary Social Theory.* Minneapolis: University of Minnesota Press, 1989.

Geras, Norman. *Marx and Human Nature: Reflection of a Legend.* London: Verso, 1983.

Giddens, Anthony. *The Third Way.* Cambridge: Polity, 1998.

Gramsci, Antonio. *Selections from the Prison Notebooks.* London: Lawrence and Wishart, 1971.

Gregg, Paul. *Realising Potential: A Vision for Personalised Conditionality and Support.* London: Stationery Office, 2008.

Hegel, Georg W.F. *Hegel and the Human Spirit: A Translation of the Jena Lectures on the Philosophy of Spirit (1805–6) with Commentary* edited by Leo Rauch. Detroit, MI: Wayne State University Press, 1983.Heller, Agnes. *The Theory of Need in Marx.* London: Alison and Busby, 1974.

H.M. Government, *The Coalition: Our Programme for Government.* London: Cabinet Office, 2010.

H.M. Government. *Giving Green Paper.* London: Cabinet Office, 2010.

Hobbes, Thomas. *Leviathan.* Cambridge: Cambridge University Press, 1996.

Illich, Ivan. *Towards a History of Needs.* New York: Bantam/Random House, 1977.

Inglehart, Ronald. *Culture Shift in Advanced Industrial Society.* Princeton, NJ: Princeton University Press, 1990.

Jessop, Bob. *The Future of the Capitalist State.* Cambridge: Polity, 2002.

Jones, Chris and Tony Novak. *Poverty, Welfare and the Disciplinary State.* London: Routledge, 1999.

Jordan, Bill. *Welfare and Well-Being: Social Value in Public Policy.* Bristol: Policy Press, 2008.

Jordan, Bill. *What's Wrong with Social Policy and How to Fix It.* Cambridge: Polity, 2010.

King, Desmond. *In the Name of Liberalism: Illiberal Social Policy in the United States and Britain.* Oxford: Oxford University Press, 1999.

Leschke, Janice, Andrew Watt, and Mairéad Finn. *Putting a Number on Job Quality? Constructing a European Job Quality Index.* Brussels: European Trade Union Institute, 2008.

Lewis, Jane. "Work/Family Reconciliation, Equal Opportunities and Social Policies: The Interpretation of Policy Trajectories at the EU Level and the Meaning of Gender Equality." *Journal of European Public Policy* 13 (2006): 420–437.

Lødemel, Ivar and Heather Trickey. 2000. *'An Offer You Can't Refuse': Workfare in International Perspective.* Bristol: Policy Press, 2000.

Macintyre, Alister. *After Virtue.* Notre Dame, IN: Notre Dame Press, 2007.

Markus, George. *Marxism and Anthropology.* Assen: Van Gorcum, 1978.

Marshall, Thomas H. "Citizenship and Social Class." In *Citizenship and Social Class,* edited by Tom Bottomore, 3–51. London: Pluto, 1992.

Marx, Karl. *Capital.* Vols. I, II, III. London: Lawrence and Wishart, 1970.

Marx, Karl. "Economic and Philosophical Manuscripts." In *Early Writings,* edited by Lucio Colletti, 279–400. Harmondsworth: Penguin, 1975.

Mateman, Sander and Piet Renooy. *Undeclared Labour in Europe: Towards an Integrated Approach to Combating Undeclared Labour.* Amsterdam: Regioplan, 2001.

Offe, Claus. *Contradictions of the Welfare State.* Cambridge, MA: MIT Press, 1984.

Offe, Claus. *Modernity and the State: East, West.* Cambridge: Polity, 1996.

Peck, Jamie. *Workfare States.* New York: Guildford Press, 2001.

Pierson, Paul. "The New Politics of the Welfare State." *World Politics* 48 (1996): 143–179.

Pochet, Philipe. *ETUI Policy Brief—Issue 2—What's Wrong with EU2020?* Brussels: European Trade Union Institute, 2010.

Polanyi, Karl. *The Great Transformation.* New York: Rinehart, 1944.

Powell, Fred. *The Politics of Civil Society: Neoliberalism or Social Left?* Bristol: Policy Press, 2007.

Putnam, Robert. *Bowling Alone.* New York: Simon and Schuster, 2000.

Rawls, John. *A Theory of Justice.* Oxford: Oxford University Press, 1972.

Ritzer, George. *The McDonaldization of Society.* Thousand Oaks, CA: Pine Forge Press, 2004.

Rose, Nikolas. *Powers of Freedom: Reframing Political Thought.* Cambridge: Cambridge University Press, 1999.

Sandel, Michael J. *Justice: What's the Right Thing to Do?* London: Allen Lane, 2009.

Seebohm Rowntree, Benjamin and G. Russell Lavers. *English Life and Leisure: A Social Study.* London: Longmans, 1951.

Sen, Amartya. *Commodities and Capabilities.* Amsterdam: Elsevier, 1985.

Sen, Amartya. "Human Rights and Capabilities." *Journal of Human Development* 6 (2005): 151–166.

Sennett, Richard. *The Corrosion of Character: The Personal Consequences of Work in the New Capitalism.* New York: Norton, 1998.

Sevenhuijsen, Selma. *Citizenship and the Ethics of Care.* London: Routledge, 1998.

Shue, Henry. *Basic Rights: Subsistence, Affluence and US Foreign Policy.* Princeton, NJ: Princeton University Press, 1980.

Social Accountability International. *Guidance Document for Social Accountability 8000.* New York: SAI, 2004.

Social Justice Policy Group. *Breakdown Britain.* London: Centre for Social Justice, 2006.

Social Justice Policy Group. *Breakthrough Britain.* London: Centre for Social Justice, 2008.

Soper, Kate. *On Human Needs*. Brighton: Harvester, 1981.

Standing, Guy. *Beyond the New Paternalism*. London: Verso, 2002.

Standing, Guy. *The Precariat: The New Dangerous Class*. London: Bloomsbury, 2011.

Taylor-Gooby, Peter. *Reframing Social Citizenship*. Oxford: Oxford University Press, 2009.

Tronto, Joan. *Moral Boundaries: A Political Argument for an Ethic of Care*. New York: Routledge, 1994.

Vygotsky, Lev. *Mind and Society: The Development of Higher Mental Processes*. Cambridge, MA: Harvard University Press, 1978.

Walzer, Michael. *Spheres of Justice*. Oxford: Blackwell, 1983.

Williams, Colin and Jan Windebank. *Informal Employment and the Advanced Economies*. London: Routledge, 1998.

9 Quality of Employment
An Alternative to Flexicurity?

Dominique Méda

INTRODUCTION

Between 2007 and 2008, 'flexicurity' became the word and concept that was most widely used to propose measures able to improve the functioning of labour markets in Europe (Serrano, 2009). This was especially the case of the European Commission, and also many governments and researchers. It was presented as a strategy designed to achieve a balance between flexibility and security. However, many authors have shown that flexicurity's main objective was to develop employability in the sense of increased adaptability to the requirements of the labour market and that, in practice, flexibility was emphasized far more than security (see also Prieto, this volume).

This chapter focuses on why the concept has been accepted by those who were traditionally resistant to flexibility, and especially on the role of economists. It discusses how the OECD has based its approach heavily on ideas that were not endorsed by the academic community. It also analyses the concepts promoted with increasing frequency by OECD and EU texts.

The first section of the chapter aims at understanding why this concept was able to be accepted and seduce some elements of both public opinion and the scholarly community. The old demand to implement a structural reform of the labour market has finally been accepted by introducing into the public debate two new elements, namely, the idea of segmentation in the labour market and the Danish social democratic model. It then analyses the uses and misuses of this concept and how it has been put into practice. It demonstrates that implementation of the flexicurity strategy in Europe has resulted in greater flexibility than security.

The second section explains why we do not need a new version of flexicurity, but rather an alternative to this notion. In fact, the crisis has revealed the economic and structural shortcomings of flexicurity. It has drawn attention to the importance of a new model of development demanded by a planet that is threatened by social explosion, depletion of natural resources, and damage to the environment. The concepts of decent work and quality of employment lie at the heart of this new model.

THE REASONS FOR THE SUCCESS
OF THE FLEXICURITY CONCEPT

In 2007, the European Commission's paper entitled *Towards Common Principles of Flexicurity: More and Better Jobs through Flexibility and Security* was published (European Commission, 2007), and the use of this concept was formalised. Since then, the term has been used as a veritable *panacea*. It is believed that this concept can miraculously reconcile—as numerous articles have pointed out—any number of contradictions and should become a goal for all member states. At the same time, it respects the specificities and traditions of each member state, and is flexibly adapted to the specific features of national labour markets. This idea is based on the premise that there exist 'national pathways', as the report of the European Expert Group on Flexicurity (2007) argues. The first section of this chapter seeks to understand how this concept was able, initially at least, to generate considerable appeal and interest on the part of the public and a large number of researchers.

Context of the Design and Implementation of the Concept

I should like here to develop three hypotheses. The first is that the concept of flexicurity was the new label for the labour-market reform policies proposed beginning in the mid-1980s by the OECD. Even more crucially, it was the product of the economic theories that a number of economists propounded during the 1980s and remodelled in the mid-1990s. They successfully incorporated the role of institutions into their reasoning and equations. In this regard, I should like to examine the decisive role played by economic ideology in the creation of this term in the perspective explored by B. Jobert in *Le tournant néo-libéral en Europe* (2004). It shows how decisive economic ideologies—and, in turn, their propagators (in France, high-ranking civil servants)—were in the dissemination of the new neoliberal injunctions in France and in Europe. The second hypotheses is that the addition of the 'security' aspect and, more importantly, the use of countries offering a high level of social protection as 'models' have made acceptable a series of measures whose implementation was strongly opposed by several member states during the 1980s. They won over opinion shapers, researchers, and unions previously opposed to increasing flexibility. The third hypothesis is that the neologism 'flexicurity', which might otherwise have simply been a piece of short-lived jargon, offered an opportunity and an extraordinarily apt resource to achieve an attempt at reorientation towards the liberal model of the Mediterranean and continental countries. This was done by emulating two models of countries offering a high level of social protection, belonging more to the universalistic social democratic system.

Structural Reform of the Labour Market: An Old Demand

Increasing criticisms by economists and international institutions of the rigidity of the labour market and the emphasis they have placed on it date back to the mid-1980s. In 1990, in *Labour Market Policies for the 1990s*, the OECD declared that it was necessary to "achieve sufficient flexibility in the labour market within a socially acceptable framework" (21).[1] It went on to say that legislation in the matter of employment and redundancy "influences employment levels by restricting, directly or indirectly, the freedom of employers to take on and employ workers" (23). In 1994, in the *OECD Jobs Study*, the doctrine appeared to be definitively established. Globalisation, technological change, and the nature of growth had turned the old regulations, protective measures, and institutions into so many obstacles to the process of creative destruction that it was important to accept profound deregulation. Policies had made markets rigid, particularly labour markets. Consequently, it had become urgent "to look across the full range of policies that have been put in place over the last 30 years to see where, and to what extent, each may have contributed to ossifying the capacity of economies and the will of societies to adapt" (25). The study concludes with a series of nine policy recommendations. Regarding employment protection legislation (EPL), which can "make employers more reluctant to hire new workers" (34), the OECD advocated that "mandatory protection for regular contracts could be kept relatively 'light'" (34). It indicated that "*a balance* has to be struck between allowing employers greater freedom in decisions to hire and fire, and ensuring both sufficient employment security for workers and firms to be willing to invest in long-term training and protection for workers against unfair dismissal" (35).

It is important to understand the nature of these recommendations and the academic knowledge they are based on, as well as the network they could rely upon to be disseminated and converted into precepts that in practice were just as rigid. It is clear that these proposals, which are presented as the result of academic studies, were based in the purest form of neoclassical economics. The first lines of the study's introduction were devoted to structural unemployment and the adaptability required to fight it. The main problem is that "the policies and systems in place have made the economy rigid and paralysed the ability, even the will, to adapt" (4). Box 4 in the study, entitled "Cyclical Unemployment and Structural Unemployment", shows that structural unemployment "probably affects 7 to 10 percent of the labour force" in the European community (29). Thus all ills stem from an inability to adapt to change, and more particularly, to take full advantage of the numerous available innovations. Technology "destroys lower wage, lower productivity jobs, while it creates jobs that are more productive, high-skill and better paid" (30). So it is essential not to oppose this process, to allow unproductive jobs to be delocalised and to allow this process of creative destruction to run its course. This means eliminating the obstacles found in the product market and the labour market. The above lies at the heart of the theory relentlessly championed by the OECD from the mid-1980s to the present.

During the same period, academic studies on these issues were not nearly as conclusive. On the one hand, economists incorporated the role of institutions into their arguments and some studies asserted that the institutional changes, which had been affecting the European labour markets for the last twenty-five years, were the chief cause of the lamentable European performances in terms of employment (Siebert, 1997). However, on the other hand, other studies—which were published at that time and regarded as highly reliable—significantly nuanced the argument that the labour market and its rigidities were exclusively responsible. By addressing only these factors, they helped to orient and focus research on this single issue. In 2003, in a major review article, Edmond Malinvaud, a highly influential French economist, returned to the question of the labour-market institutions' role in poor European performances and to the OECD study on employment. He highlighted that the causal link between labour-market institutions and the unemployment rate was not proven and questioned the need for structural reforms. "It is natural to ask how the authors of recommendations as detailed as those of the OECD could be certain that their implementation would be beneficial. Quite frankly, one might well wonder whether the assurance with which these recommendations were made is based more often than not on the *belief* that the problems would all disappear if the labour market worked in the same way as the product market. Perhaps, but as this will never happen, as we have seen in section 3, such a belief is *irrelevant*. And once discarded, we have to admit that our knowledge of the effects to expect from the structural recommendations is *vague*" (2003: 15). The article ends with the idea that "we do not have a pertinent model that includes in particular an accurate representation of all the relevant institutions. It is difficult to estimate exactly the effects on employment of any very simple change in the structures of the labour market" (26).

Despite this very significant (but hardly unorthodox) stance on the part of an expert, who shows how little the positions of the OECD are justified and are more a matter of belief, they continue to be imposed in all the OECD's publications and converted into precepts that must be followed. This is the case in several respects. The OECD is one of the only organisations to have a detailed, comprehensive database on the principal elements, institutions, and policies of the labour market, social protection, and the major economic trends. This database is used to make precise comparisons and longitudinal studies. The OECD teams are empowered to send questionnaires to governments and publish national reports. They also construct their own variables and create their own indicators, which are then applied in economic circles (see also Salais, this volume). Thus they have all the means they need to create and show correlations, and even causalities, which subsequently are very difficult to criticise or reconstruct. Hence the OECD can perform ongoing benchmarking activities, which started well before those of the European Commission. They are designed to unremittingly compare the relative performances of the different member states and correlate them with certain selected variables. The publication of annual reports, in which the situation of each country is described precisely and compared with that of the other countries, is in itself an incentive for the other member states. Every year, the OECD has an official meeting with those responsible in each country for presenting a preliminary report on its employment situation. This is a very important occasion, for which the different national departments make very serious preparations—the report must not be unfavourable, the country disparaged or its policies criticised. This provides a further incentive to follow the OECD's precepts, either in reality or by camouflaging the policies actually pursued.

The Emergence of a New Argument: Segmentation in the Labour Market

Gradually—while evidence of a close link between the "rigidities of the labour market" and the unemployment rate was struggling to impose itself—another controversial argument emerged. It was born of the neoclassical economists' reinterpretation of the theory of segmentation of labour or of the dualism of the labour market. Piore and Doeringer first proposed it in 1971 by speaking of *insiders* and *outsiders*. Only those workers with a job would have a say in wage negotiations, to the detriment of outsiders who would take no part in them, namely, the jobless. A theoretical model of this nature explains the paradoxical coexistence of high rates of unemployment and high rates of wage increases (Lindbeck and Snower, 1988). During the 1990s, the OECD and various economic studies used this model to explain high rates of unemployment by attributing them to the downward rigidity of wages, due to insiders, buttressed by the unions, who defend only their own jobs and are hence responsible for the labour market's imbalance. The reluctance of those with jobs to agree to the changes necessary in terms of wages, working hours, the organisation of labour, and mobility was now given as the chief explanation of labour-market maladjustments, unwillingness to adapt, and thus high unemployment rates and insufficient job creation.

At the end of the 1990s and the beginning of the 2000s, the argument concerning segmentation intensified. It was argued that the rigidities caused by labour market institutions resulted in a double segmentation, not only between those with jobs and the jobless, but now also between employees on open-ended contracts and those on fixed-term contracts. The large number of fixed-term contract employees was due to reluctance on the part of companies to take on open-ended contract employees. Such reluctance was understandable, given the weighty obligations attaching to open-ended contracts. That was the argument developed by the OECD in early 1999 in its report *Employment Outlook 1999*. The primary argument raised among the "potential costs" of EPL was that of segmentation: "Even if EPL has the desired effects of improving the access of some workers to stable jobs that provide ample training opportunities, it may simultaneously disadvantage workers who fail to gain access to these sorts of jobs. In other words, EPL may enhance the dualism between protected workers (so-called "insiders") and jobseekers and temporary workers (so-called "outsiders") (. . .) to the extent that EPL reduces overall hiring in the economy" (68). The argument in favour of segmentation was used on a massive scale from this point on. From the moment it emerged that the effects on unemployment rates and the length of unemployment were not clearly in evidence, the argument shifted towards the fact that EPL was the cause of segmentation in the labour market and hence of confining a certain number of workers to insecure employment.

That was the central argument of Blanchard and Tirole (2003) in their report for the French Economic Analysis Council entitled *Protection de l'emploi et procédures de licenciement*. They emphasise at the outset that many economists and the majority of multidisciplinary bodies, from the OECD to the IMF, have "a position close to that of companies: the employment protection systems are ineffective" (8). As for employment protection pertaining to open-ended contracts, nothing changed: "these reforms have engendered a dual labour market, with major inequalities between employees and doubtful effects on effectiveness" (8). Their recommendations stemmed from this evaluation: Replace employment protection by a tax and return to a single employment contract system.

This would avoid what is now seen as the predominant threat, namely the threshold effect preventing employers from converting a fixed-term contract into an open-ended contract. *Employment Outlook 2004* drives this point home: EPL and, more importantly, "the differences in the rigour applied by EPL between permanent and temporary jobs might help to explain the increase in temporary employment among young and/or poorly qualified populations" (67). The objective was still to ensure protection under the conventional contract. This obsession reached its peak with the French studies of Cahuc and Kramarz, who in 2004 submitted to the French Ministry of the Economy and Finance a report entitled *De la précarité à la mobilité: vers la sécurité sociale professionnelle*. The report places at the centre of its rationale the question of segmentation and suggests a tax on redundancies to replace all the current regulations as well as the introduction of a single contract. In this way, insecurity would be replaced by security.

Advent of the Danish Model and the Link between the Analyses in Terms of Welfare State Systems and EPL

In 2005, a document by André Sapir (2005)—a member of the Bruegel Center who had published a controversial report two years previously—succeeded in bridging the arguments for growth based on innovation and creative destruction and those emphasising the braking effects of EPL. It also established a link between the relative performance of the different welfare state models, measured in terms of sustainability (rate of employment) and equity (rate of poverty), and labour-market institutions. This reinterpretation produced two extremely important results. Instead of making them both the object of criticism, as in the previous studies, employment protection and the generosity of unemployment benefits were now seen as opposed to one another. Thus inefficient countries prioritise employment protection, whereas efficient countries are notable for the generosity of unemployment benefits. Further, countries belonging to the continental and Mediterranean model are condemned. The text extends and refines the Esping-Andersen typology (Esping-Andersen, 1990) and is based in particular on the works of Boeri (2002). It distinguishes four types of social models in contemporary Europe, namely, the Nordic, the Anglo-Saxon, the continental, and the Mediterranean countries. Thus if the four groups of countries are classified according to the twofold criterion of efficacy and equity, the Mediterranean countries are seen as both inefficient and inequitable, and the continental countries as inefficient. They must therefore be radically reformed. Only two models are sustainable—the Nordic and the liberal. And only one, the Nordic model, is both sustainable and equitable.

Thus the Sapir report evinces a key element of the new strategy intended to remove existing labour market protections: the establishment of the Nordic model as a paragon of virtue. The efforts made in the last few years to promote the Danish model are bearing fruit. Denmark is now seen as the model to follow, so much so that the revised strategy of the OECD (2006) developed the idea that there existed two means of achieving the same ends, namely, the Nordic route and the liberal route.

> There have been two demonstrably successful broad policy packages in the recent past: several successful performers combine low levels of welfare benefits and limited taxation to fund these benefits, as well as light EPL. Collective agreements play a limited role in these countries. The result is high employment rates, achieved at a low cost for the public purse, but also relatively wide income disparities. Other successful countries, characterised by a strong emphasis on coordinated collective bargaining and social dialogue, offer generous welfare benefits but activate jobseekers through the provision of training opportunities and other active labour-market programmes. In these countries, employment regulations are more restrictive than is the case with other successful performers. These countries have achieved high employment and low income disparity, but at a high budgetary cost. (OECD, 2006: 19)

Clearly, it was the introduction of the Danish social model—a state which belongs to the Nordic model according to the Esping-Andersen typology and which has a very extended social protection system—that seduced researchers and public opinion (particularly those on the left). It thus made possible massive dissemination of the strategy of reform of the labour market under the banner of flexicurity.

In 2006, everything was ready. The Green Book on the labour market was published, which readily led to the development of the programme of deregulation to be implemented in Europe. The concept of flexicurity became the key concept in the European employment strategy. And 'flexicurity' provided a label for the structural reforms of the labour market that both the mainstream economists and the OECD had been advocating for twenty years.

It should be noted that a small network of economists from different countries who used the same methods and worked on similar topics was central to these developments: Pierre Cahuc, co-author of the report entitled *De la précarité à la mobilité*, was among the experts in the European Commission's Flexicurity Group, as was Tito Boeri, whose analyses inspired the above-mentioned Sapir report. These economists, who used the databases and indicators created by the OECD, were the disciples or admirers of Nickell and Blanchard. They incorporated institutions in their analyses. They also recognised the advantages of the Nordic—mainly Danish—model. It was seen as the ideal model, characterised by very low unemployment rates and very high employment rates. They thus replaced the old heterodox and multidisciplinary network formed around Maria Rodriguez. The approaches adopted by its members were exclusively economic and quantitative and their postulates were clear. The obstacles to total fluidity in the labour market and the product market accounted for the disadvantages of certain European countries. The rigidities of the labour market and the allowances in the products market had to be abolished. This network now included Spanish economists, who had recently come out in favour of a single contract as being the only solution to the over-segmentation of the Spanish labour market. They advocated this in the name of the "outsiders" unable to obtain secure employment.

The Use and Misuse of Flexicurity

It is of course highly significant that the two countries that gave birth to the term 'flexicurity' were the first countries to provide high levels of social protection and were committed to a social democratic regime, fully in one case and slightly less so in the other. The story has often been repeated (Wilthagen, 1998). It is also significant that the first occurrence of the term was in the Netherlands, which in the 1990s provided a model for the rest of Europe (the 'Dutch miracle'; Visser and Hemerijck, 1997), being the example of a successful reduction in the rate of unemployment. No less noteworthy is the fact that the reforms undertaken bore directly upon employment protection. The protection afforded by the open-ended contract was reduced and that afforded by temporary contracts increased, thus constituting a complete reversal.

The Danish Model, the Embodiment of Flexicurity

What makes Denmark interesting as a textbook case is that it is open to two radically different interpretations. That is, indeed, why it was able to symbolise, for different currents of thought, a desirable model. Denmark adheres to the Nordic regime, with a very high level of both social protection and compulsory deductions, as well as a very high level of unionisation and generous unemployment benefits. The fact that the Danish model embodies the whole concept of flexicurity was a decisive factor in convincing part of the European currents of opinion hostile to flexibility and to dissemination of the precepts of the OECD. Clearly, adherence to a welfare state system, which was recognised as one of the best in Europe in terms of guaranteed protection against social risks (and increased replacement rates), was also a decisive factor. At the beginning of the 2000s, the Danish model offered an alternative to those seeking a route that was radically different from the liberal model (and from the Third Way), which risked being undermined by the continental model's problems, particularly its very high rates of unemployment. This provides a clear explanation of why several authors succeeded in arousing interest in the Danish model as an alternative to the liberal model, especially in France (Barbier, 2005; Lefèbvre and Méda, 2006; Boyer, 2006).

At one time, Denmark succeeded in reconciling the opposites, or at least achieving a balance between different tensions. It is understandable that the Danish model should have found favour with both the classical economists and the international institutions. They applauded its very low employment protection, its great insistence on employment security—, even in the absence of an employment protection system—and the active policies followed to offset the generous unemployment benefits. The Danish model began to be promoted in France in 2004 by the economists Cahuc and Kramarz, who applauded the absence of employment protection and barriers in the product market and the fact that generous unemployment benefits were offset by highly developed active policies. Cahuc and Kramarz emphasised that high expenditure on the public employment service and good unemployment benefits give employees a better feeling of security than employment protection. Lastly, the Danish model was promoted by the government itself, also from 2005 onwards, to bring in reforms intended solely to deregulate the labour market.

The Implementation of Flexicurity in Europe:
The Imbalance between Flexibility and Security

Although flexibility and security should carry equal weight, the programmes designed to implement flexibility are far more developed and have been the subject of a much greater degree of monitoring, attention and operationalisation than those devoted to security. The countries in which there existed strict rules governing the termination of employment contracts have also seen the introduction of measures designed to facilitate redundancy or the recourse to temporary contracts. In the majority of European countries, the rules governing unemployment benefits have been re-examined, the overall job offer revised, and the social welfare systems reformed (Serrano and Magnusson, 2007; OECD, 2000, 2007). The ubiquitous activation programmes initially could include provisions promoting training. However, the importance attached to training was ultimately very much eclipsed by subsidised employment or systems designed to encourage job-seekers and persons receiving the minimum welfare payment to consider a wider range of employment opportunities.

In the Netherlands and the United Kingdom, the very objectives of activation changed during the 1990s, due to the plan to promote the employment, including voluntary work, of persons far removed from the labour market (van Berkel, 2007; Lindsay, 2007). A number of authors argued for the desirability of two or even three routes or models (Lödemel and Trickey, 2000; Barbier, 2007). Moreover, there were differences of degree and philosophy between the Scandinavian nations and other countries. Nevertheless, in the 1990s and even more so in the early 2000s, the Scandinavian nations also turned to policies of activation. They themselves became increasingly oriented towards penalties and determined to bring individuals with very poor job prospects more and more quickly into the labour market, even if it meant doing any sort of work in exchange for the benefits they were receiving (Abrahamson, 2001; Kvist, 2003; Larsen and Mailand, 2007).

We made a comparative study of job-seeker assistance models in the Netherlands, Sweden, and the United Kingdom (Georges, Grivel, and Méda, 2007). There were major differences found mainly in the level of benefits and in the respective proportion of expenditure on the labour market devoted to the various services, active and passive expenditures. Nevertheless, we found a convergence in means, managerial techniques, and philosophy, specifically relating to the three principles of activation, (according to Serrano and Magnusson [2007]) namely, individualisation, contractualisation, and the emphasis on employment. In all three countries, representative of Esping-Andersen's (1990) welfare state models, eligibility requirements and conditionality of unemployment benefits were strengthened and controls and penalties increased. Greater use was made of private employment agencies. Managerial techniques, according to which the unemployed and individuals receiving minimum welfare payment were managed by private agencies that were paid on the basis of performance, became widespread. Appraisal and experimental methods were developed. We consistently observed an increasing frequency of interviews as the period of unemployment lengthened; the implementation of individualised contracts and action plans, with the appropriate rights and obligations; the systematic use, or the temptation to use, profiling techniques; and a stricter definition of a 'reasonable job offer'.

It all suggests that the work-first policy had taken precedence everywhere over the policy of social investment, which, in addition to making labour markets more flexible, had emerged as a top priority, notably in Anthony Giddens' writings and in OECD documents from the 1990s. The fact is that even in countries in which it was highly developed, long-term training declined, notably as a result of studies pointing to its relative inefficacy (Denmark and Sweden). In Sweden, where they had formed the basis of the initial policies of activation, training programmes—which in the 1990s were far from being the most widely advocated employment policies for addressing the rapid increase in unemployment—suffered a sharp decline from 1999 onwards, in terms both of the number of beneficiaries and available funds. All of this was the natural concomitant of unemployment, but the process went a step further. By the end of this period, training programmes has failed to keep pace with rising unemployment (Georges, Grivel, and Méda, 2007).

Throughout this period, training programmes in general, as well as long-term training programmes aimed at the jobless, remained neglected. This was also the case of policies that should have been implemented, had there been the will to give serious attention to the four types of security subsumed in the concept of flexicurity (job security, employment security, income security, and combination security; cf. Wilthagen and Tros, 2004), such as policies designed to promote childcare systems. Even worse—although it was fairly obvious that the balance between flexibility and security should have been achieved within each of the four key aspects—some of the measures introduced included only the flexibility component.

THE NEED FOR ALTERNATIVES TO FLEXICURITY

Unfortunately, the drift towards instrumental approaches denounced by some authors (Salais, 2004) is not the main reason for the failure of the flexicurity policies in place in Europe since the end of the 1990s. What is in question is, in fact, all of flexicurity's theoretical presuppositions, which are the basis of the policies that the European Commission has adopted on a massive scale. The question asked by Salais in 2004 has grown increasingly urgent: "the theoretical models underpinning the policies of the ECB,[2] ECOFIN (Economic and Financial Affairs Council[3]), and, as its first mainstay, the EES[4], are they the most appropriate models for sustainably increasing the rate of employment?" (Salais, 2004). And if the crisis revealed flexicurity's lack of viability in the present economic climate, it also laid bare the long-term unsustainability of the postulates on which it is based.

The Crisis Revealed the Economically and Structurally Inappropriate Nature of Flexicurity

The crisis revealed not only the inadequate, but also the unsustainable bases of flexicurity and, to a greater extent, of the general paradigm to which it belongs, fostering the absence of any link between employees and their companies, the absence of any awareness of the part of the company of its obligations regarding the future of its employees, the fragility of the social protection provided, and so on. The concept of flexicurity had laid emphasis on mobility rather than on stability; employability and security based on transitions rather than on the job or employment; the possibility of leaving a particular job; the emphasis on quickly returning to employment rather than the acquisition of new skills through long-term training and requalification programmes. In its practical application, if not in its concept, flexicurity encouraged the absence of commitment, instability, and the breakdown of the link between stability and employment. Now, the countries that best withstood the crisis were, on the contrary, those that offered a high degree of social protection and which had established strong and not easily broken relations between companies and employees. Everything happened as if the countries that had best withstood the crisis and which in one way or another had obliged companies to keep the majority of their workers (which was called retention of labour) were those that had least succumbed to the sirens of disassociation.

The Effect of the Crisis

As numerous observers have found, not all the economies of the European countries were affected by the crisis in the same way. At the beginning of the crisis, economies with the highest export activity (Germany, Finland, Hungary, Denmark, Sweden) or with highly exposed sectors (building in Spain and the UK's financial sector) were more greatly affected. Others, such as France, Belgium, or Austria, which depend less on exports and enjoy the benefit of social stabilisers that sustain demand (Husson, 2009), were less impacted. And the extent of the shocks to employment also varied (OECD, 2010; Husson, 2009; Erhel, 2010). So on the one hand there were countries in which the weakness or the fragility of the relationships between employers and employees would appear to have engendered an overreaction where employment was concerned, in other words the immediate breaking of the links binding employees to their companies. On the other hand, some European countries retained their workforce, being unwilling or unable to dismiss their employees, i.e., break the wage link, too quickly.

One might perhaps go so far as to argue that countries placing the greatest emphasis on flexicurity were also those where the reaction of employment to the crisis was strongest. They were the ones that had reformed their labour markets by reducing employment protection, encouraging part-time work, giving preference to temporary employment over any other formula, and, at the end of the day, favouring the weakest possible link between employees and companies. At the same time, they had advocated shorter unemployment benefits and the replacement of requalification and long-term training by a 'work-first' policy. This is a logical enough conclusion, the effect corresponding to the objectives sought. Moreover, is this not what the OECD recognised in its *Employment Outlook 2009*: "there does not appear to be any strong reason to expect that recent structural reforms mean that OECD labour markets are now substantially less sensitive to severe economic downturns than was the case in the past" (39)? Perhaps we could rephrase this convoluted sentence by saying that everything supports the claim that structural reforms made labour markets more vulnerable! But this absence of a strong link, this total fluidity, and this endorsement of the absence of any link—was this not precisely what was sought?

The crisis only revealed and brought out into the open what was in any case suspected. The moves seeking to weaken the links between employees and their companies led to a foregone conclusion, namely, the lone individual, denied protection and left to his own resources in the event of a crisis. In labour markets comprising an ever-increasing number of underemployed persons with little or no protection who are often caught up in a mesh of subcontractors, it is hardly surprising that the first people to be laid off were those doing temporary work or on fixed-term contracts. Moreover, reduced unemployment benefits soon caused problems. The OECD (2009) itself pointed out the effects of the policies that it had long been advocating concerning the three areas referred to above, namely, the extension of temporary employment, as well as the risks inherent in short contracts, and reduced social protection coverage. "While employment rates began this recession at a high level, trend increases in the shares of temporary jobs in many countries suggest potential vulnerabilities for the workers in these jobs, since it appears to be particularly easy for employers not to renew their contract when business conditions deteriorate" (OECD, 2009: 40).

In fact, the various effects of the crisis clearly revealed the unsustainable nature of certain methods of development, such as those practiced in Spain, based on growth which relied too heavily on a relatively under-qualified labour force and insecure jobs (also Prieto, this volume). As Catherine Vincent (2009: 109) wrote, "the performance of the Spanish labour market has been enhanced by first legislative and then contractual structural reforms designed to increase its flexibility. These reforms pursued three classic policies designed to make it easier to enter and leave the labour market: relaxation of the rules governing the use and renewal of temporary contracts; increased geographic and occupational mobility; and lower redundancy costs". The crisis further revealed the unsustainable, short-term-oriented nature of solutions intended to facilitate redundancy and 'work-first' activation policies. For whereas such policies may have 'positive' short-term effects (getting people back to work by means of every possible incentive and offering 'bits of work'), they can neither provide training leading to increased qualifications for the population as a whole nor establish stable links between employees and companies by encouraging companies to provide regular skills training, rather than dismissing their employees and relying on the labour market for their training and return to employment.

Even more surprisingly, when reviewing the employment measures introduced in response to the crisis, the OECD went so far as to approve the very measures it had been criticising for the previous twenty years, namely, measures whose common purpose was to prevent at any cost severance of the wage link. It in fact went on to advocate measures designed to safeguard employees' jobs by any means available. This was the very thing that had been so very much challenged throughout the same twenty years. In the overview it gives of the measures introduced by member states in response to the crisis, the OECD cites those intended to reinforce the guarantee of resources for persons made redundant, training programmes and subsidies for shorter working hours. All these measures were encouraged, as were all the formulas whereby employment contracts would not be terminated and employees would keep their jobs. Three measures found particular favour with the OECD, namely, shorter working hours enabling employees to keep their jobs; measures that aim at maintaining links between workers and the labour market; and employee training. As Erhel notes (2010), several previously contested policies returned to favour as a result.

Re-Evaluation of the OECD's Employment Strategy in 2009: The End of Flexicurity

The OECD policy is thus radically opposed to the recommendations that economists had been making for the previous twenty years. Two fold conclusion may readily be drawn both from the *Employment Outlook 2009* and, more importantly, from the crisis itself, which proved very revealing. First, the measures introduced to make labour markets more flexible made them particularly responsive to the crisis. And the crisis revealed the short-term, unsustainable nature of labour markets based on the absence of stable relations between companies and employees. Second, it is far from clear why measures that were beneficial in a time of crisis should not be equally beneficial at other times, as unemployment rates continued to be high. This meant a meaningful re-evaluation of the OECD's employment strategy. Its programme now made security the top priority, as a result of which it emphasised the strengthening of the wage link, making companies more mindful of their obligation to their employees, the creation of public jobs, and the sharing of work and training.

In retrospect—and in the light of the lessons to be drawn from the crisis—it would seem, in fact, that flexicurity was appropriate to a highly stressed labour market, with widespread labour shortages and a considerable ability on the part of the public services to train and accommodate employee mobility. This was the case of Denmark, since the end of the 1990s and since the exportation of the Danish model. But the European labour markets are far from this situation. Increased flexibility does not seem appropriate, and neither does the greatly diminished conception of security, seen as the ability to change jobs without difficulty. What is needed is a different conception of security.

We have seen above, in the theoretical models underpinning flexicurity, the decisive preponderance of the correlations shown since the early 1990s by a number of economists. They have been adopted by the OECD and transformed into formulas and precepts. Of these correlations, those which relate the rigidity of employment protection to the unsatisfactory performance of some countries in the matter of employment, were the most highly developed and the most widely applied. From the outset the EPL indicator took into account only the texts, and not how they were applied. Moreover, it regarded national practices, although dissimilar by definition, as equivalent. Furthermore, this approach is inadequate in many other ways, and mainly because it cannot take full account of all the variables that might explain variations in employment and unemployment. It also seeks to show correlations between the variations of only a limited number of variables. In an article entitled "Are Protective Labour Market Institutions Really at the Root of Unemployment? A Critical Perspective on the Statistical Evidence" (2006), Howell et al. refute the OECD's results. Focusing on the four countries usually considered—France, Germany, Spain, and Italy—the article shows that neither the institutions representative of EPL nor their policies can explain the success of some countries and the failure of others. None of the editions of the latest *Employment Outlook* (OECD, 2007, 2008, 2009) make any reference to this study. Thus it is essential that we abandon this principle underpinning the EES and the liberal policies pursued since the mid-1980s and replace it with an alternative approach "which does not make social security a cost for the economy" (Salais, 2004: 323).

Work and Product Quality as an Alternative to Flexicurity

The paradigm developed in the 1980s was based on the dominance of economic factors over social factors, or at least on the idea that the social and economic factors were no longer compatible. On the contrary, social factors were considered to represent a handicap, a cost, and an obstacle to economic development. It was in the name of economic development, and hence of economic efficiency and competitiveness, that restrictions were placed on social protection and on the rights of employees. Labour laws, rules, and social protection systems were now seen as rigidities, the new standard-bearer being the entrepreneur, the risk taker. The argument for the necessary adaptation of skills, companies, and employees, lower social security contributions, deregulation, and lower labour costs was based entirely on the absolute primacy given to economic development, corporate competitiveness, and the achievement of ratios prioritising short-term results. Economic development was becoming the prerequisite for social development. This new consensus, known sometimes as the Washington Consensus, replaced what was called the Philadelphia Consensus.

Social Rights Subordinated to Economic Development

In the Washington Consensus, labour was regarded as a pure disutility, as simply another commodity whose quantities and prices should be adaptable. What matters is, at the macro-economic level, the growth rate and, at the micro-economic level, corporate competitiveness, which is the guarantee of corporate performance. In a context of this nature, labour is reduced to a single dimension, namely, its instrumental dimension—the fact of being a means towards something else. Profit and the GDP are what count. The other dimensions of labour are simply not considered. We refer here to labour as the "essence of human beings" (Méda, 1995), namely, human activity enabling people to transform both themselves and the world in which they find themselves, and hence to express themselves. We also refer to labour as pivotal to the system of distribution of rights, protection, and income, in a word to the wage-earning society. It is possible for economic development and maximisation of GDP to enable the other two dimensions of labour to be promoted. However in certain circumstances—notably when there is sharp competition between the different countries and their respective systems—labour and workers can suffer. The ills of labour and workers and the reduction of the number of workers become secondary to the need for greater economic competitiveness, corporate survival, and increased growth, to which all else became subordinated.

Were the fifty years which separate us from the Philadelphia Declaration simply a parenthesis? Can social justice be the principle, the cornerstone of a new paradigm as Supiot proposes? (Supiot, 2010). This seems further removed from the primacy accorded to economic development than a number of recent proposals, centred around the idea of social investment and which, undoubtedly, correct the glaring inadequacies of the Washington Consensus, but continue to defend economic efficiency as the guiding principle. Some authors (Vielle, Pochet, and Cassiers, 2005; Méda, 2009) have attempted to demonstrate that the idea of social investment was a distant heir of the "Active Social State" and the "Active Society" advocated by the OECD. In this paradigm, the economic factor remains predominant and economic efficiency, as measured by the growth rate, remains the main criterion by which social development is judged.

As Esping-Andersen—the chief representative of this current of thought—argues, it is important to reconcile economic efficiency and social protection. For this reason, we must invest in early childhood, modernise social protection systems, and increase employment rates. A solution of this nature continues to subordinate the development of social rights and the quality of work and employment to economic development, economic growth, and achievement of high growth rates. This sort of paradigm—even though Esping-Andersen et al. (2002) state at certain moments that a new type of accounting is necessary—fails to take account both of the criticisms highlighting the limits of the gross domestic product as a central indicator of wealth and performance, and also of the criticisms regarding a type of development in which the damage inflicted on the social and natural heritage is not included. It does not escape from the primacy accorded to economic growth. Social policy should take the form of investment in the quality of human capital, which will enable economic development to be still more effective (Esping-Andersen, 2007). Social rights and social justice are subordinated to economic development. They are not suppressed, but they only remain in existence on condition of improving and increasing growth.

A number of authors (for instance, Salais in this volume) draw attention to the risk inherent in the subordination of social factors to economic ones. For several years already, they have been proposing an alternative approach, in which "social protection is no longer a cost to the economy". It is an approach based on the "politics of capabilities" in the sense ascribed to it by Sen (Salais, 2004; Salais and Villeneuve, 2004; Supiot, 2010). As Salais and Villeneuve wrote, "the domain of capabilities gives priority to the aim of the amelioration of living and working conditions, enabling their improvement *pari passu*, adequate social protection and social dialogue" (26). Whilst subscribing to this view, I should like to develop a few points. First, does not the concept of capability developed by Sen remain essentially highly individualistic—indeed, too individualistic? Is it possible to reconstruct a common world giving priority both to individual liberty and to collective wealth, with individual freedom being the main component, undoubtedly broader and more concrete than a rationality reduced to the maximisation of classic utility functions, but remaining none the less individualistic?

Salais (2004), Salais and Villeneuve (2004), and several of the contributions found in *Europe and the Politics of Capabilities*, particularly those of Deakin, reply to this objection by saying that the capabilities approach "aims at giving individuals effective means of self-development. It recognises that these means should be conceived and provided on a collective basis" (Salais and Villeneuve, 2004: 23), at the same time as replacing the concept of capability by that of ability. It seems to me that, to be fully effective, the concept of ability must therefore be accompanied by three other elements, namely, the existence of public services guaranteeing the full development of these abilities, the reality of collective wealth, and a procedure of public deliberation. Public deliberation should be the principal means by which a community (local, national, or European) decides what is important to it and what is the common and collective wealth to which it is attached (see also Salais's essay in this volume).

However, two theoretical problems remain. First, how is one to show that the principle of social justice underpinning the advocacy of a capabilities approach should have equal value with the principle of economic efficiency (a conflict of legitimacy)? And second, how is the fundamental nature of these two principles to be established? Is there not another? How is one to 'deduce' the principles that we would like to adopt, at the European level in particular, in order rationally to justify actions which could be considered as normatively good? Or rationally create a development model, which does not come up against the inadequacies revealed when the principle of economic efficiency predominates over every other principle?

What Bases for a New Development Model?

In order to establish these principles we need to identify more effectively what is important to us as a society and for our survival. It is clear that they must be sustainable over the long term (Méda, 1999; 2013). What factors are likely to impede this development, cause the fabric of society to disappear or deteriorate? Certainly, a major factor is balkanisation—that is, the division of society into its primary constituents, groups, or individuals, which often occurs as the result of civil wars and also doubtlessly due to excessive inequality. But also the deterioration of our environment and the natural heritage that we have inherited is a clear and unanimously admitted risk. Those are the two chief dangers that threaten our societies today, the cohesion of these societies being recognised as an asset, a value. We may certainly thus infer that what matters to us is at least the preservation and, better still, the improvement of the common heritage that is handed down from generation to generation. We need to make an inventory enabling us to assess developments, whether of a positive or negative nature. This heritage, its quality and evolution over time can be approached by means of certain variables that can constitute new indicators of wealth, well-being, sustainability, and development.

Then it becomes clear that progress can no longer be equated to the growth rate of the GDP and that we are forced to focus on the developments of much broader indicators (Méda, 1999, 2013; Gadrey and Jany-Catrice, 2005; Sen, Stiglitz, and Fitoussi, 2009). Thus two principles could provide the basis for a new sort of development, namely, social justice and preservation of the natural heritage. Their developments would be monitored by an indicator with two components: a natural component and a social component. The former would be, so to speak, an ecological footprint or composite indicator monitoring biodiversity, air and water quality, and renewable and non-renewable resources. The latter would be a social health indicator monitoring inequalities, life expectancy, state of health, the manner in which social risks are covered, and work-related issues. Accordingly, developments in the workplace could, along with economic security, constitute one of the chief components of the social health indicator. The adoption of these indicators involves a veritable revolution, i.e., nothing less than abolishing the primacy of economic development, or only regarding as enrichment or progress economic development cleansed of its environmental and social impact.

Each of these principles—social justice and preservation of the natural heritage—must therefore be broken down into elements whose variations can be monitored. We need to be able to replace our purely quantitative and exclusively economic objectives by much broader and also qualitative objectives. An example is the reduction of inequalities or the progress in human rights, which cannot be monitored without adequate indicators. Thus it is not so much the indicators *per se* that are in question, but the areas they evaluate and the manner in which they are defined. It is important that they should result from meaningful democratic debate, which should be organised both in society as a whole and, particularly in relation to work, in companies. Thus awareness of the huge expectations today in the matter of work (Davoine and Méda, 2008; Méda, 2010; Méda et Vendramin, 2013) could be translated into concrete objectives, as could the fight against the current ills of labour.

The expectations placed on labour are immense, but they are partially disappointed. If we want to place at the centre of the development of our societies the opportunity for self-development in work for the greatest possible number of people, we have to place work, which is man's essence, at the heart of our development. This presupposes, if not the transcendence of capitalism, at least the abandonment of management norms and imperatives, which saddle work with requirements that make it a source of ills. Putting work at the centre of development presupposes changing the reference indicator not only at the macro-social level, but also at the corporate level itself. In recent years, several concepts have attempted to promote this vision and operationalise the idea of dignified and fulfilling work—successively, the concept of decent work, of quality of employment, and then of sustainable work.

The concept of decent work made its first appearance in the report of the Director-General to the eighty-seventh session of the International Labour Conference. The concept comprises four dimensions: employment, social protection, workers' rights, and social dialogue. A number of decent work indices have been created, worked out, and tested (International Labour Review, 2003). Indicators are available, various options possible, and clear lessons to be drawn accordingly. In-depth theoretical discussions on the various solutions to be adopted to create the indicators have thus been pursued (Bonnet, Figueiredo, and Standing, 2003). In 2008, the International Labour Organisation unanimously adopted its Declaration on Social Justice for a Fair Globalisation and institutionalised the decent work agenda as being an "essential policy and operational concept enabling the ILO to achieve its constitutional objectives". But nothing has happened since. Everything carries on as if the principles set forth in the declaration remained a dead letter and decent work remained an unattainable goal. Two problems arise in this regard, namely, the articulation of the two attempts to formalise decent work and quality of employment (Prieto and Serrano, 2011) and the fact that the attempt to place decent work at the heart of the European Employment Strategy has remained a dead letter.

"The report by Win Kok in 2004 (entitled Jobs, jobs, jobs) which deals with employment and labour market policies, focuses on the quantitative aspects of employment (. . .) without consideration of their quality" (Davoine and Erhel, 2006: 3). As with decent work, definitions do exist, indicators have been created, and composite indicators and categories can be established. And as with decent work, again, the employment quality objective has remained a dead letter. It has not been converted, for lack of will, into a concrete aim, into a norm which non-compliance could have been sanctioned, if not by penalties, then at least by the regular publication in the media of the results.

CONCLUSIONS

Two ways exist today for getting Europe out of the crisis. Either we take the path traditionally advocated by the OECD, namely, low wages and reduction of employment protection, but this is likely to lead towards the impoverishment of part of Europe's population and a polarisation of the labour market and society. Or we can ensure that Europe becomes a zone of high-level qualifications, as well as high-quality jobs, work, and products, and enable workers and citizens to access high standards of living. This requires a strong political and social Europe and respect for joint social and environmental standards. *Flexicurity* has turned out to be another word for the former path—its implementation has gone along with dismantling labour law and security in Europe. That is why it is no longer an appropriate solution and must give way to the notion of decent work, which is an integral part of the new model of development that Europe needs. We now have the theoretical framework and necessary indicators for implementing decent work and a strategy based on the quality of employment. The only thing missing is political will.

NOTES

1. Translation from the French version by the author. Pagination from the French version.
2. ECB: European Central Bank.
3. ECOFIN is composed of economics and finance ministers of the member states.
4. EES: European Employment Strategy.

BIBLIOGRAPHY

Abrahamson, Peter. "L'activation des politiques sociales scandinaves: le cas du Danemark." In *La protection sociale en Europe*, edited by Christine Daniel and Bruno Palier, 123–140. Paris: La Documentation Française, 2001.

Barbier, Jean-Claude. "Apprendre vraiment du Danemark?" *Connaissance de l'emploi*, 1–4Centre d'études de l'emploi 18 (2005).

Barbier, Jean-Claude. "The French Activation Strategy in a Comparative Perspective." In *Reshaping Welfare States and Activation Regimes in Europe, Work and Society Vol. 54*, edited by Amparo Serrano Pascual and Lars Magnusson, 145–172. Brussels: Peter Lang, 2007.

Blanchard, Olivier and Jean Tirole. *Protection de l'emploi et procédures de licenciement*. Paris: Rapport du Conseil d'analyse économique, 2003.

Boeri, Tito. "Let Social Policy Models Compete and Europe Will Win." Conference hosted by the John F. Kennedy School of government in celebration of the Schumpeter program at Harvard University, 11–12 April 2002.

Bonnet, Florence, Figueiredo, José B. and Standing, Guy. "A family of decent work indexes" in *International Labour Review*, 142 (2003):, 213–238.

Boyer, Robert. *La flexicurité danoise. Quels enseignements pour la France?* Paris: Cepremap, 2006.

Cahuc, Pierre and Francis Kramarz. *De la précarité à la mobilité: vers la sécurité sociale professionnelle*. Paris: La Documentation française, 2004.

Davoine, Lucie and Erhel, Christine, « Monitoring employment quality in Europe », Communication au Colloque Etat et régulation sociale, 11, 12, 13 septembre 2006, 21p. http://matisse.univ-paris1.fr/colloque-es/pdf/articles/davoine_erhel.pdf

Davoine, Lucie and Dominique Méda. *Importance and Meaning of Work in Europe: A French Singularity? Document de travail 96–2*. Paris: Centre d'Etudes de l'Emploi, 2008.

Erhel, Christine. Les politiques de l'emploi en Europe: quelles réactions face à la crise? *Document de travail du CEE 129*. Paris, 2010.

Esping-Andersen, Gösta. *The Three Worlds of Welfare Capitalism*. Cambridge: Polity Press, 1990.

Esping-Andersen, Gösta. *Trois leçons sur l'Etat-Providence, La République des idées*. Paris: Le Seuil, 2007.

Esping-Andersen, Gösta with Duncan Gallie, Anton Hemerijck, and John Myles. *Why We Need a New Welfare State*. Oxford: Oxford University Press, 2002.

European Commission. "Green Paper on 'Modernising Labour Law to Meet the Challenge of the 21st Century." 22.11.2006. COM, 2006.

European Commission. *Towards Common Principles of Flexicurity: More and Better Jobs through Flexibility and Security*. COM (2007) 359, 2007.

European Expert Group on Flexicurity. "Flexicurity Pathways Turning Hurdles into Stepping Stones." Report by the European Expert Group on Flexicurity, European Commission, June 2007.

Gadrey, Jean and Florence Jany-Catrice. *Les nouveaux indicateurs de richesse*. Paris: La Découverte, 2005.

Georges, Nathalie, Nicolas Grivel, and Dominique Méda. *Les prestations et services d'accompagnement des demandeurs d'emploi: comparaisons internationales. Document de travail du CEE 41*. Paris: Centre d'études de l'emploi, 2007.

Howell, David R., Dean Baker, Andrew Glyn, and John Schmitt. "Are Protective Labor Market Institutions Really at the Root of Unemployment ? A Critical Perspective on the Statistical Evidence." CEPR Reports and Issue Briefs 2006–14, Center for Economic and Policy Research (CEPR), 2006.

Husson, Michel. "Le choc de la crise, le poids du chômage." In *Chronique internationale 121*, 17–39. Paris: Institut de recherches économiques et sociales, IRES, 2009.

International Labour Review. Special Issue: Measuring Decent Work 142/ 2, 2003.

Jobert, Bruno, ed. *Le tournant néo-libéral en Europe. Idées et recettes dans les pratiques gouvernementales.* Paris: L'Harmattan, 2004.

Keune, Marten and Maria Jepsen. *Not Balanced and Hardly New: The European Commission's Quest for Flexicurity.* WP. Brussels: ETUI, 2007.

Kvist, Jon. "Scandinavian Activation Strategies in the 1990s: Recasting Social Citizenship and the Scandinavian Welfare Model." *Revue Française des Affaires Sociales*, 4 (2003): 223–249

Larsen, Flemming and Mikkel Mailand. "Danish Activation Policy: The Role of the Normative Foundation, the Institutional Set-Up and Other Drivers." In *Reshaping Welfare States and Activation Regimes in Europe*, edited by Amparo Serrano Pascual and Lars Magnuson, 99–127. Brussels: Peter Lang, 2007.

Lefèbvre, Alain and Dominique Méda. *Faut-il brûler le modèle social français?* Paris: Le Seuil, 2006.

Lindbeck, Assar and Dennis J. Snower. *The Insider–Outsider Theory of Employment and Unemployment.* Cambridge: MIT Press, 1988.

Lindsay, Colin. "The United Kingdom's 'Work First' Welfare State and Activation Regimes in Europe." In *Reshaping Welfare States and Activation Regimes in Europe*, edited by Amparo Serrano Pascual and Lars Magnusson, 35–70. Brussels: Peter Lang, 2007.

Lindsay, Colin and Mikkel Mailland. "Different Routes, Common Directions? Activation Policies for Young People in Denmark and the UK." *International Journal of Social Welfare* 13/3 (2004): 195–207.

Lödemel, Ivar and Heather Trickey, eds. *An Offer You Can't Refuse: Workfare in an International Perspective.* Bristol: Policy Press, 2000.

Malinvaud, Edmond. "Réformes structurelles du marché du travail et politiques macroéconomiques." *Revue de l'OFCE* 3(86) (2003): 7–30.

Méda, Dominique. "Flexicurité: quel équilibre entre flexibilité et sécurité ?" *Droit social* 7/8 (2009): 763–776.

Méda, Dominique. *Le Travail, une valeur en voie de disparition.* Paris: Aubier, 1995.

Méda, Dominique. *Qu'est-ce que la richesse?* Paris: Aubier, 1999.

Méda, Dominique. *Travail: la Révolution nécessaire.* Paris: Les Editions de l'Aube, 2010.

Méda, Dominique. *La mystique de la croissance. Comment s'en libérer.* Paris : Flammarion, 2013

Méda, Dominique and Vendramin, Patricia. *Réinventer le travail.* Paris: PUF, 2013

OECD. *Boosting Jobs and Incomes: Policy Lessons from Re-Assessing the OECD Jobs Strategy, OECD Employment Outlook.* Paris: OECD, 2006.

OECD. *Employment Outlook 1989.* Paris: OECD, 1989.

OECD. *Employment Outlook 1999.* Paris: OECD, 1999.

OECD. *Employment Outlook 2004.* Paris: OECD, 2004.

OECD. *Employment Outlook 2007.* Paris: OECD, 2007.

OECD. *Employment Outlook 2009.* Paris: OECD, 2009.

OECD. *Employment Outlook 2010.* Paris: OECD, 2010.

OECD. *Labour Market Policies and the Public Employment Service.* Paris: OECD, 2000.

OECD. *Le marché du travail: quelles politiques pour les années 90?* Paris: OECD, 1990.

OECD. *The OECD Jobs Study.* Paris: OECD, 1994.

Piore, Michael and Peter Doeringer. *Internal Labour Markets and Manpower Adjustment.* New York: DC Heath and Company, 1971.

Prieto, Carlos and Amparo Serrano Pascual. "Les chemins de la transition." In *Qualité de l'emploi ou travail décent: les enjeux d'une controverse,* edited by Dominique Méda, David Flacher, and Thomas Coutrot, 133–145. Paris: Editions Utopia, 2011.

Salais, Robert. "La politique des indicateurs. Du taux de chômage au taux d'emploi dans la stratégie européenne pour l'emploi." In *Les sciences sociales à l'épreuve de l'action. Le savant, le politique et l'Europe,* edited by Bénédicte Zimmermann, 287–233. Paris: Editions de la MSH, 2004.

Salais, Robert and Robert Villeneuve, eds. *Europe and the Politics of Capabilities.* Cambridge: Cambridge University Press, 2004.

Sapir, André. "Globalisation and the Reform of European Social Models." Background document for the presentation at ECOFIN Informal, Meeting in Manchester, 9 September 2005.

Sen, Amartya, Joseph E. Stiglitz, and Jean-Paul Fitoussi. *Report by the Commission on the Measurement of Economic Performance and Social Progress.* 2009 http://www.stiglitz-sen-fitoussi.fr/documents/rapport_francais.pdf .

Serrano, Amparo. "Batailles d'idées dans l'espace européen. La lutte contre le chômage et le combat pour le nommer." *Revue de l'Ires* 60 (2009): 47–65.

Serrano, Amparo. "Conclusion: Towards Convergence of European Activation Policies?" In *Are Activation Policies Converging in Europe? The European Strategy for Young People,* edited by Amparo Serrano Pascual, 497–518. Brussels: ETUI, 2004.

Serrano, Amparo and Lars Magnusson, eds. *Reshaping Welfare States and Activation Regimes in Europe. Work and Society Vol. 54,* 47–64. Brussels: Peter Lang, 2007.

Siebert, Horst. "Labor Market Rigidities: At the Root of Unemployment in Europe." *Journal of Economic Perspectives* 11(3) (1997): 37–54.

Supiot, Alain. *L'esprit de Philadelphie.* Paris: Le Seuil, 2010.

van Berkel, Rik. "Activation in the Netherlands: the Gradual Introduction of a Paradigm Shift." In *Reshaping Welfare States and Activation Regimes in Europe, Work and Society,* edited by Amparo Serrano Pascual and Lars Magnusson, 71–98. Brussels: Peter Lang, 2007.

Vielle, Pascale, Philippe Pochet, and Isabelle Cassiers, eds. *L'Etat-social actif.* Brussels: Peter Lang, 2005.

Vincent, Catherine. "Espagne. Le modèle de dialogue social fragilisé par la crise." *Chronique internationale de l'Ires* 121, (2009):107–116.

Visser, Jelle and Anton Hemerijck. *A Dutch Miracle.* Amsterdam: Amsterdam University Press, 1997.

Wilthagen, Ton. *Flexicurity: A New Paradigm for Labour Market Policy Reform?* WZB Discussion paper FS I 98–202, Berlin, 1998.

Wilthagen, Ton. *Mapping Out Flexicurity Pathways in the European Union.* WPS, 1 March, Tilburg University, 22, 2008.

Wilthagen, Ton and Frank Tros. "The Concept of Flexicurity: A New Approach to Regulating Employment and Labour Markets." *Transfer* 10(2) (2004): 166–186.

Contributors

Colin Crouch is professor emeritus of the University of Warwick and external scientific member of the Max Planck Institute for the Study of Societies at Cologne. He is a Fellow and vice president for social sciences of the British Academy, and a Fellow of the Academy of Social Sciences. He has published within the fields of comparative European sociology and industrial relations, economic sociology, and contemporary issues in British and European politics. His most recent books include: *Social Change in Western Europe* (1999); *Post-Democracy* (2004); *Capitalist Diversity and Change* (2005); and *The Strange Non-Death of Neoliberalism* (2011). The German translation of this last book was awarded the annual prize of the Friedrich Ebert Stiftung for *Das politische Buch*.

Hartley Dean is professor of social policy at the London School of Economics and Political Science. His twenty-five years as a social policy academic was preceded by a twelve-year career as a welfare rights worker in one of London's most deprived multicultural neighbourhoods. His principal research interests stem from concerns with poverty, social justice, and welfare rights. Among his more recently published books are *Welfare Rights and Social Policy* (Prentice Hall, 2002); *Social Policy* (Polity, 2006 & 2012); and *Understanding Human Need* (Policy Press, 2010). He was previously editor of the *Journal of Social Policy*.

Maria Jepsen holds a PhD in economics from the Free University of Brussels (ULB). She is currently the director of the research department at the European Trade Union Institute (ETUI) and chargée de cours (associate professor) in labour economics at the ULB. Before joining the ETUI as a senior researcher in 2001, she worked as assistant professor and research fellow at the ULB from 1996 to 2001. Her main research interest is in gender studies and comparative studies of the impact of welfare states on labour supply, wages, and working conditions. In recent years she has also focused on the construction and development of social policy on the European level and how this interacts with the national settings.

Maarten Keune is professor of social security and labour relations at the University of Amsterdam and co-director of the Amsterdam Institute of Advanced Labour Studies (AIAS). Previously he worked at the European Trade Union Institute and at the European University Institute, where he did his PhD. He has published widely on industrial relations, employment policies, and the welfare state. Recent publications include *Economy and Society in Europe: A Relationship in Crisis* (ed. with Luigi Burroni and Guglielmo Meardi, Edward Elgar Publishing, 2012); and *After the Euro and Enlargement: Social Pacts in the EU* (ed. with Philippe Pochet and David Natalie, ETUI, 2010).

Dominique Méda is a former student of the École Normale Supérieure and the École Nationale d'Administration, an *agrégée* of philosophy, and accredited to direct research in sociology. She is currently a professor of sociology at the University of Paris-Dauphine. She is the author of *Le Travail. Une valeur en voie de disparition?*; *Qu'est-ce que la richesse?*; and *Le Temps des femmes. Pour un nouveau partage des rôles*. She also participated in several volumes on social policy.

Carlos Prieto is professor emeritus in sociology at the Complutense University of Madrid. director of the research group Empleo, Género y Cohesión Social (EGECO). Director of the review *Cuadernos de Relaciones Laborales*. Member of the management group of the international research group Marché et Genre (MAGE). Some of his last publications: *Trabajo, género y tiempo social* (Complutense, 2007); *Nuevos tiempos de trabajo: entre la flexibilidad competitiva de las empresas y las relaciones de género* (CIS, 2008); *La calidad del empleo en España* (Ministerio de Trabajo e Inmigración, 2009); "La flexicurité dans le cadre des métamorphoses de la norme sociale du travail: le cas espagnol," *Les politiques sociales* 3–4 (2012).

Robert Salais is professor of economics, Ecole Normale Superieur de Cachan. His main research areas include: historical economics, public intervention, employment, social fairness, and institutions. A selection of his recent publications are: *Le viol d'Europe. Enquête sur la disparition d'une idée* (Presses Universitaires de France, 2013); with Rogowski Ralf and Noel Whiteside, *Transforming European Employment Policy: Labour Market Transitions and the Promotion of Capability* (Edward Elgar, 2012); with E. Chatel and T. Kirat, *L'action publique et ses dispositifs. Institutions, économie, politiques* (L'Harmattan, 2005); with R. Villeneuve, *Europe and the Politics of Capabilities* (Cambridge University Press, 2005); with D.G. Mayes and J. Berghman, *Social Exclusion and European Policy* (Edward Elgar, 2001).

Günther Schmid is professor emeritus of political economy at the Free University Berlin and director emeritus at the Social Science Research

Centre Berlin (WZB). His expertise, focused on labour-market policy and employment, is reflected in many books and articles, among others in the *International Handbook for Labour Market Policy and Evaluation* (1996) and the monograph *Full Employment in Europe—Managing Labour Market Transitions and Risks* (2008). He has also been a member of committees at the OECD or EU level and the committee under Chancellor Gerhard Schröder preparing the German labour-market reforms. He holds degrees in political science and economics, and he was awarded Dr. h.c. at the Universities Aalborg (Denmark) and Linnaeus (Sweden).

Amparo Serrano is senior lecturer at the Faculty of Political Sciences and Sociology at the Complutense University of Madrid. Main topics of research: comparative social policy, activation policies and flexicurity, work and subjectivity, and the European social model. Some of her last publications: with P. Koistinen and L. Mosésdottir, *Emerging Systems of Work and Welfare* (Peter Lang, 2009); with L. Magnusson, *Reshaping Welfare States and Activation Regimes* (Peter Lang, 2007); with M. Jepsen, *Unwrapping the European Social Model* (Policy Press, 2006).

Bénédicte Zimmermann is professor of sociology at the Ecole des Hautes Etudes en Sciences Sociales in Paris. Her main research interests are the changing role of work in the constitution of European societies and their social organisation, with a comparative focus on France and Germany. She is the author of *La constitution du chômage en Allemagne* (MSH, 2001) and *Ce que travailler veut dire. Une sociologie des capacités et des parcours professionnels* (Economica, 2011). Together with Jean de Munck, she edited *La liberté au prisme des capacités. Amartya Sen au-delà du libéralisme* (EHESS, 2008).

Index

A

Activation, 6–9, 136–37, 182–85; paradigm of, 8; policies, 21, 137, 161, labour market, 152; active policies, 8–17, 24, 28, 75, 90, 167, 179–182; active securities, 18, 88–89, 100- 110; 188; activity agreement, 8

Alternative approaches, 15- 24, 65, 109, 120, 135, 153,159, 161, 173, 181–89

Asymmetrical power relations, 4–5, 9, 21, 63, 92

Assumptions, 2, 5, 15, 20, 23–4.

B

Balance between flexibility and security, 13–15, 20–22, 37, 73–75, 88, 91, 97, 106–9, 173–5, 183; balance of power, 3–6, 16–8, 63–64, 70; waged relationship, 5; needs, 13, 181; of class forces, 15, 38, 40–1, 45; between life activities, 20, 72, 75–76, 83, 105, 144–8, 158, 161, 164–5

Benchmarking, 1, 22, 125–6, 177

C

Capabilities , 17–20, 68, 90, 106, 116–32, 139–49, 161–2

Care services, 17, 29, 73

Citizen based labour market status, 18, 99, 102

Class, 14–5, 29–30, 33–45, 62–63, 97, 152–55, 165

Collective dimension of security, 7–9, 32, 136, 142, 148, 166, 189; collective bargaining, 27, 38, 42, 45, 52, 56, 60, 179; collective power, 15, 38, 45, 88, 106,

126, 149; collective solidarity, 4–5, 20–3, 137, 141, 165–6; collective learning, 129–30, 146, 149

concept of security, the 4

D

Danish model, 10, 36, 43, 47, 50, 64, 73, 97, 173, 178–86

Decent work 20–21, 49, 163, 166, 173, 191–192

Decommodification, 20. 153, 156

Deliberative democracy, 22, 90, 116–33; participative democracy, 18, 19

E

Employability, 1, 14, 19, 23, 75, 77, 102–4, 117, 136–49, 173, 284

Employment regimes, 16, 22, 47–66; social policy regimes, 41, 45; employment protection legislation, 12, 13, 15, 17, 28, 70, 175

Employment security, 10–3, 28, 30, 76, 83, 105, 175, 181–83

Empower individuals, 9, 16–22, 68, 78, 83, 89–90, 141, 176

Entrepreneurship, 1

Ethical theories, 1–5

Eudaimonic ethic of social welfare, 20, 159–66

European employment strategy, 1, 89, 106, 108, 180, 191

European institutions, 117, 132

European Trade Unions, 2, 12–4, 108

F

Flexibility, 2, 98- 111, 147–50, 174, 181–92; numerical flexibility, 10–11, 16, 18, 60, 71, 89, 98,

102, 109; functional flexibility, 10, 18, 89, 92, 96–8, 102
Flexicurity, 1, 6–9, 11–15, 23. 28, 69–75, 84, 88, 136, 174–187
Freedom, 9, 17–19, 57, 100, 104, 118–49, 156, 162–3, 175; freedom from want, 90, 106; freedom to act, 22, 90, 100

G
Government, 27, 35–6, 42–5, 56. 101, 121, 132, 159, 164, 173, 181

I
Income inequality, 3, 38–9; gender equality, 15–7, 68–85
Individualisation, 2–3, 99, 120, 182; individual responsibility 2, 20, 91, 137, 157, 166; Individual willingness, 19
Insecurity, 3, 29–30, 73, 107, 120, 153, 178
Institutional capacity, 22, 91; institutional frameworks, 6, 19, 130
Interdependency, 4, 9, 21, 92

J
Justice, 2–5, 15, 17, 19, 21, 88, 91–2, 106, 123, 135, 160–2, 188–92

K
Keynesianism, 27–31, 64, 116, 165–66; keynesian policy, 27, 117, 153; privatized Keynesianism, 33

L
Labour market reform, 12, 34–7, 68–9, 174, 199
Labour strength, 41
Labour market segregation, 73; insiders, 29, 37, 75, 177–8
Learning communities, 22, 101, 108
Life first approach, 161–3

M
Macroeconomic policies, 22
Marx, 120, 154–5, 159, 162; Marxist, 166

N
Neoliberalism 27
    Neoliberal societies 37
New social risks 28–29, 102

O
Outsiders 29, 75, 177–178, 180

P
Paradoxes 9
Production of public knowledge 19, 126
Polanyi 5, 152
Power relations 2, 9, 21, 24, 36
Precariousness i, 3, 12, 24, 50, 57, 117, 120–121, 153
Professional development 19–20, 110, 120, 135, 137–149

Q
Quality of employment 4, 21, 47–48, 51–65, 173, 191–192

R
Risk society 152–153

S
Segmentation 16, 21, 23–24, 49, 51, 53–54, 58, 61, 65, 83, 109, 111, 173, 177–178, 180
Self-regulation 8, 19, 129
Sen 91, 103, 111, 122, 127–128, 133, 139, 141–142, 161, 189
Situated state 19, 129–131, 133
Social bridges 18, 98
Social citizenship 152–153, 155–156, 159, 162
Social constructions 17
Social contract 27
Social justice 2–3, 5, 15, 19, 21–23, 126, 135, 151, 160, 162, 188–191
Social protection systems 4, 24, 80, 112, 187–188
Social rights 3, 9, 18, 21, 48, 73, 88, 99, 106, 108, 152, 155–156, 188–189
Social risk 5, 28–29, 31, 33, 98, 102, 137, 181, 190
Sustainable transitions 17, 89

T
Transitional labour market theory 89
Trade Unions, Europe 37, 51–2, 56, 64, 101, 147, 149

U
Uncertainty 29–31, 34, 36, 38, 98
Unity of life 22

Unpaid work 16–17, 68, 72–74, 83–84,
     90, 159

V

Vulnerability 2–5, 9, 16, 21, 24,
     49–50, 60, 138

W

Weakening of labour 24
Welfare states 3, 136, 153, 160
Welfare state dependency 6
Workfare 28, 89, 99–101, 152, 156,
     171

Printed in the United States
by Baker & Taylor Publisher Services